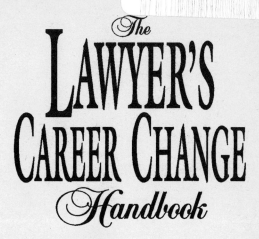

The
LAWYER'S
CAREER CHANGE
Handbook

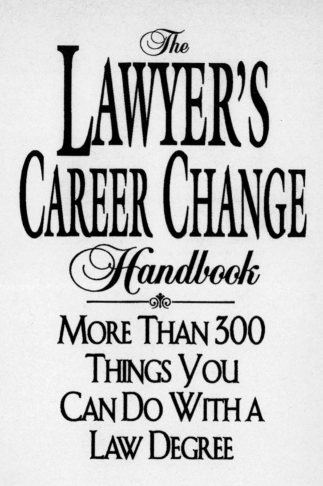

The LAWYER'S CAREER CHANGE Handbook

MORE THAN 300 THINGS YOU CAN DO WITH A LAW DEGREE

HINDI GREENBERG

AVON BOOKS NEW YORK

AVON BOOKS, INC.
1350 Avenue of the Americas
New York, New York 10019

Copyright © 1998 by Hindi Greenberg
Interior design by Kellan Peck
Back cover author photo by John Lannertone
Published by arrangement with the author
Visit our website at **http://www.AvonBooks.com**
ISBN: 0-380-79572-8

Library of Congress Cataloging in Publication Data:
Greenberg, Hindi.
    The lawyer's career change handbook / Hindi Greenberg.
        p.   cm.
    1. Law—Vocational guidance—United States. 2. Practice of law—United States. 3. Career changes—United States. I. Title.
KF297.Z9G74   1998   98-28856
340'.023'73—dc21   CIP

First Avon Books Trade Paperback Printing: December 1998

AVON TRADEMARK REG. U.S. PAT. OFF. AND IN OTHER COUNTRIES, MARCA REGISTRADA, HECHO EN U.S.A.

Printed in the U.S.A.

OPM   10   9   8   7   6   5   4   3   2   1

Work is love made visible.
And if you can't work with love but only with distaste,
It is better that you should leave your work
and sit at the gate of the temple and
take alms of the people who work with joy.

—KAHLIL GIBRAN, *The Prophet*

Acknowledgments

If you're lucky, life is one problem after another.
When you're not, it's the same one over and over.
—ANONYMOUS

I have been working with lawyers who are thinking of changing jobs and looking at career alternatives for thirteen years. As probably the first person in the U.S. to both counsel and provide programs for these lawyers, I have been encouraged by many people, for many years, to write this book. Although I have had a written manual since almost the beginning, I finally agreed that it was time to develop and expand that manual. While there are a number of people to whom I owe a debt of gratitude for either encouraging me to write this book or cheering me on while I did so, the following individuals, in particular, deserve my heartfelt thanks:

To Suzi Cohen, for listening on and on and on while I railed against deadlines, lack of sleep, or anything else I felt like complaining about;

To Walter Caplan, for keeping me on track and on time;

To Tama Greenberg and Eva Roza, for generosity with their computers when I needed them;

To Dr. Jeff Prince, for his wonderful and creative ideas, and his excellent analysis and information on the Myers-Briggs inventory;

To my agent, Betsy Amster, for finding me and proposing that I write this book and then being patient with me;

To my editor, Chris Condry, for her words of encouragement; and

To Pip and Edie, for their playfulness and warm affection.

Contents

Introduction

It isn't work unless you'd rather be doing something else.
—PETER PAN

The practice of law has changed so dramatically from what it was twenty, ten, and even five years ago, that those of you who are thinking of entering law school, are already in school, or who have been out in law practice for two, eight, or twenty years can't necessarily base your career decisions on the legal career progressions of your older relatives or friends. The extreme changes in the profession and the increased uses for a law degree mandate that you look afresh at various career considerations and options, whether you intend to continue practicing as a lawyer or move into a career outside of law.

The Lawyer's Career Change Handbook is intended to provide you with a lot of information and a number of tools to help you decide:

1

1. whether you should become a law student or lawyer, if you're not already;
2. if you are a law student, whether you should finish your studies; and
3. if you are now a lawyer, whether you should continue in practice or seek a less traditional or out-of-law career.

To help you decide which of these various career moves would serve you best, this handbook is divided into three sections: Taking Stock, More than 300 Things You Can Do with a Law Degree, and How to Find the Job You Want.

The first section, Taking Stock, begins by addressing the changes in the legal profession, then explains how to either mitigate aggravations in your current work situation or, if need be, make career adjustments to alleviate those aggravations. If minimal changes aren't sufficient, this first section will then help you decide if a complete job change is best for you, and if so, how to determine what work styles and adjustments you would be willing to undertake. This section also defines different types of personalities and then discusses which personality types do best in certain styles of legal practice. The first section ties up these issues by helping you assess your skills, interests, and values in order to enable you to choose your next career step so that it fits comfortably.

Once you have an idea of how you would like to work and what assets you bring to the marketplace, the second section of this handbook, More than 300 Things You Can Do with a Law Degree, will give you ideas about the many career options available to you as a holder of a juris doctor degree. These options are divided according to whether you want to maintain your active bar license, work in a field where your J.D. is important but you don't need a license to practice law, or actually move away from the legal field completely and never think like a lawyer again. All of the jobs listed within this second section have been performed by one or more law school graduates—they aren't fantasy. Once you select a job option that interests you, the numerous resources in each section will help you begin your research into a particular field, so you can determine whether that job will really fit for you.

The third section of this handbook, How to Find the Job You Want, will cover what you need to know about networking and informational interviewing, resumes and cover letters, and job interviews and self-presentation. This last section is at least as important as the previous two because while you may be the best qualified candidate for a particular type of work, if you don't find out about the opening, don't make the appropriate contacts, or don't present yourself well on paper or in person, you still won't get the job.

You may want to skip around within this handbook, reading the parts that are applicable to your situation at present. However, the tendency for most of my clients is to immediately seek out the list of job options, without giving proper consideration to their particular skills, interests, values, previous experience, or personality type—all important factors in creating job satisfaction. A certain job title may sound sexy in the short run—screenwriter, for instance—but in the long run, the initial allure will quickly vanish if the job has the same time pressures, big egos, excessive critique from bosses, and unstable nature, all of which you catalog as negatives in your current work.

Therefore, in order to make the most satisfying job selection, you should give at least passing attention to the first section of this handbook, doing the exercises contained in the early chapters. After selecting a few interesting career options from the second section, spend some time perusing the third section, learning how to network, conduct informational interviews, and prepare resumes. Those individuals who have made the most successful career transitions either within or out of law are those who know themselves, decide what they want, research and select appropriate career options, then pursue a planned and systematic approach to achieve their desired job. This is an approach that you can accomplish. It may take some time, and you may need to stretch yourself out of your normal comfort zone and do a lot of hard work in learning, researching, talking, and interviewing, but many, many lawyers have already made successful changes, and you can do it too. Are you ready to start? Then read on.

PART ONE

TAKING STOCK

Trust your hunches. They're usually based on facts filed away just below the conscious level.
—DR. JOYCE BROTHERS

From conversations I've had with literally thousands and thousands of lawyers over the past thirteen years, I can break them into roughly two groups—those who think their practice of law should be abandoned, the sooner the better, and those who feel that using their legal skills is desirable but wish they could lessen the aspects of practice that they dislike, or find new meaning, or rekindle lost excitement in their work.

Although the information in this handbook should be of assistance to either group, I wish I could greatly simplify the job and career change process for you. However, no one has ever indicated to me that I resemble a fairy godmother. It would be wonderful if I had a magic wand that I could wave to turn all those jobs that feel like useless, sluggish, or uninspiring pumpkins into vibrant, sleek, new carriages. But the reality of career change is that it's hard work.

For those of you serious about making a job or career change, the approach and techniques you will need to apply in order to find fulfilling, meaningful work, whether within the legal field or outside of it, are really quite the same. Whether you are looking for increased career satisfaction in work similar to what you currently do, or you are seeking completely new challenges, the necessary steps are outlined in the career evaluation checklist set out immediately below. For most effective results, I advise that you give *at least* passing attention to each step. Each step will be more fully explored in subsequent chapters in this handbook.

CAREER EVALUATION OUTLINE

1. Objectively evaluate what you like and dislike about your present job.
2. If you're less than 75 percent satisfied with your current position, proceed to the self-assessment exercises (good to do any time).
3. Do self-assessment.
   a. Identify your interests. Pick three that no job should be without.
   b. Assess your skills (abilities/aptitudes). Pick three that no job should be without and two that you must absolutely avoid.
   c. Identify your values. Pick three that no job should be without and two that you must absolutely avoid.
   d. Assess your own personality traits/style and those desired in your coworkers; identify any traits in yourself or others that you must have and must avoid; determine your preferred work style (solitary/teamwork/large or small groups); determine your management style (consensus/sole decision maker).

    e. Identify any absolute work environment "must haves" and "must avoids" (casual/formal/indoors/outdoors/aesthetics/size).

    f. Identify your lifestyle needs (location, income, etc.).

4. Research the career options that will accommodate the interests, skills, values, personality traits, and lifestyle needs you identified in step 3.

5. Reduce the list of options generated by Step 4 to those that provide the environment, coworker type and number, and work style you prefer.

6. Research the remaining career options in depth.

    a. Develop a network and use it.

    b. Conduct informational interviews.

    c. Read relevant publications, attend organization meetings.

7. Market yourself in the fields you've chosen.

    a. Develop one or more effective resumes.

    b. Prepare a cover letter to highlight your transferable skills.

    c. Learn how to interview to show yourself off to best advantage.

    d. Work your network.

8. Periodically review your answers to step 3 and apply them to whatever your current job is in order to ensure continued career satisfaction.

CHAPTER ONE

Where Did That Perfect Legal Job Go?

I'm too old to learn to do something else,
too greedy to give up the money I make,
and too burnt out to deserve it.
—MACK MALLOY; SCOTT TUROW, *Pleading Guilty*

The legal and lay communities are finally waking up to an issue that many lawyers have known for some time—we do not all want to be like Perry Mason. Although there are many lawyers quite satisfied with their choice of profession, not all law school graduates want to appear in court, work for a big firm, handle large or complex cases, spend the majority of their waking hours in their offices, or even earn top dollar. Instead, many want the opportunity to explore and pursue alternative options, both in and outside of the law. They want to do work that they love, or at least work that they feel good about.

Law is an excellent career choice for some individuals. It challenges their intellect, it utilizes their analytical reasoning, it allows them opportunities to write and speak and negotiate and counsel. If you are one of these individuals and are just looking for a different position within the legal field, you may want to skip this chapter and move on to the chapters on self-assessment, career options, and interviewing skills.

Unfortunately, many lawyers are not satisfied with their chosen career. If every lawyer in the country were sitting in a (very) massive auditorium, and I asked who really, *really* liked their legal practice, studies show that less than one-half would raise their hands! Although the maxim "No job is perfect, that's why you get paid" is as true in law as it is in other fields, a growing number of lawyers are questioning their career choice. If you are thinking about entering law school, or are a current law student, or are waiting to pass the bar exam—questioning where you might find a satisfying and productive job either within or outside of law—the following discussion of the changes in the profession may stimulate you to think through important considerations before you decide to get into law. Some of the changes are encountered primarily in law firm practice rather than in jobs in less traditional legal practice areas, such as government offices, the courts, or corporations, but many of the issues permeate the practice, how ever and where ever it is done.

• Changing Expectations

> *After people make enough for food and shelter,*
> *they don't work for money, they work for acknowledgment.*
> —LOU SMITH

A fifth-year business litigation associate from a large law firm— I'll call him Bill—recently phoned me at Lawyers in Transition^SM to set up a career counseling session. He told me he'd gone to a good law school and done reasonably well, clerked for a year, then took a position at his current firm. The first few years at the firm were fine, since he was learning a lot of new things. Then the work became routine and the time commitments overwhelming.

Over this past year, Bill began to dislike the numbing details and repetition that practice required, as well as the voluminous paperwork, contentiousness, stress, competition between the firm's attorneys, and long billable hours. He now has to force himself to get out of bed in the morning to go to work, and he doesn't have time for any life outside the office. He looks at the partners in his firm and sees that they don't seem very happy; he doesn't want to be like them. But he feels trapped in his job because it pays well—he just bought a house and is still paying off student loans—and he doesn't know what other work he could do and still earn good money. His legal training narrowed his focus and made it even more difficult for him to envision an alternative career.

Unfortunately, like many lawyers who contact me, Bill admitted that when he chose to attend law school, he had not talked to many lawyers or given much thought to what the actual practice of law would entail. He went to law school because he was finishing his undergraduate work and didn't know what else to do. He thought that legal training would give him credibility, useful knowledge, and a good general background for any work he chose. Now he's not so sure. He says he hasn't a clue what his work experience qualifies him for, if anything, other than legal work. He's definitely narrowed his perceptions of himself and his abilities since entering law school.

Bill's attitude is similar to a large percentage of the more than 10,000 lawyers who have called me over the past thirteen years, expressing dissatisfaction with some aspect of their own work or the practice of law in general. Of those who contact me, a majority say that since they already have their legal degree, they would like to continue to use their legal skills if they could find some less stressful or frustrating position. My own unscientific study indicates that approximately 80 percent of the people who call me either make job changes within law or make no change at all; only 20 percent leave law completely. But a poll taken by *California Lawyer* magazine in 1993 found that over 70 percent of the respondents said they would not go into law again if they could begin their careers anew. This poll was reinforced by a study published in the *California Bar Journal* in 1995, which found that more than half of the lawyers participating in the study were at least somewhat dissatisfied with their legal work.

What's going on here? What's happened to that epitome of professions, the one that every mother and father dreamed their child would enter? The one that would provide high income, power, and prestige?

• The Changing Profession

> *Only babies with wet diapers appreciate change.*
> —LIZ GREENBERG

Although there are many lawyers who greatly enjoy practicing law—in law firms, in corporations, in nonprofit organizations, for the government, and in the many other areas where lawyers work—there is a growing discontent among the legal ranks. Many lawyers feel that the practice of law has dramatically changed over the last twenty-five years; it no longer provides the collegiality, intellectual depth, job security, and lofty ethics that had been the hallmarks of the profession. Although some practitioners earn high incomes, the median income of attorneys in the United States is only about $60,000, not the grand sums claimed by the media. Furthermore, work hours and clients' demands have expanded dramatically, as has the public disdain for lawyers.

In "the old days," lawyers would aggressively argue a motion in court, then have lunch with opposition counsel. This was possible because effective lawyering did not mean accosting the other attorney with personal attacks. A spirit of cooperation with other attorneys used to be the foundation of law practice. Today, more than a few lawyers seem to use the pit bull as a role model for their legal personas. Steven, a solo practitioner who handles real estate deals, small business transactions, and litigation, cringes when he looks at the return address on certain envelopes or is informed by his secretary that one of several other attorneys is on the telephone line. He knows that he is in for a confrontation, because that is the style these individuals choose, believing that intimidation and bullying are effective methods for dealing with other attorneys. Steven says that there are, unfortunately, a growing number of such practitioners, and that these individuals make the practice of law a whole lot less fun than when he first began more than twenty years ago.

However, when Steven first began practicing, the community of lawyers was much smaller, and so there was more accountability to one's peers. Because practitioners in each specialty knew most of the other attorneys in their field, a particularly hostile or unfriendly lawyer could be singled out and shunned or pressured to reform. But with the greatly increasing number of lawyers—the American Bar Association predicts that there will be more than one million by the year 2000—and the vast increase in interstate and multinational law practices, there has been a breakdown in personal relationships. It is impossible now to know all, or even most, of the attorneys practicing in a given city or area of law.

Litigation, n.
A machine which you go into as a pig and come out as a
sausage.
—AMBROSE BIERCE, *The Devil's Dictionary*

Law is the only profession in which a bright and well-trained individual is expressly paid to counter another bright and well-trained individual's every move and to prove that the other is wrong. In litigation, the opposition attorney is hoping to make the other lawyer look foolish. In transactional deals, the lawyers representing each party advocate their client's interests, always alert for a winning edge. In either case, lawyers must always be on the defensive so that another attorney won't trip them.

One of my clients recently wrote a stinging evaluation of law practice, listing the things he dislikes. In his words: "I dislike (1) the interpersonal nastiness of litigation, (2) the combativeness of litigation, (3) the win-at-all-cost attitude of litigation, (4) the crisis mentality of litigation, (5) that my goal is to defeat my opponent and my opponent's goal is to defeat me, (6) the pressure of being expected to do work that my opponent can never criticize—an absolutely unrealistic expectation, (7) that I am always around people who are angry at someone, (8) that I cannot be fair or reasonable, as I see fairness and reason, but have to fight for every advantage I can get out of a situation, (9) that I cannot spend my life working with a group of dedicated people to achieve a common goal but instead must constantly fight other people to achieve success."

Relationships with clients have also changed dramatically. Previously, lawyers primarily represented individuals or small businesses. There was often a warm working relationship between the lawyer and the client; the outcome of the case mattered to the lawyer, and the reason for the legal work and its meaning were obvious. Now lawyers complain that the work they do has little meaning. As they represent progressively larger national and multinational companies, lawyers become more and more removed from anyone who is directly affected by their legal work; it seems that the work merely takes money from one pocket and puts it into another. Also, the individuals within the client companies often change, so there is less continuity in personal relations. The result is that when some practitioners consider the meaningfulness of the work, earning top dollar to represent a faceless entity loses some of its glamour.

Other lawyers are looking for more creativity and freedom in their work. After her graduation from law school in 1985, Tamara practiced at two different large law firms. Although she began thinking about law alternatives in only her second year of practice, she kept telling herself that she "wasn't giving law enough of a chance." But she felt stifled and longed for more creativity in her work. "With work consuming all my time," she notes, "I found it difficult to grow as a multidimensional person." To alleviate that situation, she eventually became president of a small publishing company, cowriting two books and working to cultivate other authors.

Some lawyers feel that the litigation process itself is too adversarial and wasteful. After Michael graduated from law school in 1973, he worked as a personal injury and business litigator. But he decided he would prefer to work as part of a team rather than in competition against others, and he wanted to facilitate business and real estate transactions, do deals, be an advisor, and have one client rather than many. So he actively networked, was invited to join a bank as staff counsel, and was promoted to general counsel three years later. As counsel within the bank, Michael was exposed to many nonlegal business issues and didn't have to deal with what he saw as the wastefulness of litigation.

• Changed Relationships and Increasing Competition

The relationship between lawyers and law firms has greatly changed. Firms are busy inventing new categories such as "permanent associate" or "special counsel" to be given to associates who are not offered a piece of the partnership pie but who are "good enough" to be kept on staff. For some associates these are promising developments, alleviating the stress caused by partnership track competition and client development requirements. But for others, it is an insult to the countless hours they billed for the firm at the expense of their private lives.

With the increasing number of licensed lawyers and the shrinking number of traditional legal jobs, competition for jobs, clients, and billable hours is increasing. In past years, most lawyers felt there was enough work to spread around, but now lawyers are worried about having enough clients and income. In almost every law firm, both associates and partners must meet minimum billable hours requirements, and those requirements keep increasing, from an average of 1,800 billable hours per year in 1980 to over 2,000 in 1996—and some firms are now requiring more than 2,400 per year! In fact, the leading partner at a Silicon Valley firm told a group of associates that any lawyer who couldn't bill 2,500 hours a year had no business being a lawyer. Be wary of a law firm that touts its on-site exercise facility, complete with showers and cots for resting—you just may end up living at the office, sending out for clean underwear, and paying someone to walk your dog and water your houseplants. This worrisome climate encourages attorneys to pad their billable hours, fosters pressure to keep a case from settling so that more work may be generated from it, and increases "ambulance chasing" in order to obtain new clients. (Many lawyers know the joke about the young lawyer who dies and goes to heaven; at the heavenly gate he protests that he's too young to die, but the gate guardians say that, according to the number of billable hours in the lawyer's time sheets, they figured that he was at least 85 years old.) Additionally, in most firms, there is continuous pressure to cultivate new clients, a process that takes additional time over and above the billable hours requirement.

In more than a few law firms, there are partners who hoard their clients and the billable work that those clients represent, refusing to pass enough work on to the associates working under them. This creates a dual pressure on those associates—the need to expand their work in order to bill the required number of hours set by the firm while adhering to their responsibility to charge clients only for time actually spent on their cases. This ethical dilemma and the resulting tension—to watch the clock and not overcharge, yet to bill as many hours as possible—is one of the most common complaints I hear.

Related to that stress is the fact that lawyers' hourly fees are increasing; a number of practitioners express feelings of guilt for charging per hour what the average person takes two or three days to earn. Many lawyers would like to perform legal work for free or at reduced cost, if only they could afford to do so. However, there are often large amounts of unpaid receivables, especially in solo and small firms, which usually represent individuals and small businesses rather than large corporations. These unpaid bills lessen lawyers' income and preclude them from doing much pro bono work. As Steven said of his solo practice, "If I could collect all the money that my clients owe me, I could perform legal services for free for the next five years."

• Changing Populations

Another change in the legal profession is the influx of a more diverse population. In 1969, most law school classes were less than 5 percent female. By 1995, many classes were at least 50 percent female, resulting in a growing number of women attorneys and judges. Although the influx of minority law students has not been as dramatic, there is a marked increase in nonwhite legal practitioners. The perspectives that women and minorities bring to legal practice, while not always different from traditional views, often reflect their respective life experiences. Those experiences can influence their professional expectations and their relationships with other attorneys.

A good example of changing relationships is illustrated by Suzi's experience when she began legal practice in 1977. Over the next six years, she worked in three small litigation firms, but her experiences weren't pleasant. Because she was the only woman lawyer in each of the three firms, she frequently found her relationships with the other attorneys to be uncomfortable. In one firm, she was treated as an outsider, who was never included in business discussions, invited to lunch with the other attorneys, or spoken to unless she was given an assignment. These working arrangements were unsatisfactory enough that they resulted in Suzi deciding to become self-employed; she has worked as a contract attorney since 1983.

Women (and a smaller number of men) with children have made demands on their colleagues for some recognition of, and accommodation for, their child-rearing responsibilities. These demands have not always resulted in alternative work arrangements. In fact, some firms have expressly rejected requests for part-time or other alternative work schedules for any reason. For example, at a program sponsored by the Young Lawyers' Section of the State Bar of California, a partner from a medium-size, prestigious national law firm was asked what a law firm's response should be to a request for a reduced work schedule from a fourth-year male associate who wanted to write a book. The partner said the associate should be fired, because the associate obviously was not dedicated to either the interests or work of the firm! Of course, the partner was oblivious to the fact that this response neither exhibited much dedication to the associate nor much willingness to be flexible in order to accommodate his personal career goals.

For many women of childbearing age, an alternative work schedule policy is a major priority. Additionally, many lawyers express a desire to work temporarily on non-law projects, such as writing a book, volunteering at a non-profit organization, or running for a political office. To remain competitive, get the legal work done, and attract and retain the best lawyers, firms will be forced to accept part-time workers, hire independent contractors, and make accommodations for individual choices. This is developing, but slowly. (The topic of alternative work schedules, such as part-time, contract legal work, job sharing and telecommuting, is discussed in detail in chapter 4.)

• Lost Loyalty, Lost Trust

Previously it was presumed that a law graduate would go to work as an associate for a firm, work hard for five to seven years, make partner, then ease up a bit and enjoy the fruits of past labor and continued good work. That presumption has now died with the downsizing, restructuring, and merging of law firms. Not only are many law students unable to find jobs but even associates who work hard aren't always offered partnerships, and partners who don't have large client lists wait for the knock on their office door that announces their forced departure.

Twenty-five years ago there was still a bond of loyalty between the lawyer and the law firm. In 1973, when Harriet, a third-year student at Hastings College of the Law in San Francisco, was trying to decide whether to renege on a job offer she had already accepted so that she could instead take a job with a different, more prestigious, firm, she sought the advice of one of her professors, a man in his late forties. She vividly recalls that her professor's advice was that loyalty and honor counted, and since she had already accepted the first position, it was the one she should stick with. "My professor had been educated and practiced law during a time when people believed that a lawyer's word was to be relied upon, not to be broken. He felt that if I was honorable, I would fulfill the commitment I had made when I accepted that first job, even though the second job would be to the advantage of my career." At the present time, it is doubtful whether a student in this situation would receive the same advice. Now most law firms and lawyers act in their own best interests, without much consideration for the problems or inconvenience their actions might cause others.

In our current atmosphere of job instability, with lawyers hopping from job to job and firms merging, closing, and downsizing, loyalty has been lost, and with it, I believe, much of the trust lawyers previously had in their colleagues. Partners now switch firms, not necessarily because they didn't like their former colleagues but solely to earn bigger dollars. Firms choose not to elect an associate to partnership for reasons known only to the partnership but not necessarily understood by—or even communicated to—the associate. This all causes the legal world to feel excessively competitive and unforthcoming to most attorneys, resulting in a lack of trust between lawyer and law firm, and between lawyers themselves.

This lack of trust is exacerbated by those lawyers who practice on the ethical edge. Sharon has for the past ten years been a partner in a small civil litigation firm. She states that she is tired of lawyers who say one thing but write a letter to "memorialize the conversation" that sets out a completely different scenario. Or who, purposefully and with impunity, make actual misrepresentations to the court or their clients. According to Sharon, this happens more than occasionally. She expresses regret that she has become a bit cynical, but these negative encounters with opposition attorneys have damaged her trust. She now documents everything in writing. This increase in paperwork naturally takes more of her time, increasing her resentment toward untrustworthy practitioners.

An older lawyer recently phoned me to say he "wanted out" and offered his perception of lawyer relationships: "I have practiced law for forty years. I never had a lawyer lie to me during the first thirty years. And I haven't had one tell me the truth for the last ten"—a ringing condemnation.

Often it is these same unethical lawyers who rate media attention, causing the public to believe that improper conduct is the daily course of the law profession, rather than an aberration. This feeds the growing disdain with which the public views lawyers. Formerly, the public generally held lawyers in esteem, honoring them for their hard work and respected position within the community. In the current climate, many lawyers say that if they tell a person their profession, they can expect to be assailed with either cruel lawyer jokes or tales of woe about the terrible experience the person had with a lawyer or the legal system.

Among many "funny" but cruel jokes that people send me, I recently received one that read, "If an attorney and an IRS agent were both drowning and you could save only one, would you go to lunch or read the paper?" This attitude is hurtful to many lawyers. They studied hard, spending three or four years and countless dollars on law school; they work hard, often averaging fifty or more hours per week; and they believe they do the best they can for their clients. After all that, to be disparaged in the press and at public and private functions is a real slap in the face.

Since client respect for lawyers has diminished, the incidence of malpractice claims has greatly increased. Clients no longer hesitate to file a claim if they believe they were not treated fairly or if they did not get the result they expected. However, client expectations are often entirely unrealistic, caused by media promotion of the gigantic sums recovered by plaintiffs for seemingly minor grievances. Some clients, no matter what the outcome of a case, will believe that the result is deficient enough to warrant a malpractice complaint. Additionally, some clients use the threat of malpractice as a lever to force an attorney to back off from a claim against the client for unpaid fees. Brett, an experienced solo practitioner, says he has written off a lot of money owed him by clients over the years rather than be subjected to a State Bar disciplinary complaint or a malpractice lawsuit, however unjustified.

• Warp Speed Practice

The pace of practice has been increased to warp speed by facsimile machines, computer modems, and beepers. Many lawyers are troubled by the "shoot from the hip" mentality that currently pervades legal practice, since clients often expect instantaneous responses to their questions. No longer do lawyers have the time for concentrated contemplation and reflection or the luxury of producing a finely crafted brief or memorandum. On-line legal research provides a quick turnaround, and this puts pressure on lawyers to have answers at their fingertips. Contributing to the increased speed of practice, many courts now require "fast-track" processing of lawsuits, where response times for various motions and procedures are greatly reduced.

• Staying in or Leaving the Law

Our biggest regrets aren't things we've done,
but things we haven't done.
—GREG REIS

There have been numerous changes in law practice over the past years. Some have benefitted the public, the practice, and individual lawyers. Others have not. Many of these changes have resulted in practitioners' choosing to change jobs or careers.

Many dissatisfied practitioners initially believe that they need to quit the practice of law. However, simply obtaining information on how to stay in law and develop career satisfaction—with only a minor adjustment to a current working situation—will often suffice to remedy the frustrations. Perhaps all that you need is to move to a different firm, a different area of law, or a different type of client. Or maybe a more drastic change is necessary. Whatever you decide to do with your work life, remember that the choices are many and varied, limited only by your creativity, desire, and willingness to spend the time and energy necessary to cultivate your next professional incarnation. To help you decide whether to enter the legal field or change jobs or careers, in the next ten chapters I will present relevant information, helpful self-assessment exercises, career resources, and anecdotes about other lawyers who have found satisfying work in or out of law.

CHAPTER TWO

Finding a Better Fit in a New Legal Job

I'd rather be a failure at something I enjoy than a success at something I hate.
—GEORGE BURNS

For many of you, starting or continuing to practice law in some manner is your favored alternative. After all, you are studying or have studied the subject for three (or for some of you, four) years, will take or have passed a bar examination, and a number of you have now practiced law for a few or more years. That's a large commitment. In fact, many of my clients have spent so much time obtaining their legal credentials, that they now feel they "need to give *it* one more chance." When I ask them what "it" is, many cannot articulate exactly what they mean—perhaps "it" is law practice itself, their current career path, the title of "lawyer," sometimes even the relationships they have with their law firm or partners.

Before you decide whether to continue on in your legal career or change to another field, it is important to recall and examine your motivations for going to law school and practicing law in the first place. These may have changed over the years, but recalling your early motivators will help determine whether they continue to inspire your vision or whether you are just going through the motions.

For example, when Carolyn was in junior high and planning to become a sculptor someday, she became privy to the employment tribulations of a friend's father. Hearing about this man's negative treatment by his employer and witnessing the resulting emotional fallout, Carolyn resolved that she wanted to become a labor lawyer and help employees receive justice in their workplaces. After several years of representing wronged employees, Carolyn has moved away from the practice of law because she found that her early motivation to practice law has waned in comparison to her renewed interest in fine art.

Similarly, Carl was a '60s kind of guy, without interest in money or material goods, who wanted to make the world better for everyone. After law school, he began lawyering with various nonprofit organizations, earning only a meager living. When Carl turned forty, he married, and over the next several years had two children. He now finds that his early motivation is gone, although he may stay in law if he can earn a better income. Helping his family financially has become a stronger motivator to him than helping others.

However, while it is important to honor your feelings about continuing on in law, make sure you aren't doing so in order to fulfill someone else's expectations of you. Did your parents pay for your schooling and now want you to get their money's worth out of your degree? Does your family (or you) like the status you achieve from being a lawyer? Although the law profession as a whole is too often derided by the public, lawyers are still generally given respect on an individual basis. And this is particularly true for women and minorities, who are received more attentively when they indicate they practice law than they would be if they said they worked in an office or were a nurse or a teacher.

Do you come from a family with many lawyers, where leaving

the profession might raise some eyebrows? Are you the first person in your extended family to go to law school, or maybe even receive a higher education? Do you feel pressure to continue as a role model and not be a "quitter"?

It is important for you to continue practicing law only if it feels right and can be made to work for who you are, what you believe, the way you like to work, and how you want to live your life. I don't want to get too depressing, but keep in mind that parents eventually die, significant others can leave, and law partnerships often split up, as the rest of us continue to get up in the morning and go to work. A lawyer-turned-entrepreneur told me that his father, on the older man's deathbed, said to his son that "since everyone has to make a living and it takes up so many hours, months, and years of your life, you may as well invest that time in something that you can look back on when you are old and feel you accomplished something and had a bit of fun doing it." A solid piece of advice. As a friend of mine is fond of saying, "This lifetime is not a dress rehearsal."

The problem for many lawyers is that they "fell into" law—they were graduating from college without knowing what to do next. Because they weren't ready to go out into the work world without a high-ticket credential, they had to select one. These people entered law school merely to pursue an advanced degree that they presumed provided good employment potential, not necessarily to become lawyers.

When they entered school, they did not really know what the day-to-day practice of law was like nor did they know about the various law practice areas (even over three years, most law schools fail to enlighten their students on those topics). Then early in their third year of school, these same students joined with other aspiring law graduates in the feeding frenzy of interviewing and got caught up in acquiring the most offers from the most prestigious firms, whether or not those firms and the work they do fit with the individual's unexamined aspirations. More important initially was the pressure to obtain high salaries in order to repay large student loans; for many graduates, there were few other options. Many students liked the ego gratification of being invited to join a large, prestigious firm. Then some of these lawyers woke up three years later and said, "What am I doing here in this big firm, litigating securities fraud cases for $95,000 a year, when I had intended to use my legal training to work with disabled children and abused women?" Now it's more difficult to make a big switch; it would require a marked change in office environment, a perceived prestige loss, and certainly a drastic pay cut.

But if you have been questioning your job satisfaction for more than six months, maybe it's time for a change. Here are questions to ask yourself, to clarify your attitude toward the practice of law and toward work in general. Circle one letter for each question.

1. How important is your legal career?
   a. My work is what fulfills me and gives life meaning.
   b. My career is important but not the only thing of impor-
      tance to me.
   c. I work to make a living, to pay for a home, my kids, or
      a vacation.
2. Did you enjoy law school?
   a. I loved law school, with its theory and analysis.
   b. Law school was okay, as a means to an end of becoming
      a lawyer.
   c. I couldn't wait to finish law school. It was too theoretical
      and abstract.
3. How do you feel about your current job?
   a. I am repeatedly invigorated by my work and find it
      compelling.
   b. I am tired of what I'm doing, but a shift in emphasis may
      improve it.
   c. I am sick of the people, projects, and issues I'm working
      on.
4. Does your work utilize your strengths?
   a. It causes me to stretch and grow.
   b. Some of my strengths are used, some are atrophying.
   c. No, not at all.
5. Are you proud that you are a lawyer?
   a. I wear my credential like a red badge of courage.
   b. It is a good way to make a living, I just wish the jokes
      would go away.

    c. At parties, I say that I work as an animal attendant at the zoo.

6. Does your work allow you to have a quality of life sufficient for your needs in the following categories?

Financially?

    a. My remuneration is more than adequate.

    b. I earn as much as I need but not as much as I want.

    c. I don't earn enough to keep myself out of debt.

Time-wise?

    a. I have time for a balanced life.

    b. I have to juggle more balls than I would like to.

    c. I'm drowning and I don't have time to come up for air.

7. Does the work you do feel meaningful to you?

    a. My work is very emotionally rewarding.

    b. I feel that some of the things I do resonate for me.

    c. All I am doing is shifting money from one business's pocket to another business's pocket.

8. Are you able to work on projects you enjoy, in subject areas you find interesting?

    a. Yes, usually.

    b. Sometimes.

    c. No, hardly ever.

Score the previous exercise by counting how many a, b, and c responses you checked. If you checked at least four of the a boxes and none of the c boxes, you most likely are in the right work, maybe just needing some adjustment for small irritants. If you checked more than four of the b boxes, your work is probably just a job and most times doesn't bring you much joy—although not much misery either. But if you checked more than two of the c boxes, you have a problem and should consider moving on to other work.

Here is another exercise to check your job satisfaction. On a scale of 1 to 5, with a score of 5 being the most satisfied and 1 the least, estimate your present level of satisfaction with your job and write a number next to each of the following phrases.

____Varied responsibilities
____Interesting work
____Challenging work
____Sufficient salary
____Opportunity for professional growth
____Opportunity for personal growth
____Respect/fair treatment from superiors
____Sufficient autonomy/ independence
____Personal/organization values compatible
____Adequate leisure time
____Reasonable work hours
____Opportunity for friendships
____Adequate resources to do job
____Physical environment
____Worthwhile work
____Sufficient authority
____Sufficient status/prestige
____Lack of pressure
____Desirable location
____Adequate evaluations
____Client appreciation
____Able to use special skills
____Ability to use creativity
____Can regulate own work
____Limit on unrelated work

Add your score. The highest score you can get is 125, but you probably wouldn't be reading this book if you scored that high. If your score is higher than 90, you probably are reasonably satisfied with your work, needing only a few minor adjustments.

A score between 60 and 90 indicates that you have some noteworthy aggravations that need remedying if you are to continue in your current job or even in the same practice area. Examine which items scored low and evaluate whether there is any way to improve your satisfaction level. For example, if the location is bad, maybe transferring to a branch office nearer to home or a closer, similar firm will improve the commute. Or if you no longer feel challenged by your work, perhaps changing your practice focus will once again stimulate your gray matter.

Greg, a litigator from Georgia, initially scored 75 on this test. He was unhappy that he had such an unpredictable schedule— with a new baby, he wanted to be home in the evening. Additionally, he really disliked the contentiousness of litigation. But he enjoyed and felt challenged by the research and writing, so he proposed to his firm that he develop an appellate practice so that the firm could keep its cases in-house from start to finish. When his firm agreed and Greg began working on appeals, his score increased to 115!

Andrew scored 70 and thought he would have to quit practice because he really disliked his clients, their workers' compensation issues, and the atmosphere of the neighborhood law office where he worked in a big city in Ohio. But when he parlayed his employer-employee relations experience into a labor defense practice with a more sophisticated, downtown law office, his score rose to 100.

Many lawyers feel that if they are unhappy, they must give up their legal career, without realizing that perhaps only a slight adjustment is needed. At this point it might be helpful to peek ahead into the next chapter under the subheading Should You Stay Where You Are? to see if any of the issues raised there are relevant to your job satisfaction and ability to mitigate the problems. However, if your score is below 60, you should definitely consider switching jobs and perhaps think seriously about looking at alternative career options. With a very low score, mitigation attempts will probably be insufficient to improve your job enough to be tolerable.

• How Do You Select a Satisfying Practice Area or Style?

If you are a new lawyer or have worked in only one or two areas of law, you may not be aware that different practice specialties often require extremely different work styles and personality types. The lawyer who enjoys and is successful in personal injury defense, handling intense negotiations and conducting trials, may be bored with the detail and documentation of an estate planning practice. The gregarious lawyer who loves talking to, counseling, and interrelating with clients would feel very isolated and unconvivial working as a writer for a legal publisher. A quiet, methodical, contemplative thinker would be repeatedly traumatized by the fast footwork needed as a public defender or district attorney. Therefore, it is important to analyze both yourself and the work you think you want to do so that you consider your personality and your style in relation to the work and its style: do they mesh rather than grate?

ANALYZE YOUR PERSONALITY AND STYLE COMPARED TO YOUR DESIRED WORK

If your personality and style aren't suitable for certain types of work or for dealing with certain kinds of people, you will be like a badly aligned auto, able to function but bumping along painfully, possibly damaging both internal and external systems. To avoid this situation, it is important to consider your personality and style in relation to those of your coworkers and the requirements of your work.

An interesting career assessment instrument that can help you analyze your personality and communications style is the Myers-Briggs Type Indicator (MBTI). The MBTI is administered in companies (and a growing number of law firms) that want to foster clearer, more effective communication and teamwork among their members. The MBTI is also increasingly being used to correlate personality types and career satisfaction. It describes several basic personality preferences that indicate where you prefer to expend your energy, how you prefer to acquire information, and how you make decisions. While no career assessment "test" can give you a definitive answer as to what work you should do, your MBTI results may steer you toward work roles that may be more satisfying and away from those that do not draw on your strengths.

The following brief explanation of the MBTI may help you decide whether the information you can gain from it would be beneficial. The MBTI is based on psychologist Carl Jung's theories of personality types. Jung believed that there were two principal dimensions of personality that guide life. He presented these two dimensions as two opposing personality preferences at each end of a continuum: sensing/intuition and thinking/feeling.

The sensing/intuition dimension refers to an individual's preferred way of gathering information. In Jungian theory, people who have a sensing preference focus on concrete information drawn from their five senses, and they look at life from a practical, live-in-the-here-and-now approach. People with an intuitive preference are more visionary and look at new ideas and possibilities.

The thinking/feeling dimension refers to an individual's preferred way of making decisions. People with a thinking preference are logical and analytical, basing decisions on objective analysis of cause and effect, whereas people with a feeling preference are more concerned with interpersonal relations, values, and harmony. This is not to say that people with one preference don't also engage in some of the behaviors of the opposing preference. Indeed, we generally need to use all of the preferences at various times in our daily routines. Jungian preferences are similar to left versus right handedness; we strongly prefer to use one hand rather than the other. We can, if necessary, use the non-preferred hand, but doing so is often awkward, slow, and uncomfortable.

The mother-daughter creators of the MBTI elaborated on two additional personality dimensions, again each having two poles; extraversion/introversion and judging/perceiving.

The extraversion/introversion dimension refers to an individual's preferred way of interacting with the world. People with an extraversion preference (maintaining Jung's original spelling, since the term as used in the MBTI does not have the same connotation as the more common "extroverted") focus externally, preferring to gather their energy or stimulation from the world outside of themselves, whereas people with an introversion preference search inside themselves for ideas and rejuvenation.

The last dimension, judging/perception, refers to an individual's preferred way of organizing her daily activities. People with a judging preference like life to be planned and organized, reaching closure on issues, whereas people with a perceiving preference like to keep their options open, with a more spontaneous and flexible approach.

The MBTI takes these four sets of personality preferences and breaks them down into sixteen possible combinations or personality types, then ascribes certain overall characteristics for each type. What is interesting is that each combination has its own interests, skills, and values—that's what makes the world go 'round. However, various career fields and job descriptions seem to attract a disproportionate number of some types. Law is no different in that regard.

Larry Richard, a trial lawyer turned psychologist, administered the MBTI to 3,000 practicing attorneys, all active members of the American Bar Association and, therefore, presumably somewhat happy with their work. His results indicated that 57 percent of lawyers are Introverts (versus 25 percent of the general public), and 57 percent are Intuitors (versus 30 percent of the general public). This may surprise those of you who stereotype the average lawyer (even if the stereotype doesn't fit you or your friends) as outgoing and gregarious, one who deals with facts and not hypotheses. While preferring introversion does not mean that a lawyer dislikes public speaking or being with others, it does mean that time has to be allocated for quiet reflection. Similarly, while preferring intuition does not mean that a lawyer will disregard practical realities—since any good attorney worth her salt must address factual issues continuously—it does mean that she will often look to the future and plan for possibilities.

In the other two categories, the lawyers' scores are not at all surprising. Seventy-eight percent of the respondents were Thinkers (versus 48 percent of the general public), and 63 percent were Judgers (versus 55 percent of the general public). Again, this doesn't mean that lawyers haven't any concern or capacity for harmony (feeling) or spontaneity (perceiving)—it just means that their preferred mode of dealing with the world is through logic and decisiveness. For information on Richard's study of lawyers and the MBTI, see "Testing" at the end of chapter 5. You can read more about the MBTI itself in the books listed in that same section.

If you decide to take the MBTI, you may find that your type is comparable to that of the majority of lawyers—or not. Either way, the results do not mean that you will or won't be a happy and successful practitioner simply because you do or do not fit the norm. All they mean is that if you differ from the lawyer norm, you may have to stretch a bit to adjust your preferred style to fit with that of your colleagues. But the results of your MBTI are of interest to see both how much of a stretch you might have to make and also what practice areas might fit better for you, since certain personality types are more often in sync with one style or practice area than another.

According to Dr. Jeff Prince, clinical director of Counseling and Psychological Services at the University of California at Berkeley, specific lawyering skills may work best with certain personality preferences. The chart below from one of the workshops he presented for Lawyers in Transition^{SM} will give you an idea about how preferences may complement the various skills.

Skill	MBTI Preference
Problem solving	Intuition and Thinking
Legal analysis and reasoning	Thinking
Legal reseach	Intuition and Thinking
Factual investigation	Sensing and Thinking
Communication	
Written	Introversion
Verbal	Extraversion
Listening	Introversion
Counseling	Intuition and Feeling
Negotiation	Extraversion and Intuition and Feeling
Litigation	Extraversion and Intuition and Thinking
Organization and management	Sensing and Thinking and Judgment
Ethics	Intuition and Feeling

Thus, if you do an analysis of some of the legal practice areas or styles of practice and compare them to your MBTI results, you may be able to select a focus that fits you more comfortably. For example, if you are an Extravert, you may want to work with groups of other people, or at least be at the center of the action. Marketing your own law practice or becoming your law firm's rainmaker will get you out among the hordes. You will want to work where your ability to think on your feet and formulate your thoughts under pressure is appreciated—trial or hearing work, as a district attorney or public defender, taking depositions, as a negotiator, appearing at regulatory or administrative hearings.

If you are an Introvert, you probably prefer communicating in writing, and listening rather than talking. So look for jobs where you get to spend quiet time doing research—with the courts, legal publishers, legal research services, contract research for other lawyers, working in real estate or intellectual property law, or other practices where a lot of time is spent alone drafting documents. Jobs where listening skills are important are in a probate, estate planning, or tax practice, or as a hearing officer or administrative law judge. You may also be more comfortable in a small office or in a firm with smaller practice groups.

If you are a Sensor, you are probably more concerned with tangible, practical results and the facts and data found in some general business and corporate practices, as well as real estate and tax law. Certain types of environmental, financial planning, and intellectual property practices also will provide you with tangible results.

If you are an Intuitor, abstract meaning and conceptual relationships are most important, so you may do well in some general litigation areas, labor and employee relations, international or criminal law, conceiving trial strategy, or business planning.

If you are a Thinker, you generally value logic, objectivity, and making the "right" decisions without consideration of your personal preferences. While Thinkers are prevalent in all law practices, areas such as litigation, structuring large business deals, tax and estate planning, or complex class action lawsuits should engage your penchant for problem solving.

Feelers are in the minority among lawyers—only 22 percent in Larry Richard's ABA study. But if you are a Feeler, you base your decisions on your personal values and are sensitive to harmony and humane solutions. You may want to consider family, adoption, environmental, elder, immigration, criminal, or employment discrimination law. Mediation may feel right to you.

Lawyers with a Judging preference like to live and work in a planned, orderly way; I would recommend those practice areas where the Judger has some control over scheduling and where there is closure of issues, such as probate, tax, and real estate law. If you are a Judger, look for a firm where your organizational skills—and ability to timely produce your assignments—will be admired, or set up your own practice with your own format. Be sensitive to visual and auditory cues when interviewing—look at the arrangement of the office to see if it is organized and functional, and listen for decisiveness in the interviewing attorney. Do not take a job with, or stay assigned for long to, an attorney who is disorganized or indecisive. You will quickly begin to tear your hair out.

If you are a Perceivor, you like to be spontaneous and keep your options open until the last minute, which is sometimes difficult in law practice. You are curious and like to learn as much as possible; client interviewing, investigation, and research would probably interest you as long as you know when to stop. Litigation practice can have benefits and detriments for you—you will respond to surprises well, but you will perhaps have a difficult time meeting all the deadlines. Your prodigious capacity for taking in information can be used in appellate and securities work.

To clarify the components of the various preferences and how they differ, I have taken the following four charts, prepared by Dr. Prince for a Lawyers in Transition[SM] workshop, and added my comments wherever I thought they might be useful. Dr. Prince's material is in boldface.

I.
INTROVERSION vs. EXTRAVERSION

Communications/Meetings:
Preparation vs. Spontaneous

Introverts like to reflect before making a decision or voicing an opinion—send them a memo. Extraverts usually think as they talk. They need to hear themselves speak in order to solidify a thought—corner them at the water cooler. Introverts, while they can function well in groups for short periods, find it necessary to retreat in order to replenish their energy and refocus their thoughts. They are inward-directed. The more people that Extraverts are around, the more energized they become. They thrive as the center of attention—they are outward directed.

Developing Clients/Practice:
One-on-one, writing vs. Networking, public speaking

Introverts prefer developing in-depth, individual relationships and communicating through e-mail, fax, or letters. They often do best in office-based practices, with quiet for concentration. Extraverts prefer developing relationships with many people through telephone calls, networking and oral presentations—they would be happy never to read a memo or receive an e-mail. They like activity and to have other people around. They are the rainmakers.

II.
SENSING vs. INTUITION

Job Duties:
Fact finding, information gathering vs.
Legal concepts, problem solving

Sensors gather their information though sight, smell, taste, sound, and touch. They are very attuned to the real world and the realities of its activities. Intuitors are often said to have a "sixth sense," prefer to follow their hunches, and like to look at the broad picture.

Job Focus:
Practical implementation vs. Future project focus

Sensors thoroughly and systematically focus on what works now. Intuitors, always considering possibilities, prefer to focus on new ways to do things.

Name Calling

Sensors can be called **"Bean Counters"** because of their focus on detail and precision and their lack of inspiration. Intuitors may be called **"Head in the Clouds"** because of their inattention to detail, always daydreaming of possibilities.

III.
THINKING vs. FEELING
(this is the most important predictor of lawyer dissatisfaction)

Values:
Seek truth and justice vs. Follow personal values

Thinkers respond more to ideas and logic than to feelings. If the firm's bottom line requires it, they can fire a close friend. They are tough-minded and may unknowingly hurt people's feelings. Feelers can usually see how a choice affects others; they ask how a layoff would affect the morale of the firm.

Adversarial vs. Harmony

Thinkers have no problem taking an opposing position based on logic. Feelers want to please others and dislike dealing with unpleasant situations.

Tasks:
Legal analysis vs. Counseling, ethics

Thinkers are excellent analysts and can predict the logical outcome of a choice. Feelers often have their finger on the pulse of an organization and are the moral rudder. They want to know the person; the Thinker wants to know the fact.

IV.
JUDGING vs. PERCEPTION
(this is a frequent predictor of work-related conflicts)

Workstyle:
Planning and milestones vs. Last minute changes

Judgers like to plan; they set a due date and plan their work to finish accordingly. They love making detailed checklists—and love even more when they can check off items. Because they prefer to resolve things quickly, they often make overly hasty decisions. Perceivers hate feeling hemmed in by calendar items—they have a great capacity to "go with the flow" and take last-minute changes in stride. Their checklists, if they even have one, have reminders of the things they want to accomplish "someday." Because Perceivers want to know as much as possible, they may have difficulty ending their information gathering and come to a decision.

Name Calling:
"Inflexible" vs. "Not Serious"

Judgers can be seen as rigid, planned too tightly with no ability to improvise. They plan their goals and keep to them. On the other hand, Perceivers can be viewed as flighty. If they set goals, they often don't accomplish them, and they often start too many projects and finish too few.

Job Tasks:
Organizational management vs. Crisis management

Judgers put a calendaring system to effective use; they like to schedule every step of a project. They hate last minute changes. They are great organizers, of both people and things. Perceivers are great at working under pressure and adapt well to changing situations. They often have the ability to see opportunities and seize them.

If you feel the MBTI would benefit your self-assessment and career analysis, you will need to locate a counselor or a counseling center that is licensed to administer and interpret it for you. You might find it helpful to locate a counselor who has experience interpreting the MBTI for lawyers.

• How Can You Change Your Job or Practice Area?

If you are a brand-new attorney, you should exercise the option to pick a practice area (family, business, probate, tax, or environmental law are examples) and style of working (litigation, transactional, research and writing) that fits with your personality, interests, skills and values. See chapter 5 for a more complete discussion of these issues.

If you are either an attorney in your first few years of practice or a partner in a law firm, you can change your practice focus with relative ease. The somewhat inexperienced lawyer could, for example, request a transfer from litigation to transactional work, or from the real estate to the tax department. But before making this request, you should assess how satisfied your superiors are with your work. If you are already on shaky ground, you may immediately be given your walking papers. If your request is honored, you may be required to take a year or two backstep on your partnership progression in order to learn the new area of law. But if you're more satisfied with your job, you'll probably do better work and eventually make partner anyhow. Roy was a second-year business litigation associate in a midsize firm. Although he received very good evaluations, he knew he wasn't happy as a litigator. So when his request to transfer to the business transaction group was accepted, he was willing to accept his firm's contention that his training was beginning anew. He lost credit for his two years on partnership track and had to start as if he were a new associate. Seven years later he made partner, two years behind his class, but Roy has never regretted his choice to switch practice styles.

If you are already a partner in a firm and want to make changes, it is necessary for you to determine how supportive your partners will be. It is also important to anticipate their concerns and present solutions. For example, because your billable hours may drop while you are trying to cultivate business in a new area of the law, you could agree to reduce your income share accordingly. However, your new specialty may prove to be financially beneficial to your partners' work—your decision to target corporate employment issues may meld well with the general business consultation that several of your partners offer their clients, creating a more full-service feel to your firm.

If you are a solo practitioner, you can change your practice focus at any time, as long as you are prepared to endure a possible reduction in income until you have cultivated new clientele. However, a drop in income is not always necessary if you watch for appropriate opportunities. Alan was a general practice attorney, focusing mainly on business litigation and patent law. When he won a large judgment for a client in an age discrimination lawsuit against a major employer, he took full advantage of the resulting publicity by touting himself as a successful employment lawyer. As a result, he received several new employment law clients, and he was then off and running in this new practice area.

Although it's not easy to change the focus or style of your law practice, the following five steps have proven effective for some people who have made these changes:

1. Ask for work from a partner who is in the practice area you want to learn. As you develop some abilities in the new area, ask for more work to develop more skills and confidence.

2. If you are on your own, affiliate on a case with another lawyer who works in your desired practice area. You should be willing to do the "grunt" work in order to learn from an experienced

practitioner. This is a great way to develop a mentor and scope out the new area without making a complete commitment until you decide you really like it. Thom had practiced criminal law for eighteen years and wanted a change. Because his daughter has cerebral palsy, he decided he might have an interest in disability law. After researching which firms in town handled that practice area, Thom proposed that he would assist, for free, on a few of their cases, in exchange for some mentoring in disability law and the experience of working on an actual disability case. One firm accepted his proposal, and he is now spending about ten hours a week learning disability law and meeting other lawyers practicing in this area.

3. Volunteer for your bar association's pro bono panel and request to be assigned to work with a lawyer experienced in the area you'd like to move into. You will then receive both education and possible contacts. You probably shouldn't go it alone on a pro bono case as a beginner—that would not be training and it might be terror.

4. Attend legal education classes in your desired practice area, as well as meetings of relevant bar associations. You'll learn new information and meet lawyers working in this field.

5. Combine new growth areas with previous experience—for instance, moving acquisitions and mergers experience into corporate reorganization or bankruptcy work, or using a business litigation background as a springboard to mediate business disputes.

• Career and Job Hunting Books, Newspapers, and Web Sites

Spend some time in a large bookstore or library, browsing through the titles in its career section—there are hundreds! You will be amazed at the diversity of ideas and career possibilities presented. There will be "how-to" books with suggestions for options you never knew existed (and some of them may be exciting to you). Go to the career services office at your law school—many have printed resource materials as well as access to on-line career resources. Also, if you have access to the Internet, browse the Web—there are numerous job hunting and career information resources on-line. Type in the word "career" in a search engine such as Yahoo or Excite.

Dictionary of Occupational Titles, U.S. Department of Labor, updated periodically, most recent is 1996. Contains descriptions of more than 12,000 jobs. Available at most career centers, law school placement offices, bookstores or public libraries.

Occupational Outlook Handbook, U.S. Department of Labor, 1998. On-line at stats.bls.gov/ocohome.htm. Updated every two years, with over 200 career descriptions divided into occupational clusters to facilitate review of similar positions. Available at most career centers, law school placement offices, and public libraries.

The Three Boxes of Life (And How To Get Out of Them), Richard Bolles, Ten Speed Press, 1978. No routine or preconceived life or work plan allowed here. A nice perspective on the topic of work/play/learning balance in your life. Still current and a best-seller after all these years.

Your Money or Your Life: Transforming Your Relationship with Money and Achieving Financial Independence, Joe Dominguez and Vicki Robin, Penguin USA, 1993. A good look at work, life, and financial priorities for those of you who feel you can't take a financial backstep.

What Color Is Your Parachute? A Practical Manual for Job-Hunters & Career Changers, Richard Nelson Bolles, Ten Speed Press, generally updated yearly. The "bible" of career change; you will definitely know who you are and what you want if you can get through all the many excellent written exercises. Has an extensive bibliography and a section on using the Internet for job hunting. Can be accessed on-line at www.washingtonpost.com/parachute. Once at the website, you can access the many excellent links to career resources webwide.

Wishcraft: How to Get What You Really Want, Barbara Sher, Ballantine Books, reissue edition, 1986. A book that encourages the reader to dream, then gives guidelines to achieving those dreams and goals. Highly recommended for attorneys, who tend to have a narrow focus on life and work.

I Could Do Anything I Want If I Only Knew What It Was, Barbara Sher, Delacorte Press, 1995. Excellent examination of the quandaries faced when trying to choose a new field, along with exercises and specific ideas.

It's Only Too Late If You Don't Start Now: How to Create Your Second Life After Forty, Barbara Sher, Delacorte Press, 1998.

Do What You Love, The Money Will Follow, Marsha Sinetar, Delacorte Press, reissued 1989. An inspirational guide to reexamining one's attitudes toward life, love, and work.

The Complete Job-Search Handbook, Howard Figler, Henry Holt, 1988. For the reader who knows what he or she wants and is ready to develop opportunities in a targeted area of work.

For salary information on the Internet, go to jobsmart.org/tools/salary/index.htm.

Transitions: Making Sense of Life's Changes, William Bridges, Addison-Wesley, 1980. Deals with the various transitions in life and how to get through them and even appreciate them. An all-time best-selling book, and highly recommended.

When Smart People Fail: Rebuilding Yourself for Success, Hyatt & Gottlieb, Penguin Books, 1993. Helps you kick-start a new move.

Career Shifting: Starting Over in a Changing Economy, William Charland, Jr., Bob Adams, Inc., 1993. Describes developing new fields and how to shift into them.

Creating You & Co.: Learn to Think Like the CEO of Your Own Career, William Bridges, Addison-Wesley Publishing, 1997. "The key to constructing successful careers," says Bridges, "is to think not as an employee in a job but as head of a small independent company supplying an employer."

Amazon On-Line Bookstore (at www.amazon.com) lists 2.5 million titles, a number of which relate to career and job hunting. Search under the word "career" to locate many useful books that you can order on-line, or find these publications at your local bookstore or library.

Jobs '98 (annual), Kathryn Ross and George Petras, Fireside Press, 1997. A complete guide to jobs, from entry to executive level, in numerous career areas, including industry trends, job descriptions, and salary levels.

Adams Electronic Job Search Almanac 1998, edited by Emily Ehrenstein, Adams Publications, 1997. For job hunting on the Internet, with information on techniques to find job listings and create and post a resume.

The U.S. Bureau of Labor Statistics has a website (stats.bls.gov) which offers job market trends and salary information.

CareerNet is a website that has information and links to other career-related sites. Access it at www.careers.org/.

Getting Unstuck: Breaking Through Your Barriers to Change, Sidney B. Simon, M.D., Warner Books, 1989. Examines barriers to change and sets out exercises to help overcome them. Audio version, issued in 1996 by Simon & Schuster, is available.

Preventing Job Burnout: Transforming Work Pressures into Productivity, Beverly A. Potter, Crisp Publications 1995. Discusses the causes of burnout and gives strategies to beat it.

The Whole Work Catalog contains descriptions of numerous books and videos on every facet of career selection and change— options, resumes, interviewing, etc. You can order any of the books/videos that are in the catalog. To receive a free catalog, contact The New Careers Center, P.O. Box 339, Boulder, CO 80306; (800) 634-9024.

110 Biggest Mistakes Job Hunters Make and How to Avoid Them, Linda Sutherland and Richard Hermann 2nd edition, 1994, $19.95. A guide to avoiding job hunt problems, with a bibliography of job sources and reference books. Order from Federal Reports, 1010 Vermont Avenue, N.W., Suite 408, Washington, D.C. 20005; (800) 296–9611.

The Career Development Resources Catalog contains descriptions of books and videos covering career change, self-assessment, resumes, and more. Contact Career Research & Testing, P.O. Box 611930, San Jose, CA 95161-1930; (800) 888-4945, e-mail info@careertrainer.com for a free catalog.

Balancing Acts: Juggling Love, Work, Family and Recreation, Stautberg & Worthing, Master Media, 1992.

Breathing Space: Living and Working at a Comfortable Pace in a Sped-Up Society, Jeff Davidson, Master Media, 1992.

Comfort Zones: Planning Your Future, Elwood Chapman, Crisp Publications, 4th edition, 1997. A retirement planning workbook.

The Wall Street Journal and its *National Business Employment Weekly* have a listing of nationwide professional positions, plus a calendar of events of upcoming programs on job/career change. Call (800) JOB HUNT or check on-line at careers.wsj.com/ or www.nbew.com/, respectively.

Parting Company: How to Survive the Loss of a Job and Find Another Successfully, William Morin and James Cabrera, Harcourt Brace, revised 1991.

Between Opportunities: A Survival Guide for Job Seekers, Robert Riskin, Aar Dee Aar Publishing, 1993.

There are a number of job–hunting sites on the Internet that have job listings, career resources, and other information useful to someone who is evaluating career options; for example, try the Online Career Center at www.occ.com or The Monster Board at www.monster.com. See also the websites listed in chapter 8.

The Only Job-Hunting Guide You'll Ever Need: The Most Comprehensive Guide for Job Hunters and Career Switchers, Kathryn and Ross Petras, Fireside Press, revised 1995. Includes all the basics: how to write a resume, research a company, get an interview, prepare for it, follow it up, and agree on an employment package.

Job Smart, at jobsmart.org, was developed by a librarian and is an extensive and well–organized on-line catalog of useful career information sites, directed to California jobseekers, but with good general resources as well. It is updated every thirty days. It has diverse sections, including one called Salary Information, which now registers 50,000 hits a day.

Hook Up, Get Hired!; The Internet Job Search Revolution, Joyce Lain Kennedy (nationally syndicated career columnist), John Wiley, 1995. Shows how job seekers can view 100,000+ on-line job ads, and put their resumes on-line. No Internet experience is assumed.

• Career Counselors and Career Counseling Centers

Some of you may decide to work with a career counselor. Be sure to ask what his or her credentials, training, and experience are. Ask for a few references and call them. Also trust your intuition—if you don't feel comfortable with the person, don't work with her.

When selecting a career counselor, it is important to inquire whether the individual has previously worked with attorneys. Most career changers are attempting to climb the corporate ladder, whereas lawyers who leave traditional legal jobs or the law are often perceived as descending in prestige. A counselor who has not worked with attorneys may spend time attempting to discourage a transition and will not have information on relevant resources or options.

Do not expect a counselor to give you "the answer" to your career quest. If someone promises to tell you what to do or help you find the one perfect job, immediately proceed to a different career counselor. Just as in psychological therapy, a good counselor can help you find answers and direct you to relevant options and resources, but no one but you knows which career choice is best for you.

Avoid counselors who charge an up-front flat fee for career counseling, rather than an hourly rate. If you decide you do not like working with that counselor, you are out of luck, but you can terminate your relationship with an hourly fee counselor at any time. Additionally, beware of expensive, up-front, flat-fee organizations which advertise that they will counsel you and then, "because they are so well-connected," will find you jobs with big salaries (and the BIG money is always pushed). They generally have no secrets not known by more reasonably priced and hourly rate counselors, and most do not have connections— instead they give you library books and show you how to research your own connections. Buyer beware!

RESOURCES

The National Board for Certified Career Counselors will provide you with a list of NBCC certified career counselors in your area. Contact the NBCC at 3-D Terrace Way, Greensboro, NC 27403; (336) 547-0607, www.nbcc.org.

The International Association of Counseling Services, 101 S. Whiting Street, #211, Alexandria, VA 22304; (703) 823-9840, mason.gmu.edu/~iacs has a directory containing listings of non-profit and private counseling centers nationwide.

Career services offices at some law schools offer counseling to their students and alumni. Most of these offices also know of other local counselors or career centers that work with lawyers.

Career counseling centers at community or junior colleges may be more appropriate for entry-level applicants, but their services are, by and large, free, and they can administer various self-assessment and career evaluation tests at relatively low cost to get you started (including the Myers–Briggs Type Indicator). Additionally, many colleges and universities run career counseling offices for students and alumni and, at times, the public (for a fee).

There are **Experience Unlimited groups of the Employment Development Department** in many states; these are free job clubs for professionals. They are located in many communities and have career resource books, support groups, and services for job hunting professionals. Contact your state's unemployment office to see if it sponsors an employment office for professionals. Also inquire whether that office has a directory of other non-profit career counseling centers.

Forty-Plus is an excellent self-help career counseling and net-working organization for white-collar and professional workers over forty years old. There are branches in major cities around the country.

Many larger communities have non-profit career centers that often coordinate their information and resources with the local business community. Most cities, and even many smaller towns, have for-profit counseling centers. Ask around for recommendations to a good center.

CHAPTER THREE

———⇒●⇐———

Taking the Plunge and
Leaving the Law

You may fail, but if you don't try, you surely will fail.
—FROM THE MOVIE *Sounder*

Have you ever thought of leaving law, just to find out if the grass is *really* greener somewhere else? Michael often daydreamed about becoming a chef. He finally quit his legal work and trained at a culinary academy in France, returning to the United States to cook for a few years in several sophisticated restaurants. However, Michael is once again practicing law; he found that working as a professional chef in an upscale restaurant made law practice feel easy.

We lawyers somehow think that we are the only workers, professional or otherwise, who experience stress, work under severe time constraints, or have demanding clients. Michael learned that a chef has to deal with these issues on a continual basis, and generally for a lower salary!

For lawyers, our profession is often an identity—we don't say we "practice law," we say, "I am a lawyer." Being a lawyer is an identity that confers status, a badge of achievement paid for with perseverance and hard work. Therefore, for many lawyers, contemplating leaving the law altogether is quite frightening. It creates a feeling of deprivation—a loss of identity—and makes them feel as if they've "given up" and become unsuccessful.

Additionally, many lawyers are afraid of the accusation that they are "quitters," not capable of successful law practice. That fear overlooks the fact that many of my clients have had successful practices or worked well in various jobs for several years before they decided to make a change. Others knew from the time they were in law school that the traditional practice of law was not for them, that they wanted to use their legal training as a stepping-stone to other fields. Others chose to go into law without sufficiently knowing what the practice entailed, and once into it, they realized it was not to their liking.

Leaving law for any of these reasons should be seen not as "quitting" but as merely shifting direction, because lawyer career changers will continue to use the information and skills they gained from their legal training and practice. So they are not quitting, just using their skills differently. Bob, who opened his own gourmet Chinese restaurant after seventeen years of legal practice and cooking for friends on the weekend, said that his legal training didn't help his stir-fry, but it certainly continues to inform his negotiations with vendors, landlords, and employees. He doesn't feel he "quit" practicing law. Instead, he applies his legal skills when needed, rather than on a daily basis.

Many of my clients cling to their legal job because of the credibility it gives them or because they feel they have spent many years learning the field and should therefore give it one more chance. But for some, a move to work outside of law would be more productive, and certainly more satisfying.

Obviously, a large number of new law graduates feel that work outside of the legal profession is a better choice for them; according to the National Association for Law Placement in Washington, D.C., nearly 10 percent of the 1996 class graduating from the 179 American Bar Association–accredited law schools— 37,152 graduates—did not take a legal job.

How do you know if you should avoid a legal job? When does it become time to divorce yourself completely from the law? And what does it take to make the mental and actual transition from "lawyer" to "something else"?

• Should You Stay Where You Are?

Are you really so unhappy that you need to quit your job immediately and rush off to Tahiti? If you haven't been at your present position very long, maybe what's bothering you can be overcome by making some adjustment at your current job. The following are some points you should consider:

The grass is not always greener outside the law. Ask Michael, the former chef. Or perhaps Albert, who left law to manage a large, publicly traded printing company. Overseeing the work and personnel issues of numerous employees, developing budgets and adhering to them, meeting impossibly short deadlines for printing jobs (yes, other fields also have unreasonable clients), and working under the scrutiny of a board of directors made him rethink his career change. Albert, too, is now back working in a law firm, and happier for it.

Additionally, it is very important to ask yourself candidly whether your perceived dissatisfaction with your work and your desire to graze in greener pastures are actually a reflection of other dissatisfactions in your life, which you project onto your working hours. Job change does not adhere to the Cinderella fantasy, where a fairy godmother can wave a wand and immediately create a gorgeous dress and makeup job, causing all other aspects of her protégée's life to immensely improve. A new job will not magically transform your marriage/weight/love life/hair/ finances/bowling score/golf game from a pumpkin into a golden carriage.

Stick with your job if it provides good training and you continue to learn. You may find that you eventually discover a niche—keep in mind that it takes at least several years to become a good trial attorney or negotiator or estate planner. Clarence Darrow was not a first- or second-year associate! Or as Eddie Cantor, the vaudeville, singing, and film star once replied when asked the secret of his rise to fame, "It takes twenty years to become an overnight success."

If your unhappiness is caused by the fear of not knowing the law or procedure in your area, with increased practice you will develop more expertise and comfort. Perhaps this additional training will eventually help you move to a corporate counsel position, since most corporations want their new attorneys to have some prior law firm experience.

Or use the training to open your own office, with solid knowledge and a community contact base acquired on someone else's dime. Sally did that. She worked at a fifteen-person firm for three years, knowing that she would eventually practice on her own when the time was right. During those three years, she requested and was given work on cases in a number of practice areas and was fortunate to receive good instruction on unfamiliar issues from members of her firm. She performed valuable work in exchange for the training and salary she was paid, but when she felt that she had sufficient legal knowledge and contacts in the community, she left to open her own office, able to service her clients immediately, with confidence in her legal abilities.

If your firm is expanding and taking on new clients and you take the opportunity to be involved in business development or maintaining clients, you will become very valuable to your firm. If client involvement and business development are areas that interest you, be assured you will become an asset at your firm and be encouraged to do more of what you like. If you are consistently bringing in new business you will also position yourself for bonuses and promotions.

If your firm or company has good clients, your work should progressively get more interesting and challenging. When your work does develop in substance, especially as you are given more responsibility, you might then feel sufficiently engaged. For example, for the first year that Barry worked in a 150 lawyer firm, he spent much of his time doing legal research and writing. When he came to see me, he complained that he wanted more complex work with increased client contact. When we discussed the career paths of several of the senior associates in his firm, he realized that if he stayed with his job, he would gradually be given more client contact and responsibility. As his experience grew, so would the complexity of the issues he handled.

Because a good mentor is not always easy to find, reconsider leaving your job if you have such a mentor. One of the chief complaints I hear from new attorneys is that they are flung in the deep end of the legal pool, given major assignments to weigh them down and then left to flounder unassisted. They complain that no one takes the time to explain, let alone guide them. So if you have found a good mentor, you are fortunate, and you may want to rethink a change, at least while the relationship continues to develop and remains fruitful.

If you are given good client contact, it means your supervisors view you with respect. You can then anticipate that eventually you will be able to request and exercise more authority over your work, both in content and style.

If business at your firm is good, and if associates are being made partners there is opportunity for you to grow along with the firm. Room for expansion, along with opportunity for growth, are two major considerations before deciding whether to quit your job, balanced by an examination of whether any other work will allow for the same responsibility and remuneration. Remember, if your firm grows and you proceed up the responsibility ladder, you can sometimes shape your job with your own vision of what you want it to be. Dwayne did. He had decided that he wanted to become an administrative hearing specialist and help his firm cultivate legal work that would require his appearance before administrative bodies or judges. When he started at his firm, Dwayne probably would have been shown the door if he had suggested he wanted to work so narrowly. But once he was a senior associate with a proven track record, his presentation to the partnership about the benefits to the firm of developing an administrative hearing department, with him as the rainmaker and primary specialist, was given a warm reception.

• Should You Get Out?

So you've looked at whether you should stay with your current job or change jobs and/or careers. Maybe, after considering the above points, you've now decided that you don't want to make any changes at this time, even though you don't really love your work. However, perhaps you should still consider changing jobs if:

1. **You are not excited by what you are doing even though the monetary rewards are high.** Although the majority of lawyers don't earn the enormous sums that the public thinks they do (remember that the median income of lawyers across the United States is about $60,000), many do earn well above the average income paid to other white-collar and professional workers. However, if every day is drudgery or if you can't imagine spending another year in your job (let alone another ten), a large income probably isn't enough recompense. Perhaps when you were first hired at your job, the large salary or impressive status of your firm kept you going. But once the initial excitement of a new position wears off, if there isn't something other than money to give you satisfaction, you should probably begin to look elsewhere. Keep in mind that realistically there are few jobs that are exciting every day (fire fighting? skydiving?), but it *is* important to feel positive about your work. A public defender once told me that she had loved her work for six years—but she had now been in the P.D.'s office for eight years, and that was two years too long. She was bored, and it was time to move on.

2. **Advancement is blocked.** Moving to another job or field may be advisable if your firm is laying off partners, the company is closing offices, or there is only one general counsel position and the holder of that job has been there for fifteen years and is only forty-five years old.

3. **You don't like rainmaking and client maintenance.** If it is necessary to engage in these tasks in order to succeed at your firm, you may want to look elsewhere. However, to avoid these requirements, you don't necessarily have to move out of law,

but just out of a law firm. Lawyers in government, corporate, public interest, or legal publishing jobs, for example, don't have to cultivate clients, although maintaining good relationships and good customer service is a requisite for any good lawyer in any job.

4. The company or firm is badly managed and is losing clients. You should probably move on fairly quickly, since you could be associated with the failure. Or worse yet, in a smaller firm, you could be held jointly liable for the mismanagement of the clients' cases. And you will probably soon be out of work anyway if the firm or company is doing so poorly. It is better to leave by your choice than to be fired or laid off, since less emotional baggage attaches to a voluntary decision to quit.

5. You are not adequately rewarded for your work. If you are not sufficiently compensated, you don't receive adequate benefits, your work is not given the recognition it is due, or you are not treated with respect, you should think about moving on to a new opportunity that does give you these basic elements of meaningful work.

6. You are not fulfilling your dreams. If you have had a special dream forever in the back of your mind and are not pursuing it, it may be time to do so. While there is a pervasive myth that "somewhere out there is the perfect job," it *is* just a myth. If your job were perfect, you would probably be willing to do it for free. Lawyers, who are taught to be perfectionists in their legal practice, dotting every i and crossing every t, think that their career should also be perfect. But even those who love their work are said to give it a "complete satisfaction" rating only 75 percent of the time, which means that they have less than complete satisfaction with their work 25 percent of the time. Every job has irritations and dissatisfactions—the reality is that you won't find a job without them.

• Career Myths

Just as there persists the myth of the perfect job, most people unconsciously carry around other myths that negatively affect their ability to manage career change. If you have a subconscious belief that prevents you from taking a risk, making a change, or having the confidence to explore an alternative job, you will always find a reason not to look for a new job. Your myths tell you in advance that you won't get it or can't have it. Those myths that put extreme pressure on a new job choice will likewise stop any exploration: If you feel that the right job will make everything in your life run smoothly, then selecting the "right" job becomes almost too scary, since the "wrong" job will make your life terrible. That's why it is so important to recognize, clarify, and respond to the myths you carry.

The statements below are "myths" because they are incomplete pictures of reality.

- **MYTH:** Finding the right job will make my personal and professional life complete.
- **MYTH:** Only artists, musicians, and athletes are lucky enough to do work they love.
- **MYTH:** I'm too_____(old or young, over or under qualified, experienced or inexperienced, etc.) to be thinking about changing careers.
- **MYTH:** It's who you know, not what you know, that is the basis for career success.
- **MYTH:** I have only a few marketable skills as an attorney.
- **MYTH:** Somewhere out there is the one career that will fit perfectly with my values, skills, and interests.
- **MYTH:** Once I've selected a goal, getting there is mostly a matter of luck.
- **MYTH:** Each and every job requires one specific set of talents and skills.
- **MYTH:** Once I've decided on my career path, the decision is final, and my future is secure.

All of the above are false. But we often believe them because they either allow us to avoid the effort of moving ahead or relieve us of the responsibility for the poor choices we might make. What are your career myths, and how do they impact your ability to manage career change?

• Barriers to Making a Change

If you are contemplating leaving law, it is important to acknowledge and confront the barriers that many career changers erect for themselves. These barriers can make any change more difficult, or even impossible. Which of these barriers block *your* forward movement?

An overload of "I don't want to." Every person has things they don't want to do, even if those things would be beneficial— becoming more organized, losing weight, maintaining an exercise program. Here's a sampling of "I don't want to" attitudes that can stymie job hunters by narrowing the opportunities they will consider.

• "I don't want to work at a temporary job." Temp jobs are an excellent way for you to preview a law firm or company and show off your skills at the same time. Often temporary jobs become permanent.

• "I don't want to make less money." Consider the entire package, including benefits and perks, before deciding if the new opportunity nets you less. Also, when changing careers, it is often necessary to take a step back in income until you prove your mettle and pay your dues.

• "I don't want to work for a small (or large) company (or law firm)." Small offices can be collegial or stifling, and large companies or firms can have small departments or practice groups that are like those small offices. It is best not to generalize but instead to investigate the individual opportunity.

• "I don't want to take a step back in authority (prestige, control, etc.)." However temporarily disquieting a "step down" might be, the opportunity it provides may allow eventual access to increased satisfaction or success.

An unrealistic agenda set by yourself or others. You may have decided to become a lawyer to be like Perry Mason or those practitioners on *L.A. Law,* or maybe you went to law school to please a relative or because you sat as a juror in a moot court trial when you were in high school. But you must now come to terms with the fact that law practice isn't a moot court trial or *L.A. Law* with its glamorous, sexy, well-coiffed and well-clothed attorneys. It's not Perry Mason either, where cases resolved within an hour, misanthropes always confessed on the witness stand, and legal documents appeared, magically researched and written by some scribe who was never seen. You need to reconcile your underlying agenda with the reality of your situation so that the former doesn't block changes in the latter.

Your family's agenda may require (or at least you think it requires) you to continue practicing law for the status or money or lifestyle it provides. Your spouse likes the Mercedes or the golf course at the country club. Your kids like the designer clothes you buy them. But you can't foresee earning a similar income in the several alternative career fields you are interested in pursuing.

Are these agenda sufficient to keep you from making any changes? They are if you can't see yourself revamping your earlier, misinformed, vision of law practice, simplifying your lifestyle, or explaining to your family your career/lifestyle dilemma and including them in your decisions.

Your mind-set. What you think about your opportunities and capabilities for change or advancement greatly impact what changes you can make. If you believe you don't have the ability to perform certain work, then you won't apply for that work; people seldom attempt what they believe is impossible to achieve. If you believe that you have the ability only to practice law and nothing else, then you may feel stuck in it but will continue to grind away. If you are afraid your colleagues will resent or talk poorly of you, you will worry about it and stay where you are. If you believe you have no choices about or control over your career direction, you won't make choices or take control.

The perfectionism that must be cultivated to be a thorough

legal practitioner can often work to a job hunter's detriment. That person has an unspoken belief that if the new job can't be perfect, why bother making any change. But as noted earlier in this chapter, even individuals happy with their work dislike aspects of their jobs 25 percent of the time. Realistically, perfection is as unattainable in work as it is in life.

Everyone has performance and job-related fears. But some fears, and the intensity with which you feel them, are not grounded in reality. When they swim around in your subconscious, they can sabotage the career moves you might want to make. Some of those fears, and the internal messages you may be receiving, are:

• Fear of failure. What if I don't succeed at my new job? If I can't do it right, I shouldn't do it at all. What if I don't make enough money at my new endeavor?

• Fear of success. If I do really well at my new job, my former colleagues and friends will resent me. Success may negatively change my relationship with my family and friends. What if I upstage my best friend/brother/sister/husband/wife/mother/father?

• Fear of the unknown. At least I know what I have to contend with in my current job and field, but what about a new job? I just don't know what a new job or field would be like.

• Fear of disappointment. What if a new job is no better than the one I have now? Maybe the field I'm looking into isn't all that exciting.

• Fear of embarrassment. What will my old colleagues or friends say when they find out I'm leaving law to become a carpenter? A fund-raiser? Or an insurance salesperson? Will they think I'm a fool? (To overcome this fear, it might be helpful to remember my wise mother's good advice: "You wouldn't worry so much what other people think of you if you realized how seldom they do.")

Practical realities. The fact that lawyers often do make a better-than-average living can often be an impediment to career change. If you want to earn an income in excess of $100,000 per year, there certainly are other fields you can pursue and still bring home that amount, but fewer than if you were willing to accept, for example, $50,000. Lawyers can often be bound very tightly by what are called "golden handcuffs." Sidney, a sole practitioner with a gross income of $275,000, informed me that he had no choice but to continue his lucrative but unhappy law practice, because he "couldn't afford to earn less money." When I inquired as to his fixed expenses, he shocked me by stating they were $265,000 per year! Those turned out to include, among other expensive commitments, a mortgage far in excess of $10,000 per month. Because Sidney apparently didn't consider his housing cost an extravagance and truly believed that it couldn't be reduced, since he and his family "loved where they lived," he was erecting an unassailable financial barrier to career change.

Other practical realities to be considered are your age, years of experience in law, areas of legal practice (since the skills and knowledge acquired in some specialties are more readily transferable to other fields), professional incarnations prior to attending law school, geographical location, realities of your local marketplace, and willingness to relocate. Each of these issues can have a bearing, positive or negative, upon your job choices and chances.

Unwillingness to compromise. My experience as a legal practitioner allows me to say the following: we lawyers tend to be elitists, and as such, we are reluctant to consider career opportunities that are thought to be "below" the dignity or income-generating capability of a lawyer.

For example, a number of years ago, a client embarrassedly confessed his love of carpentry, but admitted that he could not envision turning his passion into his career. Fortunately, I was able to link him up with a few other professionals who had moved into trade jobs, and after talking to them, he finally decided to make a career change. After undertaking an apprenticeship and working for a few years as a carpenter, he bought a cabinetmaking shop and now happily fashions fine cabinets for interior designers, netting about $125,000 per year. The moral here is to refrain from presupposing what income you can make in any given field, since that presupposition may keep you from taking a closer look at an otherwise attractive opportunity.

Along that line, did you know that legal book and CD-ROM salespeople can earn more than $100,000 per year, or that insurance and financial planning consultants are considered low grossers if they don't bring in at least $150,000? And if income is important to your ego, think about this. If you are working fifty hours per week, fifty weeks per year, and earning $80,000, your gross hourly rate is only $32 per hour. Not so impressive when compared to the numerous management, career, marketing, or design consultants who bill upwards of $75 per hour. Or even auto mechanics or plumbers who can earn more than $50 per hour. It is true that certain professions have a higher perceived status in our society, but career satisfaction is based on doing interesting, fulfilling, meaningful work and earning an income that can sustain you, so don't exclude options simply on the basis of status and income—at least until you investigate them more fully.

Lack of creative career ideas. A client of mine succinctly illuminated a major roadblock for lawyers who are considering new options when he said, "We lawyers have been trained to rely on precedent, so it's now difficult to rely on imagination." If you can't imagine a new field for yourself, perhaps you need to work with a career counselor, join a networking group, read career change books, and immerse yourself as much as possible in the idea of career change in order to stimulate your creative thoughts.

• Approaches That Do and Don't Work

Some thought processes and methods of approaching job and career change will work better than others. If you are contemplating a major change, you will want to avoid the following approaches that don't work, and instead actively pursue those approaches that do work.

APPROACHES THAT DON'T WORK

Hanging on to the idea that you owe a lifetime commitment to your colleagues or your work. If you believe that you must give "it" another chance, that your work owns you, you will not let go of it enough to seriously contemplate changing jobs, let alone careers. If you think that you have a commitment to your employer, partners, or legal colleagues that is forever binding, rather than severable, you will not be able to free yourself to make change. You must begin to think of yourself as a free agent, capable of selecting the best team to play on whenever an attractive opportunity arises. Be assured that your law firm, company, or partners would have little hesitation in moving on without you if their business exigencies required them to leave you behind.

Intellectualizing where to go. Because lawyers tend to be logical, linear thinkers, an unhappy practitioner might ruminate on career change in this fashion: Because I'm a construction defect litigator, I guess I should become a construction company manager if I want to get out of law practice, even though I don't want to be a manager or work in the construction industry. Rather than considering what feels right, what jobs sound interesting, and what skills she or he does or doesn't have (maybe lousy management skills), our practitioner draws a straight line from current experience to unimaginative career change. But a person's motivation for change is internal—almost a "gut" feeling—rather than logical or practical.

Coming from a place of desperation or depression. Don't wait until you are completely burnt out or financially pinched to decide what job or career field you want to pursue. Your choice will then be based on expediency, not on potential success.

Expecting employers to offer you a job solely because you have a J.D. The entitlement mentality that I find in some lawyers—"I've gone to three years of law school, passed the bar, and practiced family law for eighteen years, so I should easily be able to get a job as a corporate manager and get paid a lot of money"—belies the reality of the job market, which is that a lawyer merits prestige, respect, and a big salary for skills and relevant experience, not for obtaining a J.D. and working in a non-applicable field of law. Although many employers are impressed with a J.D., you can expect to be given special consideration only if you are applying for a job that requires that degree. In fact, you may have to "pay your dues" once again; if you go to work at a newspaper, for example, you may have to start out writing obituaries or neighborhood news rather than immediately covering breaking stories.

The important thing to keep in mind is the "stepping-stone" approach to change, where each move lays a foundation for the next and isn't necessarily in and of itself the end step. Thinking in these terms takes a lot of pressure off your next move, allowing it to be "in the right direction" rather than the absolute right job. Just make sure you are moving forward, toward an end goal, keeping on track rather than taking a side step, learning new information and enhancing your resume.

APPROACHES THAT DO WORK

Building a strong sense of yourself. Having a clear vision of who you are, what you want, and what you do well gives you a sense of confidence. It also allows you to answer interview questions well. Therefore, it is important to do a thorough analysis of your skills (see chapter 5 for relevant exercises and information on skills assessment) so that you can present yourself effectively to an employer.

Expecting and accepting an emotional roller coaster. Recognize that there will be days when you have a great interview or receive some exciting new information, and everything seems easy. Then there will be days when it all crashes, when you are told that they hired someone else. The job hunt process goes up and down. During this time, it is important to either join a support group with other job hunters or have someone you can talk to about the frustrations and excitement of the search.

As Alexander Graham Bell once said, "When one door closes, another opens; but we often look so long and so regretfully upon the closed door that we do not see the one which has opened for us." Remember that what you may consider a negative could become a positive if you keep your eyes open.

Reducing expenses and saving money. Career counselors previously told clients that it took about three months to find a new job within their field and about six months to find a job in a new career field. However, for budgeting purposes, I usually advise my clients to double that estimate. This is especially true if you are working full-time and can only make a few networking or informational calls and visits each week.

Therefore, unless you are independently wealthy or have a friend or family member who is willing to give you financial assistance, it is important that you reduce your expenses when you begin to contemplate changing your job or career. That way, if there is a hiatus between your current job and a new position, you will have a nest egg. If your new job pays less, you will already have learned to live on a reduced income (and if the new job pays more, you can buy yourself an extravagant gift). Of course, if you have been laid off or fired from your job, you won't have the opportunity to save money. In that case, it is imperative that you cut your expenditures to the bone, so that you allow yourself the optimum amount of time to find new employment without the necessity of taking a job just for the income. You might also consider doing contract legal work to bring in some income while you look for other work. (See Chapter 4 for information on contract lawyering.)

Investing time and energy into planning. Many of my clients tell me they don't have the time to plan a career move, that they work too many hours to read information or talk to people in order to decide and set their career goals. I tell these clients that lawyers spend more waking hours at their office than at home, so if those hours are spent unhappily, isn't it worth investing some of their free time to plan a strategy to remedy the dissatisfaction? Even very busy people take an hour to play tennis or swim or read or garden or hike or watch TV. Until you find a new job, you need to capture those leisure hours and apply them to your job hunt.

I counseled a litigator who spent a number of hours gathering information about a new cellular telephone and a new computer, both items with a useful life of barely three years. Amazingly, she kept complaining that she didn't have time to make net-working calls or go on interviews. I suggested that she needed to rearrange her priorities; she had spent a lot of time on technology research that she could have devoted to job hunting. I pointed out that she probably wouldn't take a case to a two-week trial without spending hours and days and weeks on thorough preparation and planning, yet she couldn't see the need to put that same amount of effort into preparing and planning for a new career that could last for years.

Being persistent. I often receive dejected calls from lawyers who tell me that they made several job hunt–related phone calls and sent out several resumes over the previous few months and hadn't received any responses. My reaction is "Only several? Over a few months?" If I were a bookie, I'd say those are lousy odds. As Josh Billings once said to his offspring, "Consider the postage stamp, my son. It secures success through its ability to stick to one thing till it gets there."

While it is generally not effective to blanket a market with unsolicited resumes (see instead the techniques set forth in chapters 9, 10, and 11), it is absolutely necessary to be persistent and continuously cultivate and pursue new contacts. There is a bene-fit, at least early on, in having large numbers of contacts. Once you have effectively and thoroughly developed your network, you can be more selective about the future contacts you make. But unless you are one of the very few lucky job hunters, sending only one or two resumes isn't going to get you the job you want; the odds are against it.

There is a nationally known salestrainer who tells salespeople that, on average, they must contact nine prospects and receive nine rejections to allow for an acceptance on the tenth contact. He goes on to say that salespeople should thank those nine who issue a rejection because it brings the salespeople closer to the "yes" they are waiting for. That's probably good advice for job hunters. The more contacts you make and the more targeted resumes you send, the more likely you will finally receive that desired "YES!"

• Other Issues to Consider

You don't necessarily have to follow traditional steps to obtain the job of your dreams. Without either a degree or work experience in journalism, Shelly secured a coveted job writing for a newspaper in Dallas because she had collected a clipping file of the various op-ed articles she had written and published while she was practicing law. Don was able to obtain a job as the manager of a real estate company because he promoted the fact that he had numerous real estate companies as clients, even though he himself had never managed a company or worked in real estate.

You have more than one income-producing skill. Keep your eyes open for other possible uses for the various skills you have. If you are asked to speak at a program about an article you wrote, perhaps you could develop and market a seminar on the topic. A client of mine displayed a fine design and color sense in the clothes she wore and always received compliments on her style; she took a short course of study on fabric design, took a job as an apprentice in a design studio, and is now designing fabric for a large company.

It is possible to establish a career based on your solutions to your own problems. A lawyer in New York became the "Noodge [someone who pesters] Lady," advocating with bureaucracies and companies on behalf of disgruntled clients after learning for herself how to navigate their labyrinths. If you often customize the computer software you use to expedite your office procedures, perhaps you could design legal programs for a software company.

How you structure your work may be as important as what you do. Marilyn, who is both a lawyer and a certified massage therapist, does contract legal work, teaches a law class, does massage, and teaches a massage class. The content of her work is important to her, but so is the fact that law and teaching exercise her intellectual and communicative side, whereas massage uses her nurturing and physical side.

• Look Long Term

Although most career changers are looking for current satisfaction in their work, looking at the long-term potential of a career choice is even more important. The potential of your new field will influence your career longevity, professional development, income, satisfaction level, and challenges. When looking at any new opportunity, it is very important to consider the following:

1. Look at both the type of work you might be doing and the opportunity for growth in the job or field under consideration. Short-term, the specific projects may be what attracts you, but it is the long-term potential of the job and its related aspects that should merit your interest.

2. Evaluate the initial training and guidance you will be given in any job, but focus on the commitment of the employer or industry to long-term education and development of its employees.

3. The individuals who supervise you can make your work life happy or miserable, so evaluating these people when you interview is important. Jobs and supervisors change, however, so a more important factor concerns the quality of management of any organization you are considering. A company or law firm's philosophy of management provides the framework within which all employees and supervisors work.

4. While the environment in which you work, whether casual or formal, structured or unstructured, must fit with your style in order for you to be comfortable, these environmental indicators also offer clues to the values of the organization. These values, in turn, usually influence all aspects of an organization's operations. Often people find that a company and a job that are in sync with their values have as much bearing on their job satisfaction as the actual work they do.

5. Although the salary and benefits that you may be able to obtain in a new job or field are important considerations, even

more important is the compensation philosophy of the organization or field you are exploring. What is the potential for economic growth in the job or industry? What achievements are rewarded, and when and how?

Your research should not only look at present benefits to your career opportunities but it should also be based on long-term considerations that will help you achieve your career goals.

CHAPTER FOUR

———⟫●⟪———

How Much Change Can
You Take?

CLIENT: *But I can't go back to school to study a new field now, it's too late. I'll be 50 before I graduate in four years.*

HINDI: *And how old will you be in four years if you don't go back to school and graduate?*

—HINDI GREENBERG AND A COUNSELING CLIENT

The world of work is changing. In past years, employees were praised, as well as given gold watches upon retirement, for working at the same job for forty hours per week for twenty, thirty, even forty years. That world no longer exists.

As a wise person once said, "The only constant in life is change," that precept now applies to the work world, too. Current studies indicate that an individual graduating from college will, on average, change jobs every two to three years, and change careers at least three times during her work life.

For some of you, this concept is terrifying. Others take it as a challenge. I remember reading several years ago about a man who died at the age of 103. He had retired at 65 from his career of forty years and vowed that he would thereafter pursue a new career every ten years. During the ten-year segments of his life after retirement, he became a noted expert in astronomy, then geology, then mycology, and was well into research and writing in his fourth career—architectural history—when he died. Perhaps that's why he lived so long: Making exciting discoveries, meeting new people, and feeling useful, challenged, and acknowledged certainly helped fuel his internal fires.

For those of you who are seeking to restoke a fire by evaluating your career options, this chapter will cover some of the ways to make those changes, both within the same work you are currently pursuing (for example, work style and schedule alternatives, salary reductions, relocation), as well as in completely different fields (retraining, becoming self-employed).

• Work Style and Time Alternatives

Perhaps you've decided that you basically like your work well enough, whether you are currently practicing law or not, but you don't want to do so much of it; you want to readjust your time commitment or workstyle. Maybe you need time for family or health-related issues. Maybe you want to write a book, run for political office, start a family, travel more, grow a garden, start a business, or develop some of the numerous other interests that cut into your traditional work hours.

If so, you are investigating time and workstyle alternatives at an auspicious period. Many experts in these fields (see chapter 6, beginning at page 153, for relevant articles, publications, and the names of organizations that specifically address workstyle and time alternatives) predict that, in the near future, a business will generally consist only of a core group of full-time employees. The rest of the company's tasks will be outsourced to vendors with expertise in a particular field (i.e., payroll, human resources) or executed by independent contractors or part-timers. In fact, Peter Drucker, the management guru, has said, "By the year

2005, 35–50 percent of the U.S. workforce will be contingent workers"—working on an hourly rather than salaried basis. And the experts say that the core employees will more often telecommute or job share, and certainly work on a flexible schedule. These alternatives are slowly being accepted within the legal field and becoming work-time norms in most fields outside of law.

Law firms are gradually revamping their attitudes and policies about less-than-full-time attorneys. No longer are these lawyers thought to be "less worthy." In fact, good part-time and contract attorneys are often envied for their ability to organize and handle complicated legal matters in a shorter time frame, which saves money for the firm and time for the lawyer. While some entrenched law firms are trying to resist implementing alternative work schedules, contending that proper lawyering cannot be achieved with a less-than-full-time commitment, these firms will stand to lose excellent lawyers if they do not eventually accede to the realities of the marketplace. This bodes well for those of you who desire quality time outside as well as inside the law office.

So what are the benefits and detriments of these work alternatives—job sharing, telecommuting, part-time, flextime, independent contracting—that we are reading about more and more?

PART-TIME WORK

Part-time work is just that—work performed in less than a forty-hour week. It leaves you more time to engage in other endeavors or quality of life activities. However, in law firms, "part-time" can mean something a bit different. Several years back I was called by a headhunter who was seeking to place a lawyer on a part-time basis at a particular law firm. When I asked what the firm considered to be part-time, the headhunter responded, "Forty hours a week." Now, I don't know what your interpretation of part-time is, but that certainly doesn't fit with my concept (although for those of you currently working sixty to seventy hours a week, forty probably sounds like a vacation)!

Here are some negatives about working less than full-time. Many part-time workers are not covered by the employment benefits provided to full-time employees, such as health insurance, paid vacation time, sick leave, and pension plans. Or if they are, those benefits are provided according to the number of hours worked in proportion to what a full-time schedule would be—that is, a half-time schedule would provide fifty percent of benefits. Therefore, if you have a serious medical condition, not having adequate medical coverage could be a great detriment.

Unfortunately, in law firms it isn't unusual for a part-time lawyer to receive less than proportionate salary and benefits—for 80 percent time, the lawyer may receive only three-quarters or two-thirds salary and benefits. All percentages, of course, are negotiable, so run your time/income/benefits estimates very carefully and be prepared to give the firm a counterproposal. If you later find that you are regularly working more than the negotiated number of hours, you should present an altered salary and benefits proposal based on the actual hours you are working.

For example, Carol, a fifth-year associate in a general litigation firm in Kansas City, initially requested a reduction in her work schedule to two-thirds time so that she could more easily take care of her aging and infirm mother. She and I prepared a proposal for her to present to the firm, indicating how her part-time status would be a win-win situation for the firm, by using contract lawyers to cover any work she was unable to accomplish and by reducing her benefits to correspond to her reduced billables.

Although her fifteen-attorney firm had not previously had a part-time lawyer, they valued Carol's work enough that they didn't want her to leave if they said no to her proposal. They agreed to allow her to work two-thirds time (which at her firm meant approximately thirty-five hours per week) in exchange for two-thirds salary—but they allowed for only 60 percent benefits. Although Carol wasn't truly satisfied with this result, she reasoned that the deal she got was better than no deal at all. She anticipated revisiting the figures with the firm's partners after six months to a year; if things went smoothly with her work, she felt she would be in a good position to then request higher benefits.

However, a problem arose when a case she was working on heated up and she had to put in additional time, as she had agreed to do if she was needed. After a number of weeks of working more than forty-five hours, with no end in sight, she began to feel taken advantage of, since she was only being paid for thirty-five hours. Unfortunately, there wasn't a provision in her agreement with the firm for overtime pay. And she was still receiving benefits for only 60 percent of the negotiated thirty-five hours, not the forty-five plus hours she was actually working. When she finally made another presentation to the firm for a revised arrangement, which would acknowledge and compensate a number of the excess hours, the partners, who apparently had given little thought to her dilemma, realized that they had been taking extreme advantage of Carol and agreed to the new arrangement. But the bottom line was that Carol wanted to return to thirty-five hours a week. This reduction in hours took approximately three months to do; Carol believes that the firm felt pressure to reduce her hours because of the increased costs to the firm from the revised arrangement.

The lesson here is to be aware of "hours creep," so that you don't work a lot more hours than you're getting paid or receiving benefits for. You will find that the issue of billable hours in excess of your agreed salary will never be brought up by your firm—it is your responsibility to monitor your time. In some cases, you may even have to make a decision to leave your firm if they are not willing to compensate you equitably.

You should also be aware that in both the corporate and legal markets, part-timers may not be considered for promotion or partnerships. And at times, work assignments aren't as choice and client contact isn't as involved, because part-timers may be looked upon as less integral—almost peripheral—to the firm's business. Jacob, a third-year associate on the "Daddy track," is working an 80 percent schedule (and is relatively unavailable for any additional hours) in order to spend time with his young daughter. Although he hasn't actually been told that he won't progress up the partnership ladder, Jacob is well aware that his prospects for advancement have been stunted. In fact, he isn't often invited by the partners to "go out for a beer" along with the fast-track associates.

Law firms are especially concerned with "face time"—having you available in the office as many hours as possible "just in case something comes up." Although we all know that with telephones, fax, pagers, and voice mail a part-timer can be reached off-hours in an emergency, legal employers are nervous that you won't be available. The wise individual will address that concern as part of a part-time proposal and agree to be flexible when work requires more hours (but not so flexible that you will gradually find yourself working fifty hours every week as Carol did) and offer solutions for potential problem situations when you may be away from the office. Remember, most people go on vacation at some time, and the law firm doesn't fall apart because that individual is away.

TELECOMMUTING

Law firms have been slower than the business community to accept the newest workstyle innovation—telecommuting. Telecommuting is work done from a location other than the main office—usually the telecommuter's home—using voice or data communications to stay in contact with the office. One of the great advantages of telecommuting is that you can live in one locale and work in another. More and more businesspeople and lawyers are spending several days of each week at home offices in, say, Arizona, and the balance of the week in their Chicago office.

Chris's young daughter and his wife, a well-known tenured professor at Harvard, live in Boston, where Chris spends his weekends and part of the work week, communicating with his colleagues and clients via telephone, fax, and e-mail. But his law office is located in San Francisco, so he travels to the West Coast for at least three days a week to handle any meetings and problems that need to be resolved in person.

Yet for the same reasons that law firms are suspect of part-timers, they also are concerned that an employee who is not physically in the office won't be readily accessible if a problem comes up or a client has a question. The response to these concerns is obvious. When you are doing legal research at the law library or are at a lunch meeting with a client or are waiting around the courthouse, your firm doesn't fret about wasted time or inaccessibility. Why should those issues be any more of a problem if you are at your home office, where you are readily available by telephone or pager and can review documents just as easily on your home computer screen as you can on your office unit?

To ameliorate your colleagues' concerns, you need to keep in close contact with the office and agree to be reasonably available during business hours when you are working from home. Chris carries a cellular telephone and is available by pager as well. And never give your firm cause for alarm by choosing to return a phone call or a fax later rather than sooner! Response time is everything in establishing your colleagues' comfort level with your physical absence. Chris's rule of thumb is to return all cross-country phone calls within three hours maximum! He uses the telephones in airplanes to very good advantage.

Firms are also nervous about your independence from their scrutiny. How does the managing partner know you are completing your assignments or billing legitimate hours if you are not at your office desk? Of course, sitting in your office chair doesn't ensure either productivity or avoidance of padded billings. It should be obvious to an effective supervisor if you are not producing, whether from the office or from home, or if your time sheets reflect more hours worked than the output warrants.

Keep in mind that telecommuting does not work well for every individual. Dana Shultz, a lawyer who often writes about technology and its uses (contact him by e-mail at dhshultz@ds-a.com or on the Web at www.ds-a.com.), listed several questions in the April–June 1997 issue of the *Lawyers in Transition*[sm] *Newsletter* that are important to answer before deciding if telecommuting will work for you.

"[Are you] a disciplined self-starter?" At home, there's no one looking over your shoulder if you decide to spend time in the garden instead of drafting a contract. Telecommuting can also be isolating, depriving the employee of team-building contacts with other employees. Chris told me that because he is gone from his office so much, there are times he feels left out of the social loop—he hadn't heard that one of the firm's associates had become engaged or that a secretary had given birth. To rectify this situation in order to prevent additional faux pas, he made arrangements with his own secretary to "carry tales" and fill him in on those social items everyone in the firm should know.

"[Do you] have—or will your employer provide—up-to-date computer and telecommunication resources?" You have to be accessible and able to effectively communicate by telephone, fax, or computer, as well as have adequate Internet research access.

"Is [your] manager sufficiently secure and skilled to manage faraway, rarely seen personnel?" Consider whether your manager is a laid-back or a hands-on-and-peek-over-your-shoulder type. The latter type would probably not be comfortable with your being out of the office too much.

"Will non-telecommuting coworkers accept the situation without feeling threatened or becoming jealous?" This question is a biggy, since unhappy coworkers can easily sabotage your plans and/or advancement. Do your colleagues feel put upon, believing they now have to work harder, taking up some of the slack because you are not continuously in the office?

"Have [you and your] manager established a plan for evaluating the success of telecommuting?" Without a method for evaluation, management will not know if the process is truly a success and might try to modify or cancel your hard-won alternative workstyle.

All questions must be answered in the affirmative to ensure successful telecommuting. The benefits of working from home, without long commutes that eat up time and produce stress (or in Chris's case, allowing a long commute so he can spend more time with his family), will continue to attract a growing following. For more information on this topic, see the resources listed on page 154 of chapter 6.

FLEXTIME

Flextime, where the employee sets her or his own arrival and departure times and workdays within parameters set out by the employer, is already in place in a great number of companies and government agencies and universities. For example, if an employer determines that its employees should work eight hours each day, any time between the hours of 7:00 A.M. and 7:00 P.M., an employee could choose to arrive at 8:00 A.M. and, by forgoing a lunchbreak, leave at 4:00 P.M. Or, in some cases, these employers allow a choice of four ten-hour days, giving the employee a three-day weekend.

This alternative is not widely available for lawyers in law firms, the rationale being that lawyers do not have set hours and, therefore, usually work many more than eight hours at unpredictable times. However, I do know several attorneys who are not early-morning enthusiasts; they have negotiated with their firms to arrive at work by 10:00 A.M. on days when they have neither an early meeting nor a court appearance, with the understanding that they will work until at least 7 P.M. Since I work best in the evening, I made a similar arrangement with the five-person business litigation office where I worked for two years. When I had no other reason to arrive earlier at the office, I arrived by noon and stayed until 9:00 P.M. three days a week—a definite win-win situation!

JOB SHARING

Job sharing is one of those alternative workstyles that is gaining in popularity, particularly within government agencies and somewhat in business, but rarely proposed or accepted in the legal field. In a job-sharing arrangement, two people share a job, either 50–50 or with any other division of responsibility, in order to perform the total duties of the one job. Generally, the salary and benefits are prorated according to the percentage of time each person works, resulting in only one full salary and benefits package earned between the two employees.

While many jobs can be successfully shared—accounting, teaching, auto repair—the legal community protests that it would be impossible for two lawyers to share one caseload because of strategy, confidentiality, and continuity requirements. However, that's a disingenuous contention, because in many firms several lawyers might handle substantive matters, including court appearances and negotiations, on another lawyer's cases. So long as the lead attorney adequately supervises the "case assistants," either personally or through writings, the work gets completed just fine. The same can be done between job sharers, who at the end of their workday need to leave a detailed memo either on e-mail or in the file about case developments.

In the several instances of law office job sharing I've heard about, the lawyers don't share a caseload but handle their own clients and cases as if they were part-time employees. This means they complete as much work as they can during their time in the office, then work again on those same matters when they next return. If anything heats up on a case while they are away from the office, a designated attorney does what is necessary pending return of the job sharer. The only things the two lawyers do share are the salary, benefits, and office space.

I have also talked to two attorneys working a job share in the small claims department of a state office. These two each have specific workdays and times, which are posted so that the public is notified who is on duty. Both attorneys are versed in all facets of the job of small claims advisor, and each has a designated workload and appointments that they individually handle. Their job share involves splitting office use, supplies, salary, benefits, and clerical support, but not caseloads, although each is available to help out the other if need be.

If you are interested in this workstyle and want to work in a law firm, you must *very* carefully draft a proposal that shows the benefits to the firm, such as two enthusiastic and refreshed job sharers, two heads on one matter if needed, effective use of office space, resources, and staff, and all at no additional cost. Only in this way will most law firms consider this "exotic" work style.

INDEPENDENT CONTRACTOR

An independent contractor is an individual who does work for a company on an hourly or project basis, without an employment relationship. The company and the contractor agree on the scope of the assignment, and that assignment comprises the extent of their relationship. The contractor is thus self-employed and pays for her own taxes, Social Security, health and professional liability insurance, professional dues, continuing education, and other expenses, such as a computer, fax, or copy machine.

In the business sector, independent contractors are looked

upon very favorably, since there is no expense to the business except for the contractor's billed hours. Because contractors get paid only for the hours they work, the company isn't paying for someone to hang around the water cooler, surf the net, or call the car repair shop. The company also doesn't pay for the contractor's benefits.

In fact, one of the fastest-growing segments of independent contracting is the business of consulting to corporations on an hourly or project basis, in an acquired area of expertise, such as dispute resolution techniques, marketing, effective communication and negotiation skills, stress prevention, or anything else an entrepreneurial mind can concoct. If you can promote yourself as knowledgeable in some field, there probably is a company that will be interested in purchasing your consulting services.

If meeting in the hall at the courthouse to turn in finished work, sharing a small cubicle with the bookkeeper, or managing an uneven cash flow sound like ideal work enhancements, then making a temporary or permanent living as a contract attorney may be a legal career alternative worth exploring. Independent contractors regularly move from project to project before boredom sets in, may be included in legal matters or meetings not otherwise accessible to associates or newer members of the firm, and often work with fascinating clients and cases.

The contract practice of law has become a hot topic, both for individual lawyers and for law firms. The programs sponsored by Lawyers in Transition^{SM} on this topic draw numerous attorneys looking for a way to combine their legal background with a different quality of life. Some want this "different quality of life" for a defined, short period of time, while others decide to become permanent independent contractors.

In the present legal market, there is a growing demand for contract attorneys who work and are paid on an hourly or project basis to either utilize the contractor's specialty field or do overflow work for other lawyers. Many people exploring the possibility of working as contract attorneys desire to continue to use their legal skills, but in a less intensive, all-consuming style. These lawyers want more freedom to pursue other interests or commitments.

Some become contract lawyers because they were laid off, or

fired, or quit their jobs and need supplemental income until they find another job or decide what their next career move will be. Numerous small-firm and solo practitioners, who are in the process of building their own law practices, supplement the income they receive from private clients by performing hourly work for other lawyers who are either overloaded or short on expertise in a given field. Andrea, who has made a career of contract lawyering for the past ten years, decided that she wanted to utilize her excellent client relations skills, set her own schedule, be involved in a variety of issues (rather than work exclusively in bankruptcy and tort law as she had been doing), and receive respect for her work, which she didn't feel she was getting from the small firms where she had been employed.

The reasons to pursue contract work are many and diverse, and each has as much validity as the other. I myself worked as a contract lawyer for six years while I was establishing Lawyers in Transition[SM]. This allowed me the flexibility to schedule workshops and counseling appointments at my clients' convenience, fitting the contract work into my off hours. When I had a backpack trip coming up, I didn't take on new projects. If my bank account was waning, I worked my networking list to cultivate more assignments.

However, there are numerous issues necessary for you to consider before deciding to work as a contract attorney. An effective contract attorney must be an individual who is both at ease walking into a new office with new people and new issues and comfortable being dropped into the middle of an existing case. Conscientious contract lawyers will even admit to occasional discomfort when thrown into a case with unfamiliar law, but they remedy that situation by spending time in the law library, without charge, until they feel comfortable with the new issues.

Contract attorneys are called upon to handle all kinds of novel legal and factual situations on a moment's notice. That's the reason that lawyers who seem to cultivate the most contract work usually have at least two to three years of experience under their belt. And that's both the thrill and the terror for the growing numbers of lawyers who make their living doing contract work. (At every Lawyers in Transition[SM] Program, I ask for a show of hands by those who have done contract work for other lawyers;

at times, up to half the group has performed such work in the past several years.) Although the majority of contract work is in the litigation arena, often in research and writing, appearances, and discovery, there is work available in almost every area of expertise.

There are a number of benefits and detriments to contract lawyering. Here are some to consider.

Benefits

1. A contract lawyer can earn nearly the same yearly income as a salaried lawyer in a small firm, for far fewer hours. Andrea, the career contract lawyer, averages about twenty-five billable hours per week and grossed more than $60,000 last year. Of course, the contract attorney then has to turn around and spend some of that income on expenses that a salaried attorney doesn't have, such as health insurance and bar dues.

2. Time is left for personal life choices; the work hours are flexible and can often be arranged to fit around the other important aspects of your life. But if you're not a self-starter, you may never get around to cultivating any work at all.

3. There is the intellectual challenge of picking up a file and quickly pulling together the basic information necessary to handle the immediate assignment.

4. You are responsible for only a portion of a case or just one project—there is no tracking a case for years (if you like complex, long-term cases, you may consider this to be a detriment).

5. Often there is an interesting variety of people and cases. In one of the largest cases on which Andrea has worked, a multimillion dollar libel case with more than one hundred witnesses, she was responsible for issuing all subpoenas, then martialing and controlling all witnesses over a period of several months. A number of these witnesses were truck drivers. Because their trial appearance dates changed daily, she spoke to them and their families so often that she became privy to their histories, their celebrations, and even their drinking problems, learning which

ones needed to be watched closely and which could be trusted to appear without a "designated driver."

Detriments

1. Like all self-employed people, contract attorneys must market themselves and continually cultivate business. The uncertainty about when and from whom the next job will come can be unnerving. Some individuals remedy this anxiety by cultivating freelance writing work from legal publishers. But if you left your law firm because you were offended by the requirement to become a rainmaker, you'd better either get over your reluctance to market yourself or hire someone to do it for you.

2. The quantity of work available fluctuates, causing irregular income and the need to carefully budget. If you generally live from paycheck to paycheck, without the ability to save money, working as a contract lawyer will cause you more than a little financial discomfort. Brad was such a person. He became exhausted from overwork, spending everything he earned when he worked a lot, then fearing he would become a "bag man" on the street when no clients called. Brad probably would be more comfortable working for a salary rather than attempting to budget self-employment earnings.

3. All taxes, insurance (health, life, malpractice), vacation, and sick time are paid by you—you will need to file a self-employed tax return and be responsible for Social Security as well as income taxes. However, there are numerous business-related tax deductions a self-employed person is entitled to take (i.e., technology expenses, bar dues, continuing education).

4. Unorganized client attorneys who wait until the last minute to call can disrupt your schedule, although you can refuse a job if it's too difficult or unruly. I was once asked by an attorney to read nearly five years of files, thickly scattered all over his office in no discernible order, and then write a "trial script" for him to use in a two-week trial that was to begin the next week! You can probably guess my response . . .

5. Slow-paying clients occasionally cause cash flow problems and may even have to be chased. Andrea, the career contract lawyer, found it necessary to file a small claim action against an attorney who owed her $1,500. Just before the hearing date, she was finally paid with a number of dirty, disintegrating $100 bills that even her bank wouldn't accept. So she obtained her judgment, filed a lien against some property the client owned, and eventually collected her fee. Needless to say, she no longer does work for that deadbeat lawyer.

If you are still seriously considering working on a contract basis, here are more points to consider.

If you want to be responsible for a case, have ultimate authority, or have your ego invested in the status you achieve, you should probably not work on a contract basis. Frequently the work is supplemental, often it is piecemeal, and occasionally it could be done by an experienced paralegal. Sometimes a contract lawyer works under less than desirable conditions. For example, some years ago I spent eight hours pulling books off the law library shelves and copying cases. However, I was paid $50 per hour and spent the time mentally planning my next hiking trip. Another time I spent three days reviewing complex files while sitting in one of the two stiff chairs in the reception area of a tiny law office because the solo practitioner did not want the files to leave the office.

If you are intending to cultivate contract work in a locale that is not as yet receptive to it, you will need to determine how much pioneer energy you are willing to put out to overcome the traditional objection that contract attorneys "must not be good attorneys or they would have a full-time job."

You will need to be aware of conflicts of interest when switching from case to case and firm to firm. You must always ask who the parties, attorneys, and important witnesses are and inquire about the issues in each case you work on.

There are contract attorney placement agencies in the larger cities across the country. Some of them are locally owned, and others are divisions of large employment agencies such as Kelly Services or Manpower. Some act only as brokers, matching you to firms for whom you do work as an independent contractor.

These agencies make their money by charging the law firm a broker's premium, on top of the hourly fee you have stated you want to earn, for each hour you work. You are an employee of neither the placement agency nor the law firm.

On the other hand, the larger agencies generally carry contract attorneys on their employment rolls, paying insurance and taxes. These agencies agree to pay you a set fee for each hour you work with a law firm, then negotiate with the firm for whatever higher broker's fee they can get on each of your work hours. Your decision about which kind of agency best suits your needs depends upon whether you want to maintain your independent contractor status or become an employee. From either type of agency, you might be assigned to discrete research and writing projects, be requested to make an appearance or handle a deposition, or be assigned to an ongoing project or case that lasts for several months. To locate contract attorney placement agencies, look in the classified section of your local legal newspaper or call your local bar association to inquire whether it has a list.

Although it may be fruitful to submit a resume to each of the local temporary agencies, the majority of attorneys obtain contract work through personal referrals and solicitations, not through agencies. You should call everyone you know—former employers, opposition counsel with whom you have had cordial dealings, other colleagues, classmates (this is true even if you graduated from law school some years ago)—and attend bar functions in your practice specialties to cultivate as many leads as possible. Much of the contract work comes from solo and small practices, since the bigger firms often contact their alumni about overflow projects. However, those larger firms are also more willing to pay a temporary agency to obtain help, so if you'd like to be placed with a larger firm or in a niche practice area, be sure to register with all of the agencies in your area—there is no "exclusive agency" on registration.

If you are considering a job as a full-time employee, working on a contract basis in a law firm is often a good way to preview a firm (and for the firm's lawyers to preview you). And even if you initially do work for a firm without thinking about a permanent relationship, some "romances" do develop, resulting in permanent employment.

If the firm doesn't require work to be done in its office, contract attorneys often do their research at the law library or on home computers and their document preparation on their own computers. Many contractors provide a finished product, although some firms want to have the information available on disk to have their own secretaries prepare the document.

Many contract lawyers do repeat work for the same few practitioners. Diane, who has worked on a contract basis for almost ten years, has what she calls "her stable" of about six solo practitioners who utilize her as an outside associate, contacting her every time they have too much work, a project they don't want to do, or work in one of the fields in which she specializes. Therefore, one method of marketing is to periodically call lawyers for whom you've previously worked to inform them that you are currently available.

Many contract lawyers do not carry malpractice insurance. This is a personal decision, although many insurance carriers won't insure contract workers because the companies are concerned that you may be exposing them to liability they hadn't bargained for (such as the "walking malpractice" lawyer with the disorganized files who wanted me to write his trial script). However, sometimes the supervising attorney's insurance policy will cover the "supervised work" of a contract attorney, especially if you don't sign documents but merely prepare them for signature by one of the firm's insured attorneys. Also, some contract attorneys request indemnity agreements, including lawsuit defense costs, from firms with whom they do repeat work. But most wing it and try to avoid potential problems by not allowing their names on documents of any kind.

Although there may seem to be a number of negatives to contract lawyering, detriments are balanced by the often humorous or interesting incidents encountered in journeys among many law offices and lawyers. As in the full-time practice of law, the work done by a contract lawyer can be interesting, boring, intellectually stimulating, dull, diverse, repetitive, or a combination of all things good and bad. The difference is that a contract attorney can decide with whom to work, which assignment to accept, and when to do it, a luxury not usually allowed to a law firm employee. Because of these benefits, and because the staffing needs of law firms will continue to fluctuate, contract lawyering as an alternative to the full-time practice of law will continue to grow.

WORKING FROM HOME IN LAW OR IN ANOTHER FIELD

More and more professionals, including attorneys, are deciding not to continue to work at the whim of an employment hierarchy. Instead, they are trying their own hands at their financial futures. Solo legal practice, run out of a home office, and contract lawyering are, of course, two such attempts.

I counseled with Jason, living in Montana, who has now cultivated a half dozen midsize companies that are too small to hire a full-time, in-house attorney but have numerous legal issues about which they need advice. He has negotiated a long-term consulting arrangement with each company—for a specific monthly fee, he guarantees each one a fixed number of telephone counseling hours per week, a half day per week of "face time" at the company's offices, and additional time as needed, available for an hourly fee. He now spends much of his time talking on the phone from his home office; most of his clients just need hand holding and don't even require the "face time" even though their retainers pay for it.

But other lawyers I've counseled have moved into a great number of fields besides law that allow them to work out of a home office.

For example, Sam completed mediation training and volunteered for some time in several mediation programs to obtain relevant experience and make appropriate contacts. Three years ago he finally felt confident enough about his skills to leave the law firm where he had toiled for more than twelve years, in order to make himself fully available to conduct mediations.

He set up a home office, complete with computer, modem, Internet access, fax, scanner, a telephone with several lines, and adequate file and desk space. He uses this office for everything but meeting with clients or counsel. For meetings or mediations, he either journeys to a participant's office or exercises the arrangements he has made with several law firms to rent their conference rooms. Over these three years he has developed a growing mediation clientele and a reputation for careful, methodical, fair work. Because his overhead is so much lower than his partnership expense share at his former law firm, his net income currently surpasses his law firm net and is growing. Furthermore, his pride in and enjoyment of his work greatly surpasses anything he experienced while practicing law.

• Relocating or Retraining

You must do the thing you think you cannot do.
— ELEANOR ROOSEVELT

Moving or going back to class often gets (or at least seems) more difficult as you get older and more deeply settled in your ways. This is so even if moving to a smaller town, a bigger city, another state, or a different field of endeavor could increase the career possibilities you would then have available to you.

Lower living costs would permit a reduction in income expectations. Certain opportunities are available only in selected locations—it is difficult to become a movie star while living in Keokuk, Iowa. Regional differences often influence what businesses and type of people do well in a specific locale—a bait and tackle store wouldn't be terribly successful in most parts of Arizona, while it's a very good business in the Florida Keys.

Therefore, consider the possibility of moving your physical location. Fifteen years ago and after five years of law practice, Bob realized that as long as he lived in a very large city he would never achieve two of his life goals—civic acknowledgment and a big reputation as a lawyer. He decided that, since he would rather be a big fish in a small pond than the invisible minnow he felt like when working among several million other people, he needed to move to a smaller, more rural area.

And that's what he did. He moved to a town of 15,000 people, with another 20,000 in the nearby environs, and started a law practice on a shoestring with one other person. He met a woman from a nearby town, married her, and started a family. Because living expenses were lower, he was able to eke out a living until, after ten years, and with six other lawyers, he had built the largest, most prestigious firm in town. He has been appointed the grand master of the annual parade numerous times, he is now chair of the county commission, and business leaders in the community request his advice.

If he had stayed in the big city, he would still probably be one among many. But in his adopted town, he makes a good living by rural standards and has achieved his two goals. He is a happy man who took a big risk and succeeded.

Consider the possibility of retraining for another legal practice area or an opportunity outside of law practice. Retraining can consist of as little as a few continuing legal education courses taken in the evening or on Saturdays in order to learn about a new practice area—perhaps changing focus from worker's compensation to labor law, since both practices have exposure to employer-employee issues. Or maybe you are willing to put in more time and take a two-week workshop in silk screen design, opting to produce and market gorgeous T-shirts and see how that develops.

Or perhaps you are willing to attend night school for two years to obtain your M.B.A. so that you can get a job as manager of a law firm or as financial director of a large nonprofit. Or maybe you are ready to take the big leap and go back to school full-time for several years to get your Ph.D. in clinical psychology in order to fully use the abilities you feel best about—your listening, counseling, and interpersonal skills.

Each one of these options takes both a willingness to set a goal and a commitment to follow through. You will endure some hardship fitting the retraining into your schedule, as well as find it a challenge to change your job or career emphasis after completing your retraining. But finally finding your niche has its own rewards.

Marijean is a fine example of re-creating oneself professionally; she undertook one of the longest retraining regimens I can recall. She had majored in film production in college, worked for five years, married, had a child, divorced, then returned to school to get her law degree. But don't ask her the reason—she doesn't know. When she graduated law school, she still hadn't a clue what she wanted to do with her J.D., so she accepted the first job offered to her that would pay her bills, which was litigating for a senior citizens organization. While she did feel she was helping others, especially when she had the opportunity to counsel her clients rather than fight with opposition attorneys, she soon tired of the contentiousness of her practice and realized that she preferred to work more independently, outside an organization.

At that point, she discovered mediation and concluded that she would be able to use her already-honed counseling and listening skills by working as a mediator. So Marijean took several mediation training courses and volunteered, to acquire experience, at several mediation programs, all the while continuing to support herself and her daughter by working at the senior citizens organization. But when it came time to commit herself to developing a mediation practice, Marijean realized that it still involved a number of the confrontational and bureaucratic elements that she disliked.

It was at this time that her mother died after spending a week in a hospital intensive care ward. At the hospital, Marijean met a grief counselor assigned to assist her mother and her family. Even though Marijean was greatly upset by her mother's illness, she found herself watching the counselor, observing the woman's manner and how she interacted with Marijean's family. As the week passed, Marijean became convinced that counseling was the profession that would best utilize her abilities.

After her mother died, Marijean contacted the counselor, both to thank her for her support and to ask her questions about her training, whether the woman liked her work, and what career possibilities existed in counseling. It became very clear that her next step was to go back to school to acquire a master's degree in counseling, which would allow her to lead grief counseling groups, either through hospitals or on her own. And that's what she did, spending the next few years acquiring her master's, then committing 3,000 hours to her internship training, all the while doing contract legal work for income.

Now that Marijean is involved in a counseling practice, with an emphasis on terminally ill individuals and their families, she feels she has found her niche, and is finally able to bring the intuitive, creative, and compassionate side of herself to her work.

• Taking a Step Back and/or a Pay Cut

*Money may be the husk of many things but not the kernel.
It brings you food, but not appetite; medicine, but not
health; acquaintances, but not friends; servants, but not
loyalty; days of joy, but not peace or happiness.*
—HENRIK IBSEN

Although a number of my clients express some flexibility about
the income they would be willing to accept if they change jobs
or careers, a great many more are like the thirty-two-year-old
unmarried lawyer who drove up to his counseling appointment
in a current model, top-of-the-line red Porsche and said to me,
"Because I don't have any dependents, I would consider coming
down to $125,000 a year, plus perks—but only if absolutely
necessary." Oh, how I adore an optimistic client! But, of course,
he was wrong. He definitely had at least one dependent. It was
red and parked outside.

However, that same optimism (or narrow-mindedness, depending upon your viewpoint) definitely limits a job hunter's
prospects for finding a new job or career. It isn't that other fields
or jobs can't provide more than $125,000 a year—look at what
stockbrokers or some insurance and real estate salespeople earn.
But there are certainly fewer jobs to consider if an income of
$65,000 a year is considered insufficient.

Therefore, an assignment I often give my counseling clients is
to figure out their *necessary* expenses (the expenses for items they
need, such as rent or mortgage, tuition for their children, insurance, and basic auto costs, not the items they *want,* such as a
designer silk suit, a Mercedes, a first-class trip to Jamaica).

The second thing I have them do is compute the lowest salary
they could adequately live on, taking into account their necessary
expenses and any financial contributions from other family members. Notice I use the word "adequately," and not the word
"well." I then point out that this lowest, adequate salary figure
is not a sum they would necessarily want to live on for a long
time. But it might be acceptable for a job that provides an entree
into a new field or for a job that meets all other job criteria, as
long as the income rises as the job changer acquires the requisite

skills and experience and moves up the hiring ladder. Having this "bottom line" number is important, for when you go into an interview you will know whether you can safely accept an offer of a fabulous job with "a lower salary but room for improvement" or whether you truly can't afford it. It allows you to avoid a knee-jerk refusal simply because the salary isn't as high as you'd like.

The problem with lawyers, as with many professionals, is that we often have unrealistic financial expectations; this prevents us from seeing some wonderful career opportunities simply because these new positions, at first blush, appear to be underpaid. Lawyers read about the $80,000 starting salaries paid to first-year associates at the biggest law firms and feel that they, three years out of law school, are inadequately paid at $60,000 by a five-attorney firm. Partners who considered $150,000 a great year's income in 1985, then earned $300,000 in the go-go late 1980s, overwork themselves so as not to reduce their income to the more realistic high $100,000s that the current legal market can provide. All of these attitudes preclude a nonjudgmental evaluation of career opportunities because the foremost criterion becomes the available salary rather than job satisfaction and future income possibilities.

I know from personal experience that accepting an income reduction can provide an avenue to more success, career satisfaction, and income. When I quit my last full-time legal job in 1984, after ten years of practice, I was earning what was, at the time, a good salary. Suddenly I had no income and had to live off the savings I had put away (something I fortunately do well). By the next year, I had cultivated some contract legal work and a bit of low-paying nonlegal work; I was earning under $20,000 with a mortgage to pay.

Needless to say, I was not living extravagantly, but I did find that I could still enjoy myself, going to inexpensive restaurants, cultivating the free activities in the San Francisco Bay Area, and watching my expenditures. I knew that this low-income condition wouldn't last indefinitely, so that helped me weather the two years that I lived quite frugally. Because of my own experience, I know that simplifying your expenditures can be done, without extreme hardship, as long as you have a will to make a change.

This financial reevaluation allowed me to take time to create Lawyers in Transition^{SM} and build a business that utilizes my skills, interests, and preferred workstyle, while earning a good income. If I hadn't permitted myself to step back, both financially and in job responsibility and prestige, I would not have been able to take the time to develop my business and move from the misery of my last law job in 1984 to the excitement of writing this book in 1998.

SOME THINGS TO REMEMBER ABOUT CHANGE

Faced with the choice between changing and proving there is no need to do so, most people get busy on the proof.
—JOHN KENNETH GALBRAITH

1. All change is accompanied by some type of stress.
2. The type of stress varies as we go through the change.
3. We may not be able to give as much when we are changing.
4. Change is not a smooth flowing process.
5. Often, denial of stress and frustration is the first signal we get that we are in the process of changing.
6. There are no guarantees of how long it will take to get through each phase of change or even whether we will get through it at all.
7. Other people's changes may affect us adversely.
8. The more we fail to recognize we are in a change situation, the more difficult it is to get through the change.
9. Planning is a useful part of change, but it is difficult to plan for the emotional periods that accompany change.
10. Change seems to involve the removal of old information before anything new can be accepted.
11. Much of what people call "resistance to change" probably is really change itself.
12. During the initial phases of change, we are concerned mostly with neutralizing the data, not solving the problems.
13. Being helpful to others who are changing may mean keeping some emotional distance as others experience what they must experience.

14. Your attitude toward change will directly influence your success. You can approach change as a frustration or a challenge. It can be viewed as a negative, draining experience or a time for growth and learning.
15. Change occurs periodically.
16. We all change.

CHAPTER FIVE

Assess Your Skills, Values, and Interests to Find the Best Job for You

Do not let what you cannot do interfere with what you can do.
—JOHN WOODEN

When lawyers call me, usually the first question they ask is, What are some of the career options? Although I could give them a long list of jobs that people do to earn a living—archaeologist, gardener, accountant, garbage collector—or tell them to read about the thousands of jobs listed in the *Dictionary of Career Titles* put out by the Department of Labor, I usually instead inform them that What are the options? isn't the first question to ask. The better first question is Who am I and what do I have to offer in the job market? A list of options is only a list;

after someone has answered this latter question, an inquiry into the options can be evaluated according to which jobs might be a good fit and are therefore interesting enough to pursue.

I strongly recommend that my clients devote some concentrated time to self-assessment—answering the Who am I? question—because there are various factors in job and career choice, depending upon the outcome of their self-analysis, that will make a job attractive or not to them.

• Factors in Job/Career Choice

Interests. This refers to the subject matter of the work an employee performs. Wouldn't it be more exciting to work on matters—children's issues, sports deals, environmental concerns, international relations—that are actually of interest to you, rather than working on a project just to get it done?

Abilities. When a job uses your natural abilities it doesn't feel like work, because the tasks you do flow effortlessly. For example, if you have a natural ease with extemporaneous speaking, court appearances aren't dreaded the way they would be if you lacked that ability.

Values. A job (and a work assignment) that comports with your values and ideals feels integrated and whole, rather than constantly irritating and even degrading. If you value having freedom with your time, you wouldn't want to work where you would be required to punch a clock or where your comings and goings would be monitored. You wouldn't want to be required to represent someone asserting a Second Amendment right to own a submachine gun if you believe in gun control.

Environment. If the decor, size, atmosphere, aesthetics, location, or other physical elements of your workplace concern you, a preview visit to a potential employer's office is warranted. Additionally, if the number of other employees, and whether they are creative, communicative, humorous, white- or blue-collared, extroverted or introverted is a concern, make sure that you meet as many people as possible when you interview at an office.

Personality and style. Consider whether you are a contemplative, quieter sort, who values the opportunity to reflect before responding to a question or situation (an Introvert on the Myers-Briggs scale, set out in chapter 2), or whether you are more dynamic, enjoying rapid repartee and "shoot-from-the-hip" speaking (an Extrovert on the Myers-Briggs scale). Your preferred style should greatly influence your job choice. Take David, a reflective sort. He worked as a prosecutor, then as a public defender, finding both jobs stressful and exhausting because the jobs required him to act, think, and work in a style counter to his normal personality. After several years of unsatisfying work, combined with intermittent self-assessment, David identified that he needed to work in a slower-paced, more thoughtful environment, with value placed upon in-depth analysis and reflective thinking. He is now working as a writer/editor for a legal publisher, spending his days researching, writing, and discussing his findings with colleagues—a much better personality fit.

Lifestyle/Workstyle. Consider to what extent prestige, control, and money are important to your job satisfaction. Is high prestige a motivating factor in your selection or retention of a legal career? For many lawyers, the law is more than a job. It is an identity, a badge, and for some, it is difficult to give up. This identity weighs heavy even if they are not leaving law but are considering taking a less traditional legal job—with the courts, for a legal publisher, in a bar association—often preventing a switch to what might be a better-fitting job outside a law firm.

Somehow, lawyers have been led to believe that only litigators are the true lawyers and you can't wear the badge if you are anything else. A lawyer who worked for ten years as a legal researcher with a court of appeal quit to become a litigator at a large firm so he "could try out his Perry Mason fantasies." It took him less than two months to realize he had made a big mistake, and within a year he was fortunately able to return to the court, wiser and very happy to be back.

Consider how much control you need to have in your work environment. Do you want to be in charge, to take the big picture, analyze it, and delegate its parts to other people to complete? Or would you rather be the person who gets the delegated assignments and creatively implements them? Not all lawyers are generals—some need to admit that they don't want to be in charge of the troops or the plan.

Analyze carefully how much money you *need,* not *want!* Most people want as much money as they can get, even if they don't need nearly as much. As more fully discussed in chapter 4, it is extremely important to do a thorough evaluation of your budget—mortgage/rent, insurance, student loans—to determine what your bottom-line salary would be. Then if you are offered the perfect job but it pays less than you would like, you will know if your budget will allow you to accept it.

Time investment. How much time are you willing to put into training? If the answer is not much, you had better consider taking a job very similar to what you have now. If on-job training is acceptable, you can make greater changes. And if you're willing to go back to school, you can then obtain a new credential and completely change direction.

The old adage "Know thyself" acknowledges one of the most important factors in successfully targeting a viable and fulfilling career option. A thorough assessment of who you are—your personal style, skills, interests, and values—will enable you to recognize which of the numerous career areas you may want to explore. This inventory of your personal attributes will also help you successfully promote yourself to a potential employer.

It is only after you have completed your self-inventory that the initial question, What are the options?, can be reframed. Now ask yourself, What options do *I* have? Not all options will fit into your personal style, skills, interests, and values profiles. Choosing an option that is colorful or sounds exciting won't give you job satisfaction unless it also fits who you are. Therefore, once you have those profiles, you can then more fruitfully explore potential options and select a career that fits for you.

Additionally, before undertaking either a job or career change, it is necessary to consider how the change will affect you. The ramifications can be enormous, affecting your self-esteem, emotions, relationships with others, and finances, among other considerations. Therefore, even before undertaking a self-inventory and inquiring into the potential options available, it is very important to take the time to analyze carefully what you do and do not like about the practice of law. This analysis will ensure that whatever next step you take will be based on the development of a positive focus to pursue what you like, rather than simply avoiding what you dislike.

• What Does Self-assessment Include?

> *Good instincts usually tell you what to do*
> *long before your head has figured it out.*
> —MICHAEL BURKE

A productive self-assessment includes an analysis of some personal characteristics—your interests, skills, and values—and several other preferences, including the environment in which you want to work and the people you would like in that environment. By conducting a self-assessment, you will have a clearer picture of where you might fit in the world of work and how you want to relate to that work.

Some individuals are able to undertake a self-assessment on their own, while others need assistance, either from a book, a testing service, or a career counselor. The resources listed under "Career and Job Hunting Books, Newspapers, and Web Sites" in chapter 2, "Career Counselors and Career Counseling Centers" in chapter 2 and "Testing" in this chapter may be of interest to you if you do need outside assistance. Also be sure to read the caveat about career counselors at the end of chapter 2.

To help you develop some clarity on important issues to consider, thoroughly answer the following questions:

✍
Questions to Help You Focus

• What do you really want from life?

• What are your financial needs?

• If you had six months to live, and you would be healthy and pain-free until the moment you died, how would you spend those six months?

• What do you love to do in your spare time? Or what do you fantasize about when you don't have spare time?

• What are you willing to give up to find job/career satisfaction—status or title, money, time, geographic location, certain friendships?

• What things are important to you—independence, camaraderie, money, free time, status, location, challenge, intellect, emotion, physical activity, competition, helping others?

• If you had an entire day free to do whatever you wanted, what would it be?

• If you won the lottery and suddenly could quit your job and never have to support yourself again, how would you spend your time (after you relaxed on a beach for the next six months)? What projects would you pursue?

• What other jobs or projects in your childhood or adult life have fascinated and motivated you so that time passed without your knowing it? What elements of these jobs or projects got you excited?

There should be a strong correlation between your answers and the field or tasks you ultimately pick in order to find work that interests and excites you. This correlation doesn't mean that because you enjoy throwing pottery in your spare time, you must become a professional potter. But perhaps you should consider an artistic or creative endeavor, or one where you get to use your hands as well as your head.

Many lawyers have lost or given up the ability to fantasize about their dream job. Because they feel they are unable to, don't know how to, or will be unsuccessful in a move to a new job or career, they have become rigid in their perceptions of possible jobs. Desmond was one of those who had lost his dream. He had been a litigator for six years, was now married, and had a one-year-old child and a mortgage.

By the time he and I spoke, Desmond was so depressed about

his working situation that he was beginning to drink too much. Yet he felt he couldn't make a job change, since he was afraid of losing the stability and high income he had with his current firm and couldn't think of anything he could do to earn a good living except law. When he finally relaxed into an exercise of fantasizing about his dream job, he was able to recall his long-repressed interests in teaching, helping others, and analyzing the stock market.

After several months of brainstorming with others, research, and informational interviews, he eventually obtained a job working for a large financial planning company. Capitalizing on his rediscovered interests, he now educates his clients about financial issues by teaching classes on long-range planning. Additionally he helps his clients plan for and fund their retirement and keeps current on various investment vehicles, including stocks and bonds. Not only does he actually earn more than he did when he practiced law but he also contends that his job is much more stable, since he is on commission. He says that commissioned employees are never dead wood—they don't get fired because they are not a cost to a company unless they produce commissionable income, and if do they produce income, they are worth retaining as employees. An interesting perspective on employment stability.

Here are two exercises to help you recall your fantasies and dreams.

✍

Fantasies

Pick a time when you have *at least* a half hour for this assignment. Wear comfortable clothing, do a few physical, loosening-up exercises, then sit alone in a quiet, darkened room, without distractions. Next, allow your imagination to run wild. Be impractical. Dream. This is not the time to look at things realistically—that comes later. Answer the following questions mentally, and at the end of the session, write down all your thoughts, or if you are comfortable with speaking (and if it does not inhibit the free flow of your thoughts), turn on a tape recorder and record your thoughts, transcribing them later:

If this were a perfect world and if money, age, education, health, status, training, etc. were unimportant or no problem and if no one else were dependent upon me, what would I choose to do for work and play? Not do? How would I exist, what would I do with my time, where would I go, what would I really want out of life, would I work at all, and if so, what would I do?

Do you have a fantasy of "what you want to be when you grow up"?

✍

Visualization of Perfect Day

Either right after the fantasy exercise or at another time when you can provide the same environment for *at least* another half hour, do the following:

Close your eyes and visualize your "perfect day," step by step, mentally picturing whom you are with, if anyone, what you are doing, if anything, when and where and how you are doing things. Begin with waking and end with retiring for the evening; you needn't include work unless you want it in your day. The time flow needn't be realistic—you can lunch in Paris and have dinner in China. Try to be aware of how you *feel* about your visualization while it is going on—whether it's comfortable or uncomfortable. After you have finished your day, write it all down in detail. After you write it down, analyze your day according to some of the following factors: numbers of people you are with at one time and over the course of your day; whether what you do is physical, cerebral, emotional, spiritual, etc.; whether your activities are primarily intellectual, social, aesthetic, manual, creative, etc.; whether the pleasure from your activities is a result of external stimulation of your five senses or is a result of an internal sense of well-being or fulfillment or usefulness.

After Kathy completed these exercises in a Lawyers in Transition[SM] career evaluation workshop, she became focused enough to know that she still wanted to be involved with the legal community. However, her visualization made her realize that she wanted more autonomy, liked working at her own pace, and loved being in her home office. She decided that doing work for other lawyers on a contract basis would fit with her independent lifestyle; after completing a number of other self-assessment exercises, this early evaluation still held true.

• Guidelines for Setting Goals

The tragedy of life doesn't lie in not reaching your goal.
The tragedy lies in having no goal to reach.
—BENJAMIN MAYS

Even before beginning a career evaluation, it is important to set goals to guide you in your career change, or else you can always put off for another day the thinking, networking, and researching that you must do to effectuate your search. So set short, medium, and long-range goals to help accomplish your objectives. Set targets that are beyond you, that make you reach, and that draw upon the best within you. To set goals, ask yourself:

- Do I want this goal because I think I should?

- Does it inspire me?

- Am I limiting my choice to what I think is possible for me to have or do?

- Do I really want this particular thing, or do I want to want it?

- How does this goal add to the quality of my life?

- What is the basic nature of this goal?

- Could I realize this basic nature in another way?

- In what new ways does this goal challenge me to grow?

✍

Goal-Setting Exercises to Help You Focus

The goals you set in this exercise may relate to either your career or personal issues.

    1. Make a list of short-term goals—that is, goals that are achieveable within the next month. Then make a list of slightly longer-term goals—those that can be achieved within six months. Lastly, make a

list of long-term goals—those not achieveable within one year. After you have made as extensive a list as possible for each category, go back to each list and prioritize each goal within its category.

2. Make a list of things you love to do. After exhausting all the possibilities, go back and prioritize the list.

3. Make a list of the things you are good at. Prioritize the list.

4. Make a list of what things are in the way of your a) achieving the top three goals in each category in question 1; b) spending your time doing the top three things you love to do in question 2; and c) doing the top five things you are good at in question 3.

5. Spend some time analyzing whether each barrier you listed in response to question 4 is really just an excuse or rationalization or if the barrier is capable of being overcome, and if so, how and when.

How do you determine what changes you need to make to find a better fit in a job or career? This exercise will help you think through the changes you may want to make and the goals you will need to set to achieve those changes. Complete each of the following sentences, as thoughtfully and realistically as possible.

✍

Changes and Goals Exercise

1. I now live with (spouse, parents, alone, significant other, etc.)_____
2. I would like to be living with_____
3. I now live in (house, flat, apartment, condo, etc.)_____
4. I would like to live in_____
5. I am now living in (city, suburb, rural, country)_____
6. I would like to be living in_____
7. I now work as (occupation, student, unemployed, etc.)____
_____
8. I would like to be working as_____
9. My working hours are_____
10. I would like my working hours to be_____
11. I now work in (corporation, firm, shop, etc.)_____
12. I would like to be working in_____
13. The people I work with now (names, types)_____
14. The people I would like to work with_____
15. I now travel (location, often, not at all)_____

16. I would like to travel_____
17. My closest friends now are_____
18. My closest friends would be_____
19. In my spare time I now_____
20. In my spare time I would_____

Review your responses and compare your present lifestyle, as reflected in the odd-numbered sentences, with your aspirations, as reflected in the even-numbered sentences. Then, make those aspirations that are most important to you into goals, deciding whether you want them to be short-, medium-, or long-term objectives. Next, make a list of what things are in the way of your achieving the top three goals in each category. Finally, analyze whether each barrier is really just an excuse, and if the barrier can be overcome, how and when.

✍

Too Much and Too Little

In order to get a sense of what is overwhelming you and what is missing in your life, answer the following questions in writing in as much detail as you can:

- What am I doing too little of? (Don't put down just "relaxing" or "having free time"—list more.)

- What am I doing too much of? (Don't put down just "working"—elaborate.)

- What would I like to do more often?

- What would I like to do less often?

- What takes too much of my time?

- What do I never have time for?

- What is important to me?

What can you do to remedy or improve any problems illuminated in the above answers?

If you can recall and analyze the activities and events during your lifetime that you enjoyed for the sheer joy of engaging in the experience, you can often begin to recognize a pattern of positive activity, which you can hopefully integrate into a new work situation. Wouldn't it be wonderful to work at something that you actually enjoyed most of the time?

✍

Thirty Enjoyable Experiences

Make a list of thirty enjoyable experiences in your life. Include experiences from childhood, leisure, work, and various segments of your life. Write down experiences that were fun, engrossing, and rewarding to you in some way. Acclaim or acknowledgment from another person is irrelevant; the only criterion is that *you* had good feelings about the experience.

The event can be as simple as a walk in the park or as complex as a two-week trial. If you choose a more complex event, separate the component parts of the event to establish which parts were enjoyable. For example, you enjoyed presenting your opening and closing arguments as well as cross-examining witnesses, but you hated doing the preparatory research. Be very aware of those fun experiences that you would happily repeat. Look for themes and patterns—do all your fun experiences center around physical, intellectual, or artistic activities? Are you always alone or with other people? Are the experiences structured or free form, passive or active? Are you the leader or the follower?

• What Are Your Strengths and Weaknesses?

It is very important to be aware of personal characteristics that can help or hurt your job search. It is necessary to objectively analyze your strengths and weaknesses so that you can target the appropriate jobs and, when interviewing, be prepared to tout the strengths and neutralize the weaknesses.

✍

Strengths Inventory

The objective of this inventory* is to identify the strengths you do have so you can focus on those in planning your job search. The objective is not to see how many boxes you can check off—more isn't necessarily better!

Skills—Legal Research
- ❏ I can easily conduct non-computer library research
- ❏ I understand the interrelationship of various reference materials
- ❏ I can easily conduct computerized research
- ❏ I can develop an efficient research strategy
- ❏ My Shepardizing is automatic and flawless

Skills—Legal Reasoning
- ❏ I have a solid grasp of fundamental legal concepts
- ❏ I can distinguish between primary and subsidiary legal issues
- ❏ I know how to develop a cogent legal analysis or case strategy

Skills—Writing
- ❏ I have full command of correct grammar, proper punctuation, and appropriate vocabulary
- ❏ I formulate and express ideas clearly
- ❏ My citations are accurate
- ❏ The visual presentation of my written work conforms with expected standards

Communication
- ❏ I get my point across powerfully and consistently
- ❏ People listen and respond to me
- ❏ I share my thoughts and ideas
- ❏ I hear beyond what others are saying
- ❏ I can articulate my goals and my plans for achieving them
- ❏ I am an effective communicator in advocacy proceedings
- ❏ I listen carefully

*Used courtesy of Tulane Law School, Office of Career Services, Kristin Flierl, Assistant Dean

Professional
❏ I lead a group well
❏ I handle myself well in professional situations
❏ I know appropriate deportment for my profession
❏ I meet and exceed my goals
❏ I meet deadlines
❏ I manage my time effectively
❏ I am able to set priorities
❏ I am organized
❏ I pay attention to detail
❏ I can work independently and take initiative
❏ I am on time and keep appointments
❏ My conduct is ethical at all times
❏ I accept criticism and modify my work habits accordingly

Challenges
❏ I learn from disappointments and problems
❏ I anticipate problems and handle them early
❏ I don't mind risk
❏ I adapt and make the most of changes around me
❏ I can count on myself to always survive the worst

Style
❏ People can count on me to be on time and keep my word
❏ I am organized
❏ I don't gossip; I keep confidences
❏ I am trustworthy
❏ I am energetic and enthusiastic
❏ I project a positive attitude
❏ I have and honor personal standards
❏ I make and follow through on my commitments
❏ I know when to ask questions or seek advice
❏ I exercise good judgment

Outlook
❏ I am optimistic about myself and my future
❏ I am actively engaged in creating my future

Career
- ❐ I am aware of what I can do with a law degree
- ❐ I know where I want to work
- ❐ I know what I want to do
- ❐ I am developing a sense of the skills characteristic of successful attorneys in my preferred practice areas

• What Are Your Skills?

An in-depth assessment of your skills is absolutely necessary before you can undertake an effective job or career change. Without an honest analysis of your abilities, you will probably fall into another unhappy work situation that meets neither your needs nor your wants. Once you have a clear picture of what your skills are and which ones you prefer to use, you have a focus for further exploration of which career options really would be a good fit for you.

There are three kinds of skills:

1. **Work content skills.** These are learned some time after birth—how to write a brief, how to use a computer, how to drive a car, how to sew a shirt, how to compute a math problem. Because these skills can be learned on the job or through training, you don't already need to have them when you interview for or start a job. As a law student or law graduate, you are bright and capable of learning new information, and your training alone is proof that you have the intelligence (not necessarily the flexibility, however) to learn new and complex information and skills.

2. **Organizational skills.** These are personal preference skills, such as punctuality and neatness. These are difficult to change and thus remain fairly constant from job to job.

3. **Functional/transferable skills.** These skills are innate, although often enhanced by education or experience—for instance, speaking, writing, athletic, artistic, musical, and analytical ability. Although we all have a bit of each of these skills, some of us naturally have more of one and less of another and therefore have to work harder to acquire and perfect the ones we lack.

You need to be aware of your well-developed skills because those are the ones that come naturally to you and are the most comfortable and pleasing to use. When you are using those skills, what you are doing at that moment doesn't seem like work, and you don't have to think about your actions. Everything just flows smoothly. These are the skills that you want to transfer to new work. Conversely, when you are required to use a skill that does not come naturally or that you haven't developed, the task will produce stress and feel forced. You will have to concentrate much harder to get a successful result.

PRESENTING TRANSFERABLE SKILLS

Why is an analysis of your skills important? First you will be able to explain to potential employers what you have to offer their firm or company. Second, you will be able to succinctly explain how the skills you have acquired as a law student and/or lawyer are of value to a particular employer or job. Third, you will be able to avoid using legal jargon when explaining your skills, which will communicate your skills more clearly to both legal and nonlegal employers. Particularly if you are applying for a position in a less traditional or out-of-law job, it is absolutely necessary to convey your skills in terms a non-lawyer will understand. You must clearly define your skills in language that illuminates their transferability to the desired position.

Therefore, before applying for any position, and especially before attending an interview, be sure to analyze the skills your desired position requires. For example, if you are applying for a position as a management consultant, you may determine that the required skills would be knowledge of business operations, analytical ability, ability to communicate both verbally and in writing, good interpersonal relations, facility with numbers, and so on. Then, drawing from your previous legal experience (and volunteer work and "life-before-law"), you can prepare a list of ways you've used those skills. Write those examples down in "lay" language, not legalese.

If you are interviewing for a job as a technical writer and you state that you have written briefs and made court appearances, your interviewer may well be puzzled. You not only reinforce the fact that you have narrowly focused lawyering skills but you also fail to explain what those skills are, in any manner understandable to a non-lawyer. However, if you instead inform the interviewer that you had occasion to research and analyze complex data and information, then wrote a document incorporating that data and information into a usable and understandable format, which clearly explained the issues and terminology so that your clients and the court could comprehend it, you have informed the interviewer that you have already done what a technical writer is required to do. You have made it clear that you took complex information and converted it into understandable written material and that you can make yourself understood to non-lawyers. You have demonstrated that you have the skills of a technical writer, and in a two-for-one deal, you also happen to be a law graduate.

SKILLS ACQUIRED IN LAW SCHOOL AND LAW PRACTICE

Although you may think that you have narrowed your future opportunities by training and working as a lawyer, in reality you have learned, cultivated, and utilized some very valuable skills, highly transferable and in great demand in the marketplace. Perhaps without even realizing, you have developed the ability to:

- ❏ synthesize ideas
- ❏ compile information
- ❏ listen intently and thoughtfully
- ❏ create concrete expression of abstract ideas
- ❏ write clearly and persuasively
- ❏ edit and proofread
- ❏ think and write analytically
- ❏ speak with and in front of people, including groups
- ❏ think on your feet
- ❏ work diligently
- ❏ finish projects on time
- ❏ counsel
- ❏ negotiate

- ❏ teach
- ❏ sell (persuade)
- ❏ articulate and/or advocate a position
- ❏ understand legal terminology
- ❏ understand the legal system
- ❏ work with others toward completion of a goal
- ❏ research
- ❏ develop strategy
- ❏ work effectively with a variety of people

Check off the skills in the above list that you feel are your most highly developed and be prepared to give examples of how you have used these skills.

After a thorough inventory of your skills, the next important step is to determine which of your skills you enjoy using and to what end. Satisfaction from a job often derives from using skills you are good at *and* enjoy. There are few things more stress-inducing than continually having to use skills you feel are deficient. But even if you are competent at a skill, having to continually use one you do not enjoy will soon create discontent. For example, you may be very articulate but dislike speaking in front of groups. Imagine the problem if you were given responsibility for all court appearances on your office's law and motion calendar. It is important to pinpoint not only those skills you excel at, but those you like to use as well.

FUNCTIONAL SKILLS ASSESSMENT

When assessing your skills, try to be somewhat kind to yourself and give yourself credit for skills you do possess. Pay attention to what people say you are good at. You don't have to be the best writer in the county to state that you have good writing skills. If you hang back from touting a good skill because it isn't perfect, you may never find a job that matches your skills or one that you will feel competent to attempt. As Susan Bistline emphasized, "There is nothing wrong with average. There is nothing wrong with good. Not everything has to be brilliant.

To be paralyzed because you might not be perfect is to waste a life. Go for it!"

One way to more comfortably evaluate your skills might be to assess yourself on the basis of "personal best"—the amount of potential you have actually achieved—rather than evaluating yourself on the more competitive basis of "your performance relative to all other people." The former evaluation demonstrates the effectiveness of your skills, rather than their superiority.

✍

Skills Assessment Exercise

Circle in blue each of the following skills you enjoy, then go back a second time and circle in red those skills you are good at. Take special note of the skills where the circles overlap—those are the ones you will want to emphasize when you look at job opportunities, assemble your resume, and interview. The skills you circle only in blue can become more productive job hunting skills if you take classes, read books, or perhaps apprentice or volunteer somewhere to develop more expertise. A job that uses either too many or too much of even one of the skills you circle only in red should be avoided; although you are good at those skills, overuse will burn you out, since you don't enjoy using them.

Abstracting/Conceptualizing
Advising
Anticipating events/problems/
    styles
Arranging
Auditing
Calculating
Coaching
Committee working
Confronting
Controlling
Corresponding
Creating
Dealing with unknowns
Delegating

Administering
Analyzing
Appraising programs/
    property
Assembling
Budgeting
Classifying
Collecting
Compiling
Constructing
Coordinating
Counseling
Dealing with pressure
Deciding
Designing

Developing mathematical
models
Displaying
Dramatizing
Enduring
Estimating
Examining
Explaining
Finding
Group facilitating
Handling detail work
Imagining
Inspecting
Interviewing
Laboratory work
Locating
Managing
Measuring
Meeting the public
Motivating
Negotiating
Obtaining information
Organizing
Persuading
Politicking
Preparing
Processing
Promoting
Protecting
Reading
Record keeping
Rehabilitating
Repairing
Representing
Reviewing
Selling
Setting up
Speaking
Talking

Dispensing
Distributing
Editing
Entertaining
Evaluating
Exhibiting
Expressing feelings
Fund raising
Handling complaints
Hurrying
Initiating
Interpreting
Investigating
Listening
Making layouts
Mapping
Mediating
Monitoring
Moving with dexterity
Observing
Operating
Outdoor working
Planning
Predicting
Printing
Programming
Proposal writing
Questioning
Recording
Recruiting
Remembering
Repeating
Researching
Rewriting
Serving
Sketching
Supervising
Teaching
Tolerating

Timing

Translating

Trouble shooting

Using instruments

Writing

Treating

Updating

Working with precision

CLUSTERING YOUR SKILLS

Now that you have analyzed your skills, it is helpful to visualize how they fall into certain groups. This will help you choose appropriate job categories and write a good functional resume (see chapter 10 on resumes). The following breakdown* will help you think about your skills in functional clusters. However, it's important to keep in mind that there is often a difference between a skill *category* and a skill. For example, lawyering may be considered a skill category, but that category is made up of individual skills—writing, reading, counseling, negotiating, analyzing, etc. Similarly, teaching is a skill but it is also a category, made up of the individual skills of working with groups, learning new materials quickly, writing logically, public speaking, explaining ideas clearly, etc.

MANAGEMENT SKILLS

Developing	Coordinating	Evaluating
Planning	Analyzing	Administering
Organizing	Prioritizing	Contracting
Executing	Delegating	Producing
Supervising	Hiring	Controlling
Assigning	Firing	Reviewing
Directing	Recommending	Troubleshooting

COMMUNICATION SKILLS

Influencing	Creating	Writing
Persuading	Negotiating	Interpreting

* Abstracted from San Francisco Community College, Student Personnel Services Center handout.

Helping
Directing
Leading
Reasoning
Developing
Recruiting

Arbitrating
Arranging
Mediating
Reconciling
Merging
Obtaining

Enlisting
Motivating
Manipulating
Reading
Speaking

FINANCIAL SKILLS

Calculating
Computing
Planning
Managing
Budgeting
Bookkeeping
Accounting

Auditing
Appraising
Researching
Analyzing
Record keeping
Detail
Accuracy

Speed
Allocating
Administering
Finger dexterity
Developing
Preparing
Solving

MANUAL SKILLS

Operating
Tending
Controlling
Grinding
Assembling
Setting up

Feeding
Cutting
Binding
Driving
Moving
Lifting

Bending
Pulling
Shipping
Handling
Punching
Drilling

HELPING SKILLS

Mentoring
Relating
Guiding
Leading
Adjusting
Servicing
Referring

Rendering
Attending
Caring
Sensitivity
Listening
Speaking
Directing

Perception
Intuition
Understanding
Maturity
Teamwork

RESEARCH SKILLS

Recognizing problems	Gathering	Critiquing
Clarifying	Synthesizing	Perceiving
Surveying	Examining	Collecting
Interviewing	Diagnosing	Writing
Investigating	Reviewing	Interpreting
Inspecting	Organizing	Extrapolating
	Evaluating	Deciding

CREATIVE SKILLS

Innovating	Planning	Generating
Developing	Conceptualizing	Perceiving
Creating	Synthesizing	Memorizing
Imagining	Integrating	Discriminating
Designing	Abstracting	Intuition
Visualizing	Writing	Acting
Sensitivity	Directing	Playing
Humor	Imagining	Sharing
Fashioning	Painting	
Shaping	Performing	

TEACHING SKILLS

Influencing	Explaining	Developing
Persuading	Enlightening	Enabling
Briefing	Stimulating	Clarifying
Informing	Inventing	Valuing
Encouraging	Enthusiasm	Goal setting
Communicating	Adapting	Deciding
Advising	Adopting	Initiating
Guiding	Facilitating	
Coaching	Coordinating	
Instructing		

DETAIL SKILLS

Approving	Arranging	Inspecting
Validating	Time management	Organizing
Retaining	Variety	Operating
Executing	Routine	Classifying
Dispatching	Memory	Collating
Responding	Judgment	Copying
Following through	Collecting	Retrieving
Implementing	Compiling	Recording
Enforcing	Purchasing	Processing
Responsibility	Systematizing	Facilitating
Tolerance	Tabulating	
Meeting deadlines	Comparing	

✍

Examples of Personality and Work-Style Traits

These are terms you can use to describe yourself, to show your personal qualities, as opposed to your skills. A combination of any number of these terms makes up who you are and will help give you the words to describe yourself when you are asked about your personal characteristics. Go through the list and circle the traits that apply to you.

adventuresome	concerned
adept	conscientious
alert	considerate
assertive	cooperative
astute	courage(ous)
attention to details	creative
authentic	curious
authority, handles well	dependable
aware	diplomatic
calm	discreet
candid	driven (as in ambition)
challenges, thrives on	dynamic
character, has fine	easygoing
committed	emotional stability
competent	empathy
concentration	enthusiastic

exceptional
experienced
expert
expressive
firm
flexible
generous
gets along well with others
high energy level
honest
humanistic
imaginative
impulses, controls well
initiating
innovative
insight
integrity, displays
judgment, mature
loyal
natural
objective
openminded
optimistic
orderly
outgoing
outstanding
patient
penetrating
perceptive
persevering
persistence
personable
pioneering
playful

poise
polite
precise attainment of set goals,
    to limits of standards
proficient
professional appearance
professional attitude
punctual
reliable
resourceful
responsible
risk-taking
self-confident
self-control
self-reliant
self-respect
sense of humor
sensitivity
sincere
sophisticated
spontaneous
strikes balance
strong (as under stress)
successful
sympathetic
tactful
takes nothing for granted
thinks on his/her feet
thorough
tidy
tolerant
unique
versatile
vigorous

✍

Fifteen Accomplishments

Another way to ascertain your skills is to think back on your accomplishments. In order to recognize which skills you have and which you enjoy using, it is useful to examine the skills you used in those various accomplishments. Often, it is the successful and fun application of your skills that makes an event feel like an accomplishment.

Part A

1. Think of an accomplishment, something that you did well and that gave you a sense of satisfaction. The fact that no one else knew of your accomplishment or gave you accolades is irrelevant—only your sense of achievement is what is important here. Your accomplishment may be from your work, educational, recreational, or volunteer activities. Be sure to include accomplishments from years past as well as more recent ones.

2. Describe the event in detail, using action words.

3. From your description, identify the skills you used. Use skill words that break the action down into its smallest parts. For instance, Teaching skills = assessing student knowledge and motivation, using facts to prepare appropriate lessons, performing, persuading, etc.

4. Follow this pattern of skills identification for fifteen different accomplishments.

Part B

1. Do you see any patterns among your various skills? Are there commonalities among your skills? Do certain skills or groups of skills occur frequently.

2. Group your skills into clusters, using the list of clustered skills beginning on page 110.

3. Rate the three skill clusters you most wish to use in a job.

4. Create a list of jobs that utilize some or all of your skills, being as nonjudgmental as you can (see chapters 6 through 8 for ideas on jobs).

The bottom line is that if the work you select is going to continue to satisfy you, there should be a fit between your skills and the skills needed to effectively perform the job. For example, if you want to be a litigator, you will be satisfied if you enjoy advocating a position, communicating information, telling stories, competing, analyzing complicated fact patterns, speaking extemporaneously and persuasively, and delving into situational intricacies.

On the other hand, transactional attorneys are often more satis-fied if they are detail and data oriented, enjoy analyzing and assembling puzzles, have facility with written language, have an ability to clearly convey complex information both orally and in writing, and enjoy negotiating and reaching consensus (or at least resolution of conflict).

Both litigators and transactional attorneys should have some ability to research, mentally and manually process data, digest and remember volumes of information, counsel, and listen.

But keep in mind that many of these skills can be applied as successfully outside the law as inside, so the next step to help with your career decisions is to access your values.

• Values

A thorough inventory of your values is just as important as a catalog of your skills, since you will continue to be unhappy if you are required to work contrary to your values. Much of job satisfaction is derived from the values, as well as the nature, of the work. Just because you have excellent research skills doesn't mean that you should prepare research materials for a program that is antithetical to your beliefs, or research in isolation if you desire to work on a team.

For most people, the lack or violation of a dearly held value can irreparably damage even the most exciting and otherwise well-fitting work situation. Be clear about your values when you interview for a job, and ask questions that will elicit indications whether those values will be met. Be very aware of your values, because as Howard Figler, author of *The Complete Job-Search Handbook,* said, "Values are the emotional salary of work and some people aren't drawing a paycheck."

DETERMINE YOUR VALUES

To assess your values, after each entry in the chart that follows, place a checkmark in the column that best fits the description of how important that value is to you. Once you have finished the exercise, go back through the list and circle the three most important values from the entire list. These three circled values should be used like a litmus test when examining job and career opportunities, to ensure that they fit your values.

	ALWAYS VALUED	OFTEN VALUED	SOMETIMES VALUED	SELDOM VALUED	NEVER VALUED
Advancement: opportunity to make rapid career advancement					
Adventure: doing something new or different; activities involve risk taking					
Aesthetics: involved in study or appreciation of the beauty of things, ideas, etc.					
Affiliation: recognized as a member of a particular organization					
Artistic creativity: engage in creative art work					
Challenging problems: position provides challenging problems and avoids continual routine					
Change and variety: work responsibilities frequently change in content and setting					
Community: live where I can get involved in community affairs					

	Always Valued	Often Valued	Sometimes Valued	Seldom Valued	Never Valued
Competence: doing a good job, mastering a task, being skillful					
Competition: engage in activities that pit my abilities against others'					
Creative expression: opportunity to express my ideas orally or in writing					
Creativity: create new ideas, programs, etc., not following another's format					
Excitement: experience high degree or frequent excitement in my work					
Fast pace: work is done rapidly or demands a fast pace					
Friendships: develop close personal relationships with people through my work					
Help others: directly help others individually or in small groups					
Help society: contribute to the betterment of the world					
High earnings: monetary rewards enable me to purchase luxuries					

	ALWAYS VALUED	OFTEN VALUED	SOMETIMES VALUED	SELDOM VALUED	NEVER VALUED
Honesty: able to be frank and genuinely myself with others					
Independence: able to determine nature of own work; free from constraints					
Influence people: in a position to change attitudes or opinions of others					
Intellectual status: regarded as an expert in a given field or thought of as highly intellectual					
Interest: doing something just because I like to do it, for its own sake					
Job tranquility: avoid pressure and "the rat race"					
Knowledge: engage myself in pursuit of knowledge, truth, and understanding					
Leadership: directing or showing others what to do or how to do something					
Location: live and work in an area that is conducive to my lifestyle; no long commute					

	ALWAYS VALUED	OFTEN VALUED	SOMETIMES VALUED	SELDOM VALUED	NEVER VALUED
Make decisions: power to decide courses of action, policies, etc.					
Moral fulfillment: feel my work is contributing to standards important to me					
Physical challenge: my work makes physical demands that I find rewarding					
Power and authority: controlling or influencing others					
Precision work: work in situations with little tolerance for error					
Profit and gain: probability of great material gain					
Public contact: have a lot of contact with other people					
Recognition: public recognition for my work					
Security: assured of keeping my job and a reasonable financial reward					
Stability: a work routine and duties that are predictable and not likely to change					
Status: position carries high respect with friends, family, and community					

	ALWAYS VALUED	OFTEN VALUED	SOMETIMES VALUED	SELDOM VALUED	NEVER VALUED
Supervision: directly responsible for work done by others					
Time freedom: no specific working hours, with responsibilities I can schedule					
Work alone: little contact with others, with projects I can do myself					
Work on frontiers of knowledge: involved in cutting edge information or product development, research, testing, etc.					
Work under pressure: time pressure is prevalent or quality of work is critiqued by others					
Work with others: work as a team to achieve common goals					

Once you have completed the above exercise, answer the following questions:

• Is there any conflict between your "always valued" values and your current job? List and explain.

• Is there any conflict between values in your "always valued" column, such as security versus profit and gain? List any and explain.

• Are there conflicts between what you want for yourself and what others want for you?

• Which of your values have changed over time? Which have remained constant? Which, if any, do you expect to change in the future?

• Which values does your current job/career offer?

✍

Preferences and Interests

It isn't always possible to work in a field that is directly involved with something that is a hot interest of yours. However, you probably don't want to work in a job where you are required to pursue topics you have absolutely no interest in. Make a list of topics that interest you—for example, current affairs, sports, art, jewelry, computers, home decorating, woodworking, investing, etc. Use that list as a basis for investigating possible jobs that address those interests.

• Working Environment

If you have very strong feelings about the decor, atmosphere, size, location, formality, or other factors in your working environment, acknowledge them to yourself, for the wrong environment could spoil an otherwise satisfying work arrangement. As one of my clients told me, he didn't have a suit and never intended to buy one, so he is now doing criminal appeals and writs out of his home. If an important criterion is working where you know everyone, where you can be a "big fish in a small pond," you may decide not to investigate jobs in big cities.

Be sure to give thought to what kind of people you want to work with—creative, communicative, humorous, white- or blue-collared, extroverted or introverted, etc. Everything else about a job can be adequate, but if you are working with people who are outside your comfort zone, you will not want to stay in that job.

✍

Classified Employment Advertisements

Most lawyers longingly look through either the legal or general employment advertisements, hoping to find the perfect job. As is more fully discussed in chapter 9, this is not often fruitful, since only a small percentage of jobs are advertised. But whether you intend to stay in or leave law, looking through the general employment ads to identify which ads or portions of them appeal to you can be helpful to illuminate your skills, values, and interests.

Go through a Sunday paper and read all of the job ads, circling in red any words in a listing that catch your attention, even if the balance of the ad is not of interest to you or you aren't qualified for the position. After you have completed your reading, try to identify categories of interests or skills illustrated by your circles—for instance, travel, teaching, science, healing, computers. Look for repeated themes or values, such as multiple circles around words such as "sell" or "team" or "exciting" or "independence." As an additional benefit, maybe you'll even see an advertisement that you want to answer!

✍

Data Sheet

Another method to identify your skills, values, and interests is to use the data sheet on page 124 as a template and fill out one copy for each job or volunteer experience, which can be very helpful in consolidating your prior paid *and* volunteer work. Take note that, in terms of acquired experience, and development and showcasing of your skills, volunteer work can be every bit as relevant as paid employment. If fully filled out, these data sheets can be useful for preparing for an interview, drafting a resume, or merely determining if you have the basic qualifications for a potential job.

✍

Questions for Deducing Ideal Work Situations

In order to find work that satisfies you, it is necessary to coordinate those skills you like to use, those values that are important to you, and the subjects that interest you. Try to envision an ideal job and work situation; here are some questions to ask yourself that will help you put your dream job into words:

• Are you alone or with others? How many others? If both apply, what percentage of the time are you alone?

—DATA SHEET—

DATES
COMPANY/ORGANIZATION (PAID EMPLOYMENT)
VOLUNTEER/HOBBY, ETC.
WHAT DID I DO?
WHAT INTERESTS, SKILLS, VALUES, DID I APPLY?
RESULTS (GOOD & BAD)
MAJOR TASKS I ENJOYED MOST OF ALL

• What is the nature of your interaction with others? Are you conversing with or working alongside of them? Are you engaged in some activity with (or maybe even against) them? What skills are you using?

• What are the personality characteristics of the other people around you? Upbeat? Empathetic? Analytical? Responsible? Daring? Competitive? Challenging? Smart? Artistic? Intellectual? Athletic?

• What are you doing? Is it physical, mental, both? Are you passive or active, moving or staying in one place? Conveying or receiving information?

• What is your focus in the event? Enjoyment for the sake of enjoyment, competition, personal growth, building something?

• What is the environment? Indoors or out, sunny, rainy, dark, bright, crowded, spacious, formal, casual?

• Are you relating emotionally, intellectually, physically, or spiritually to your surroundings? What values does the work evidence, and why are you drawn to it?

• Are your activities internalized (thoughtful or meditative) or external (teaching, advising, coaching, viewing entertainment)?

• What is the tempo of the event? Fast-paced, relaxed, both?

Answers to these questions may be contradictory, as you may enjoy being alone and being with others, or doing high-energy activities as well as engaging in contemplating your navel. The point of the exercise is to discover all of your important needs, skills, values, and interests, to discover what will give you enjoyment and balance in your life.

✍

Ideal Work Situation Grid

Once you have completed all of the previous exercises in this chapter, create an Ideal Work Situation Grid using the example below as a guide. Only include those skills, values, environment, types of people, and subject matter that you absolutely must have or must not have. Do not include neutral concerns—only those that could make or break your job satisfaction. Use this grid when looking at new job and career options.

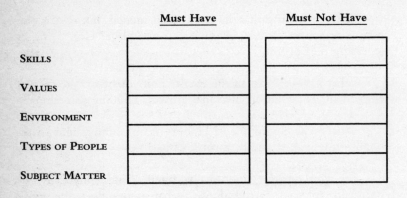

	Must Have	**Must Not Have**
SKILLS		
VALUES		
ENVIRONMENT		
TYPES OF PEOPLE		
SUBJECT MATTER		

✍

Obituary Writing

Another exercise that may help you develop focus on a new job or career area involves writing your ideal obituary. Oftentimes my clients realize, after completing their obituary, that the accomplishments they have listed in it are eminently doable and needn't remain in the realm of pure fantasy.

Write an obituary for yourself if you were to die in thirty (or if that's too soon, however many) years, setting out the accomplishments (personal, professional, volunteer, etc.) for which you would like to be remembered.

• Testing

Tests for career evaluation and individual assessment can be helpful, especially for lawyers who often need written confirmation of what their repressed emotional self is whispering. Although tests should not be used as the only means for career selection, they are informative and can provide some direction. Most career counselors and counseling centers can administer the various tests. Although community or junior colleges are a less expensive way to take the tests and receive some interpretation, that interpretation may be filtered through the perception of a counselor who generally works with young or entry level people rather than professionals.

Three of the primary tests given to career changers are listed below; however, there are other tests that might be of interest to you. Ask your career counselor or a career counseling center if they think any others would benefit you.

TESTS

The **Myers-Briggs Type Indicator** evaluates personality type to determine work and communication style preferences, which, if not in harmony with your work situation, can create discord. See discussion of this test in chapter 2, beginning on page 28. To locate a licensed MBTI administrator in your area, contact Association for Psychological Type at (816) 444–3500.

Strong Interest Inventory (formerly Strong-Campbell Interest Inventory) and **Career Occupational Preference Evaluation** both attempt to deduce interests. The former test identifies specific jobs that match interests, whereas the latter test suggests general areas of interest.

RESOURCES

Johnson O'Connor Research Foundation (national headquarters), 11 E. 62nd Street, New York, NY 10021; (212) 838–0550; for general information call (800) 452–1539. The foundation has locations in ten other cities, including San Francisco, Dallas, Seattle, Atlanta, Chicago, and Washington, DC. The foundation believes that job satisfaction results from using skills that come naturally to you; it offers a day and a half of aptitude testing designed to obtain an individualized job profile. Website is members.aol.com/jocrf.lg.

If you want to try a knockoff of the Myers–Briggs indicator on-line, try the Keirsey Temperament Sorter at sunsite.unc.edu/jembin/mb.pl. It will give you the flavor of type assessment.

Please Understand Me: Character & Temperament Types, David Kiersey and Marilyn Bates, Prometheus Nemesis Book Co., 5th edition, 1984. The authors present a simplified version of the Myers–Briggs personality indicator and apply their results to various lifestyle preferences.

Gifts Differing, Isabel Briggs Myers & Peter B. Myers, Consulting Psychologists Press, Inc., reprint edition, 1995. An explanation of the Myers–Briggs Type Indicator by one of its developers.

"The Lawyer Types: How Your Personality Affects Your Practice," Larry Richard, *ABA Journal,* July 1993. Using the Myers–Briggs analysis of personality, the author applies it to lawyers and their workstyles. Refer to the discussion of his research results in chapter 2 of this book, beginning at page 29. See also Richard's coauthored chapter, "Anatomy of a Lawyer: Personality and Long-Term Career Satisfaction" beginning at page 149 in *Full Disclosure: Do You Really Want to Be a Lawyer?* edited by Susan J. Bell, 2nd edition, Peterson's Guides, 1992, initially published by the American Bar Association. *Full Disclosure* is out of print, but would be available at many law libraries and law school career services offices.

Discover What You're Best At, Barry & Linda Gale, Fireside Press, 1990. Helps identify your interests and skills, then matches them to 1,000+ different jobs.

Do What You Are: Discover the Perfect Career for You Through the Secrets of Personality Type, Paul Tieger and Barbara Barron Tieger, Little Brown, 2nd edition, 1995. An analysis of the Myers–Briggs Type Indicator as it applies to career choice.

Once you can answer the question Who am I? You're finally ready to explore and pursue the various career options that will allow you to be who you really are so that you can actually enjoy your work.

PART TWO

MORE THAN 300
THINGS YOU CAN DO
WITH A LAW DEGREE

---

*Having it all doesn't necessarily mean
having it all at once.*
— STEPHANIE LEUTKEHAUS

Lawyers often phone me and, with a note of challenge in their voice, ask, "What *are* some of those many career options available to lawyers that I've heard that you talk about?" When I affirm that there are many, adding that I can't give them a list because those which will work for them depend on their skills, experience, interests, values, personality, and motivation, I often hear a sigh. These callers really wanted me to list three or four potential job opportunities so that they could immediately choose among the few options, begin and finish a job hunt in a week, and be done with it. We all want the easy way.

Of course, if you've read the previous chapters in this handbook, you already have been told numerous times that the process isn't easy. However, if you looked in the table of contents and turned first to this section of the handbook, let me reiterate that, for the best job and career change results, you should spend some time, after browsing through the next three chapters on options, going back and giving at least a bit of attention to the first five chapters. Selecting the job title or description of a particular career that intrigues you may give you a relieved sense that there can actually be interesting work aside from traditional law practice. But without the information about yourself that you will gain from chapters 1 to 5, you won't know if that particular career will work for you in the long run. So read on for the next three chapters, then turn back to the beginning of this handbook.

In chapters 6 through 8, I will set out and discuss many of the career options that lawyers have pursued and obtained. Chapter 6 discusses options within the law (you're required to have passed a bar exam and have your active law license); chapter 7, options related to the law (you probably need a law degree, but most often not a law license); and chapter 8, options outside of the law (your law degree is often a help, as it gives you credibility and background, but sometimes it may even be a hindrance, something you will have to explain and overcome). Although each of the career options doesn't necessarily fall crisply into only one of these three categories—writing for a legal publishing house sometimes requires an active law license, sometimes not—I have chosen to place them in the chapter where they most often fit.

Additionally, the options listed in law, related to law, and out of law are not exhaustive but are put forth as a good foundation, a base upon which to build your knowledge of other options.

One last piece of advice before you start mulling over the multitude of career options. When you're looking for work, it's important to strike a balance between accepting the very first job you are offered (and being unhappy) and waiting for your dream job (and being unhappy or financially unfit when it is too long in coming). It is pointless to attempt to make a commitment to a job you do not want to do, nor does it make sense to starve because a job isn't *exactly* what you had in mind.

Additionally, we lawyers often tend to be perfectionists, expecting our work to be wonderful 100 percent of the time. This is an unrealistic expectation; as mentioned in an earlier chapter, studies have shown that, even among individuals who state that they love their work, a 75 percent satisfaction level is considered good. Everyone has bad days, bad clients, or bad outcomes at varying times in their work year or even work week. Whether you work in law or opt for a position outside of law, you can expect nothing different.

• Option Considerations

Before you try to decide which of the numerous career options might work for you, there are some preliminary considerations that will help you narrow the possibilities. This is important, because the *Dictionary of Occupational Titles,* published by the U.S. Department of Labor, lists more than 12,000 different jobs—and, after all, you can't possibly thoroughly investigate even twenty of these many jobs. In fact, five or six is more realistic for most people, given their limited resources and lack of time. So your answers to the following questions should help you toss out some otherwise attractive options and give you a reasonable number of options to investigate.

What career style are you looking for? Are you looking for a total career, where your income derives from one source, such as your legal employer or your solo practice clients? Or do you prefer to have more of a composite career, where your income comes from a number of sources? For example, one of my counseling clients is a contract lawyer, teaches a law class on torts, works part-time as a massage therapist, and teaches at a massage school. Individuals who elect to pursue a composite career are often the people who say to me that they have too many interests and thus are having a tough time choosing which avenue to pursue. My response is, "Why choose? Why not pursue some of each interest and, combined, the income they bring in perhaps can be sufficient for your needs." For some of my clients this is an excellent resolution. However, others might feel schizophrenic, disliking the lack of in-depth focus on just one field.

Are you rooted to the area in which you live? Will you travel? Could you move to another location if you were offered a job as, say, a lobbyist, where the action is mainly in Washington, D.C., or a state capital? If you won't or can't move, there are a number of fields you can cross off. If you live in the Midwest, you can probably dismiss ambitions to be a movie star or a champion surfer. Additionally, if you aren't willing to travel much for business, there are many jobs that won't work, such as airline pilot, national sales manager, or professional golfer.

What kind of work hours do you want? Most people want or need to work full-time for the income or because work is part of their identity. However, if you want to work part-time, "reduced hours" jobs are less available in certain fields than in others. It continues to be somewhat difficult to arrange a reduced hours work schedule within a law firm, although it is not impossible. But the corporate sector is much more amenable to alternative workstyles, and it particularly likes consultants who bid a job, do it, and leave, with no remnant labor issues. See chapter 4 for a full discussion of alternative work time issues.

What kind of job environment do you want? It might not matter to you whether your job requires formal or casual attire, whether it's downtown or in the suburbs, in the city or country. But if you have certain requirements, be sure to take appropriate note and accommodate those requirements, like an East Coast client who firmly stated that he wanted to work in the suburbs, with grass and trees, and not in an area with unrelenting cement. Another client had a fabulous wardrobe and told me it was important to her to work with people who expected her to dress nicely and appreciated her style—she's now selling real estate in a very wealthy Southern community where her wardrobe fits with her job. Keep in mind that these issues are important only if they matter to you. If they don't, pass right by this question.

• How Do You Discover the Various Options?

Read magazines, newspapers, etc. to learn what people are doing both for fun and to make a living. Read about people both in and out of law, because you can get relevant ideas from many sources, whether it's an idea about a legal practice area or a job completely devoid of legal-think. Keep in mind that there are a lot of terrible jobs that people work at to pay their rent. But you are looking for the gem in the dust pile, like one of the participants in a career evaluation workshop I led, who told the group she had an "epiphany" when reading a magazine story about a woman who founded and was running a school for dyslexic kids. This workshop participant immediately knew that working with such children and running such a school was exactly what she wanted to do—by the next week she had applied to return to school and had given notice to her legal employer.

Ask anyone and everyone what they do for a living. The more ideas you get, the better informed your choices will be. You will probably be told about fields you didn't even known existed. At a party, in line at the grocery, while at the doctor's office, talk to people and ask them about their jobs. Most people are more than happy to tell an attentive listener about their work, since it is so rare that people ask—and then actively listen—to stories about the topic. For example, some time ago, on an air trip to Los Angeles, I sat next to a woman who worked for General Electric as a contract manager. At the time, I was not familiar with contract management, so by asking her questions, I learned about a totally new option. As a side benefit, you might even make an effective networking contact, who may then give you information about a great job available with her company. If you hadn't started a conversation with this person, you would never have known about this job.

Read the employment advertisements in the Sunday paper. This exercise has several benefits. First, it alerts you to fields that are hot—important information whether you stay in law (and have to pick a developing practice area or firm that is growing) or move out of practice. Second, it gives you a reality check as to what the average person earns. And third, every time I assign this exercise in a career evaluation workshop, at least one person finds at least one ad that she or he likes well enough to respond to.

Be aware that some good jobs for those with a J.D. just aren't listed in the legal papers. For example, several years ago the State

Bar of California placed an ad in the local San Francisco newspaper for a director of communications ("good writer/communicator; legal background of interest, but not necessary") but did not run it in the legal papers. Those who did not regularly read the general circulation newspaper ads never had the opportunity to apply for that choice position.

Read through all of the career options in this handbook. None are made up; they are real jobs filled by real lawyers. Perhaps one or two will spark your interest.

CHAPTER SIX

Options within the Law

Use the talents you possess. The woods would be very silent if no birds sang except the best.

—UNKNOWN

In order to work within the legal profession and practice law, whether in a law firm, the government, a corporation, a university, or the other options in this chapter, you almost always have to obtain, and maintain, an active license to practice. An inactive license is not sufficient, nor usually is a license from a state other than the one in which you work, unless you select to practice exclusively before the federal courts or work for a federal agency. To practice in the federal courts, an active license from any jurisdiction is generally acceptable. (Federal practice perhaps should be a focus if you have plans to move to another jurisdiction sometime in the future.) Some national companies don't require their in-house attorneys to be locally licensed if their legal advice is given only within the company and they are not litigators required to make appearances before local courts.

Additionally, there are numerous practice areas within law firms, and there are other entities that hire lawyers, as well as a variety of ways to practice—as a litigator or a transactional lawyer, in a large, medium, or small firm, with one or two partners or solo, in a big city or small town, representing large or small companies, individuals or public entities, and so on. The choice is yours, once you have decided that you want to use your legal skills as a lawyer and have determined what work style and environment will best suit you.

RESOURCES

The Legal Career Guide: From Law Student to Lawyer, Gary Munneke, ABA Press, 1993. The title is descriptive of what this book covers. Can be ordered from ABA, Attn: Publication Orders, P.O. Box 10892, Chicago, IL 60610–0892; (800) 285–2221 or e-mail abasvcctr@attmail.com

My First Year As A Lawyer: Real-World Stories from America's Lawyers, edited by Mark Simenhoff, Signet, 1996. Personal accounts from eighteen different lawyers who offer advice not found in most career guides.

Moral Vision and Professional Decisions: The Changing Values of Women and Men Lawyers, Rand Jack and Dana Crowley Jack, Cambridge University Press, 1989. A study of the disparities between personal and professional morality in the practice of law.

American Lawyers, Richard L. Abel, Oxford University Press, 1991. An analysis of the tensions in the practice of law, including the "tension between [a lawyer's] search for professional identity and . . . pursuit of economic success."

Lawyers: A Critical Reader, edited by Richard L. Abel, New Press, 1997. Essays that explore the rapidly changing legal profession.

Changing Jobs, The 2nd Edition, edited by Heidi McNeil, ABA Press 1994, $59.95 A practical guide for successful job searches and long-term career planning. Contains chapters by experts in career planning and lawyer placement. Also has articles focusing on job change within law or related fields. Can be ordered from ABA, Attn: Publication Orders, P.O. Box

10892, Chicago, IL 60610–0892; (800) 285–2221 or e-mail abasvcctr@attmail.com

Learning the Law: Success in Law School and Beyond, Steven J. Frank, Esq., Citadel Press, revised and updated 1997. Tells what it is to be a lawyer and succeed in law school and practice.

Turning Points: New Paths and Second Careers for Lawyers, George H. Cain, Senior Lawyers Division of the ABA, 1994, $49.95. A guide to law-related career opportunities within the legal profession for retiring lawyers or those looking for a second career. Can be ordered from ABA, Attn: Publication Orders, P.O. Box 10892, Chicago, IL 60610–0892; (800) 285-2221 or e-mail abasvcctr@attmail.com

Lawyers' Lives Out of Control: A Quality of Life Handbook, Gerald Le Van, WorldComm Press, 1992. Describes some of the problems of law practice and offers some suggestions to help achieve a balanced life. Can be ordered from the National Association for Law Placement (NALP), 1666 Connecticut Avenue, N.W., Suite 325, Washington, DC 20009; (202) 667–1666, www.nalp.org

To Be Out or Not To Be Out, NALP, 1997. This brochure was developed by the National Association for Law Placement's Gay/Lesbian/Bi Committee to provide information on interviewing, resumes, and other sources of advice for its constituent group. Order from NALP, 1666 Connecticut Avenue, N.W., Suite 325, Washington, DC 20009; (202) 667–1666, www.nalp.org

"Attorney's Comprehensive Guide to State Bar Admission Requirements," $17.95 + postage. Lists each state's requirements. Order from Federal Reports, 1010 Vermont Avenue, N.W., Suite 408, Washington, DC 20005; (800) 296–9611.

Opportunities in Law Careers, Gary Munneke, VGM Career Horizons, 1994. A discussion of jobs and practice possibilities within law.

The Legal Profession: Is It For You?, Wayne L. Anderson and Marilyn Headrick, Thomson Executive Press, 1995. An examination of the issues to consider before deciding to go into the law.

Legal magazines and newspapers that feature stories about developments, trends, and the law profession generally can be a source of information and insight, in addition to containing job listings and leads. Look, for instance, for *California Lawyer, National Law Journal, American Lawyer,* etc.

National Directory of Legal Employers, compiled by the National Association for Law Placement (NALP), 1666 Connecticut Avenue, N.W., Suite 325, Washington, DC 20009; (202) 667–1666, www.nalp.org and published by Harcourt Brace, updated annually, $39.95. Current information on size, specialties, benefits, hiring needs, and employment plans of more than 1,200 law firms and government, corporate, and public interest employers. Order from Harcourt Brace at (800) 787–8717. Also available at many law school placement offices and on WestLaw (listed as NALPLine/Directory of Legal Employers).

The Young Lawyer's Jungle Book: A Survival Guide, Thane J. Messinger, Fine Print Press, 1996. Covers a variety of topics on how to succeed in the legal field whether you're a superstar or an average law student.

Proceed with Caution: A Diary of the First Year at One of America's Largest, Most Prestigious Law Firms, William R. Keates, Harcourt Brace, 1997.

Beyond L.A. Law: Break the Traditional "Lawyer" Mold, edited by Janet Smith, Harcourt Brace, 1997. Profiles, four written by me, of 47 lawyers who have found their niche in or out of law. Excellent source for career ideas and motivation—they did it and you can too!

Life, Law and the Pursuit of Balance: A Lawyer's Guide to Quality of Life, edited by Jeffrey R. Simmons, ABA, 1996, $59.95. Published in partnership with the Maricopa County and Arizona Bar Associations, this book examines quality of life problems, then poses solutions. Order from the ABA, Attn: Publication Orders, P.O. Box 10892, Chicago, IL 60610–0892; (800) 285–2221, or e-mail abasvcctr@attmail.com

Living With the Law: Strategies to Avoid Burnout and Create Balance, edited by Julie M. Tamminen, ABA, 1996, $69.95. An A to Z guide on stress and its management. Order from ABA, Attn: Publication Orders, P.O. Box 10892, Chicago, IL 60610–0892; (800) 285–2221, or e-mail abasvcctr@attmail.com

Many law school career services offices produce newsletters containing job listings that they will send to alumni. Also check their employment bulletin boards. However, if you graduated from an out-of-town law school, you may need a letter of reciprocity from the school you attended in order to use the career services facilities of another school.

State and local bar associations will sometimes list job openings in their newsletters or magazines or take classified advertising if you want to advertise yourself.

Careers in Law, Gary Munneke, VGM Professional Careers Horizons, 2nd edition, 1997. An overview of opportunities in private practice, corporations, in federal, state, and local governments, and in teaching. Generally directed to law students, but informative for anyone looking at new areas.

"Directory of Graduate Law Degree Programs," 3rd edition, 1993, $16.95. Describes the schools and graduate legal subjects, requirements, and program descriptions. Order from Federal Reports, 1010 Vermont Avenue, N.W., Suite 408, Washington, DC 20005; (800) 296–9611.

Running from the Law: Why Good Lawyers Are Getting Out of the Legal Profession, Deborah L. Arron, Ten Speed Press, 1991. Profiles of lawyers who have made changes either within or out of law, along with some career advice. Currently out of print, but probably available at most law school career services offices.

Experience, quarterly, a magazine for "older lawyers" put out by the Senior Lawyers Division of the American Bar Association, has a partial focus on what avenues other than law a mature practitioner can pursue. Contact the Senior Lawyers Division at (312) 988–5583, or order the magazine from ABA, Attn: Publication Orders, P.O. Box 10892, Chicago, IL 60610–0892; (800) 285–2221, or e-mail abasvcctr@attmail.com

Legal Researcher's Desk Reference 1998–99, edited by Arlene Eis, $58. At bookstores or order from Infosources Publishing, 140 Norma Road, Teaneck, NJ 07666; (201) 836–7072. Lists law-related associations, law schools, legal periodicals, elected officials, etc.

Profiles of Minority Attorneys in Specialty Practices, NALP, 1995. Inspiring stories of minority attorneys who have achieved success in a variety of practices, Order from the National Association for Law Placement, 1666 Connecticut Avenue, N.W., Suite 325, Washington, DC 20009; (202) 667–1666, www.nalp.org

The Lure of the Law: Why People Become Lawyers and What the Profession Does to Them, Richard W. Moll, Penguin USA, 1991.

Breaking Traditions: Work Alternatives for Lawyers, ABA, 1993, $74.95. Essays (one by me) on changing the traditional practice of law, as well as alternatives to the traditional law firm. Order from ABA, Attn: Publication Orders, P.O. Box 10892, Chicago, IL 60610-0892; (800) 285–2221, or e-mail abasvcctr@attmail.com

Women Lawyers: Rewriting the Rules, Mona Harrington, Plume, 1995. The demands upon, and transformation of, the legal system by women.

"The Lawyers' Job Bulletin Board," a monthly job placement newsletter for attorneys interested in federal practice. Federal Bar Association, 1815 "H" Street, N.W., Suite 408, Washington, DC 20006–3697; (202) 638–0252. Newsletter is free for members, $30/year for nonmembers.

"California Law Business," a tabloid insert published alternate Mondays in both the San Francisco and Los Angeles *Daily Journal* newspapers, features topics about law firms, practice specialties, alternative practices, or law products and services in each issue, plus other articles of general interest to lawyers. Call the *Daily Journal* circulation office, in San Francisco at (415) 252–0500, or in Los Angeles at (213) 229–5300.

"What Lawyers Earn," *National Law Journal.* An annual compilation of legal salaries in law firms, corporations, law schools, judgeships, and public interest organizations.

Lawyer–Pilot Assn., c/o Karen Griggs, P.O. 685, Poolesville, MD 20837; (301) 972–7700. Members are lawyers with pilot's licenses or practicing aviation law.

"Lawyers and Career Development," a special issue of the *Career Planning and Adult Development Journal,* volume 12, number 1, Spring 1996. This issue contains a number of articles (one authored by me) on different facets of lawyer career issues and career choice. Although the journal is directed to career counselors, many of the articles have useful information for lawyers themselves. Call (800) 888–4945 for information.

Affirmative Action Register, 8356 Olive Boulevard, St. Louis, MO 63132; (314) 991–1335 or (800) 537–0655. Fee is $15 per year for 12 issues, $8 for 6 issues. Law and non-law job listings by companies with equal employment policies for women, minorities, or handicapped job seekers.

American Association of Nurse Attorneys, 3525 Ellicott Mills Drive, Suite N, Ellicott City, MD 21043–4547; (410) 418–4800. Regional chapters, with an annual national meeting. Members are lawyers who also have a nursing credential.

"ABA Publications Catalog," updated annually in August, lists the numerous helpful books, magazines, newsletters, and pamphlets published by the American Bar Association. It can be ordered from the ABA, Attn: Publication Orders, P.O. Box 10892, Chicago, IL 60610–0892; (800) 285–2221 or view the list on-line at www.abanet.org/abapubs/

What Can You Do With A Law Degree?: A Lawyers' Guide to Career Alternatives Inside, Outside and Around the Law, Deborah L. Arron, Niche Press, 1997. A career assessment and change book, with exercises and job resources.

American Association of Attorney-CPA's. National headquarters at 24196 Alicia Parkway, Suite K, Mission Viejo, CA 92691; (714) 768–0336. Members are lawyers who either practice as CPAs or hold the credential.

International Alliance of Holistic Lawyers was founded to promote the resolution of conflicts in more peaceful and creative ways. Contact the national office at Holistic Justice Center, P.O. Box 753, Middlebury, VT 05753; (802) 388–7478. There are some regional chapters.

Jobs for Lawyers: Effective Techniques for Getting Hired in Today's Marketplace, Hillary Mantis and Kathleen Brady, Impact Publications, 1996. Includes the job search process, self-assessment, networking, resumes, interviewing, using headhunters, negotiating and evaluating job offers, surviving unemployment, etc.

Guerrilla Tactics for Getting the Legal Job of Your Dreams, Kimm Walton, Harcourt Brace, 1997. Step-by-step, "you-can-do-it" solid advice for conducting a law job search primarily directed to newer lawyers.

Law v. Life: What Lawyers Are Afraid to Say About the Legal Profession, Walt Bachman, J.D., Four Directions Press, 1995. Explores the dangers and defects that are endemic to the legal profession. At bookstores or order from Four Directions Press; (800) 556–6200.

Stress Management for Lawyers: How to Increase Personal & Professional Satisfaction in the Law, Amiram Elwork, Ph.D., Vorkell Group, 2nd edition, 1997. The author discusses why the law is stressful and offers self-help stress reduction methods particularly appropriate for attorneys. This book has received numerous positive book reviews.

A Lawyer's Guide to Job Surfing on the Internet, Bill Barrett, 3rd edition, Career Education Institutes, 1998. How to look for legal jobs and where to find them on the Internet. Call (336) 768–2999 to order.

These websites might prove helpful to your job search:

—FindLaw (www.findlaw.com/) has various categories and links, such as lawyers & law firms index, career information and counseling, job listings through numerous links, information for those considering law school, and publications.

—The Seamless Website Legal Job Center (www.seamless.com/jobs/) allows you to post your resume, as well as have online discussions with other job hunters.

—Attorneys @ Work (www.attorneysatwork.com) is an on-line lawyer employment service, posting both resumes of candidates and job openings from employers.

—EmplawyerNet (www.emplawyernet.com) has teamed up with Lexis-Nexis to provide job listings, opportunities to post your resume, links to other job lists, and some headhunter listings.

—The American Bar Association (www.abanet.org) presents the services and publications offered by the ABA and a good collection of legal links (called LAWlink) for finding legal resources, including career information.

—The Law Employment Center (www.lawjobs.com) is sponsored by the *Law Journal.*

—Hieros Gamos (www.hg.org) bills itself as the guide "to everything legal on the Internet."

—Law Journal Extra! (www.ljx.com) is a free on-line legal news source put out by the *National Law Journal* and the *New York*

Law Journal. Contains headlines and also includes job information at (www.lawjobs.com), primarily for the East Coast.

—Washburn University School of Law (lawlib.wuacc.edu/ postlaw/employ.htm) maintains this list of links to various job services on the Internet.

—University of Southern California School of Law (www. usc.edu/dept/law-lib/careers/careers.html) is not a searchable database but has numerous links to other career sites. Well worth a visit.

—Indiana University School of Law (www.law.indiana.edu/law/ v–lib/lawindex.html) maintains a "virtual" law library for various legal sites, webwide.

• Private Law Firms and Traditional Practice

With the change in the economic environment for law firms— more competition, increasing expenses, clients more carefully monitoring their billings—many arrangements other than the traditional partner and associate positions have been created, each having its own responsibilities and compensation: of-counsel, permanent associate, junior or first tier partner, contract attorney, and part-time associate, among others. Some people find that the reduced pressure accompanying the step off the partnership track is welcome. Others find the offer of such a position to be an unwelcome step backward. Each arrangement has its own benefits and detriments, which must be determined on a case-by-case basis. Be sure when interviewing to ask exactly what your responsibilities will be, and what will be expected of you, when the job is linked to a title other than partner or associate.

When selecting a practice area, pick one that will have increasing business. Do your homework. Ask other practitioners, go to bar association meetings of the relevant sections, and read section newsletters and local legal newspapers to make sure that a field that might interest you isn't one that is changing and decreasing in consumer demand (for example, maritime has largely narrowed in focus and practice).

One of the anomalies of law practice, contrary to most other professions, is that the more experienced you are in your practice area, the more difficult it is to move to another law firm unless you bring with you either a good-sized "book of business" (client list with large billings) or a specialized educational and/or practice background in an area the firm wants to develop or expand. If you can't provide either and you have practiced for more than six or so years, many firms would rather not take on a highly paid lateral hire, choosing instead to bring in a more junior associate the firm can train for less cost. If you fall into this "experienced - without - book - of - business -or -specialty-practice" category, you may want to look at smaller law firms or some government agencies, which might better appreciate your extensive general experience. It may also benefit you to contact lawyers you know in firms you like—if someone appreciates your skills, they might decide to hire you even without a large client list.

How Do You Research a Law Firm?

Use the _Martindale-Hubbell Law Directory_. It's available in law libraries and on-line at www.martindale.com. (See more information about Martindale in the following resource list.) Compare volumes from the previous two years with the current year's volume to note changes in associates, partners, and practice areas. Is the firm growing or shrinking? Specializing? Branching out? Also note which associates have left the firm, then telephone the membership records office of the relevant state bar association to get those associates' telephone numbers—in most states, phone numbers are a matter of public record. Call these former associates to see if any would be willing to discuss the positives and negatives of employment at that firm.

Read through the _National Directory of Legal Employers_ (see page 146 for information on this book) to glean relevant information about law firms or other legal environments such as corporations.

Read the gossip about the firm, if any, in the legal papers. Look for information positively or negatively affecting morale (i.e., an exodus of lawyers, adding a high-profile department, etc.) reputation, liquidity, client retention, salaries.

Check with a headhunter or two. A call to one or two search consultants ("headhunters") may yield information about a firm in which you have an interest. Before you spend much time doing this, however, read the information about headhunters, especially the last paragraphs, on page 180 so that you are clear about what assistance you might expect from them.

According to the American Bar Association and other sources, the following are the law practice growth areas for the next decade:

- alternative-dispute resolution (mediation and arbitration)
- bankruptcy, including business workouts
- biomedical issues, including bioethics
- communications (print, electronic, movies and video, Internet)
- computer law
- corporate reorganization
- criminal law
- employee/employer relations (wrongful termination, harassment, breach of employment contracts, etc.)
- environmental law (water, zoning, air, wetlands, urban issues, etc.)
- estate planning
- government relations/lobbying
- health care
- immigration law (all facets, but there's a growing practice within and for multinational companies that need to move their employees in and out of the United States)
- insurance defense
- intellectual property (not only technical but also publishing, music, and licensing issues)
- international law
- litigation in selected areas
- pensions
- probate
- science & technology
- Social Security

RESOURCES

Martindale-Hubbell Law Directory, annually updated, contains listings of lawyers and law firms, along with an elaboration on specialty areas and clients for those lawyers who pay to list the additional information. Organized by state, and then by cities within each state. Found in most law libraries. Web address is www.martindale.com. Also use Lexis-Nexis (www.lexis–nexis.com) and Westlaw (www.westgroup.com) to access Martindale and to research law firms, individual attorneys and salaries.

Careers in International Law (1993), *Careers in Labor Law* (1985), *Careers in Intellectual Property Law* (1993), *Careers in Admiralty and Maritime Law* (1993), *Careers in Civil Litigation* (1990), *Lawful Pursuit: Careers in Public Interest Law* (1995), *Careers in Entertainment Law* (1990), *Careers in Sports Law* (1990), and *Careers in Natural Resources and Environmental Law* (1987). Booklets available from the ABA, Attn: Publication Orders, P.O. 10892, Chicago, IL 60610–0892; (800) 285–2221, or e-mail abasvcctr@attmail.com

The American Bar Association and many state and local bar associations have special interest sections in various areas of law practice, such as, probate, in-house, tax, environment, intellectual property, etc. Section membership benefits often include newsletters or magazines and other practice information, as well as education and networking opportunities through meetings and programs and participation in section activities. Attend meetings of the practice area(s) that interest you in order to make contacts, especially if you want to switch to a new practice area. Some local bar associations also have committees promoting specialized practices or groups, such as contract attorneys or women- and minority-owned law firms, that can serve as good networking opportunities.

National Directory of Legal Employers, compiled by the National Association for Law Placement (NALP), 1666 Connecticut Avenue, N.W., Suite 325, Washington, DC 20009; (202) 667–1666 (www.nalp.org), and published by Harcourt Brace, updated annually. $49.95. Current information on size, specialities, and benefits at more than 1,200 law firms and government, corporate, and public interest employers. Order from Harcourt Brace at (800) 787–8717. Also available at many law school placement offices and on WestLaw (listed as NALPLine/Directory of Legal Employers). NALP's website lists helpful information on resumes, interviewing, and other aspects of a job hunt.

Business Lawyer's Handbook, Clifford Ennico, revised 1997, $35. An overview of career paths in business law, the nature of the work, and skills required of business lawyers. Order from the National Association for Law Placement, 1666 Connecticut Avenue, N.W., Suite 325, Washington, DC 20009; (202) 667–1666.

For legal job hunting on the Internet, see page 142 for a sample of websites to get you started.

Making Partner: A Guide for Law Firm Associates, Robert Greene, ABA, 1992, $19.95. Available from ABA, Attn: Publication Orders, P.O. Box 10892, Chicago, IL 60610–0892; (800) 285–2221, or e-mail abasvcctr@attmail.com

American Health Lawyers Association, 1120 Connecticut Avenue, N.W., Suite 950, Washington, DC 20036; (202) 833–1100. Membership consists of lawyers and others working in the health field or practicing health law.

Environmental Law Careers Directory. Available for $10 from the *Ecology Law Quarterly.* Write Attn: Careers Directory, 493 Diamond Hall, University of California, Berkeley, CA 94720; (510) 642–0457 or order from U.C. Press at (510) 642–9129. Lists private firms and nonprofit and government agencies providing opportunities for the environmental lawyer. An environmental law careers conference is held each fall at Boalt Hall Law School at U.C. Berkeley, with information on careers in private and public interest firms. Contact the programs director at the *Ecology Law Quarterly.*

California Academy of Appellate Lawyers and California Appellate Defense Counsel are two statewide organizations of appellate attorneys with chapters in large cities. Other states would have similar organizations.

National Attorneys' Directory for Lesbian and Gay Rights includes listings of lesbian and gay bar associations, law student organizations, and attorneys nationwide. Order from Gay and Lesbian Advocates and Defenders (GLAD) P.O. Box 218, Boston, MA 02112.

1997 Associate Salary Survey, NALP, 1997, $95. NALP's annual report on compensation includes salaries of associates by years of experience and geographic location, and summer associate salaries. Includes information on both large and small firms. Order from National Association for Law Placement. 1666 Connecticut Avenue, N.W., Suite 325, Washington, DC 20009; (202) 667–1666, www.nalp.org

Each Fall *The American Lawyer* magazine publishes a survey of summer associates, with evaluations of law firms.

Hillman on Lawyer Mobility: The Law and Ethics of Partner Withdrawals and Law Firm Breakups, Robert Hillman, 2nd edition, Little Brown & Co., 1998.

Survival Skills for Practicing Lawyers, ABA Law Practice Management Section, 1994. A compilation of articles from "Law Practice Management" magazine; addresses getting and keeping clients, time and case management, malpractice prevention, etc. Available from ABA, Attn: Publication Orders, P.O. Box 10892, Chicago, IL 60610-0892; (800) 285–2221, or e-mail abasvcctr@attmail.com

The Insider's Guide to Law Firms, Sheila Malkani and Michael Walsh, 3rd edition, Mobius Press, 1997. Evaluations of large law firms by summer associates.

National Employment Lawyers Association, a nationwide plaintiff's bar organization, publishes a quarterly newsletter and has a lawyer referral panel. The national headquarters is at 600 Harrison Street, Suite 535, San Francisco, CA 94107; (415) 227–4655.

Computer Law Association, 3028 Javier Road, Suite 402, Fairfax, VA 22031; (703) 560–7747. A nonprofit educational association that deals with computer/legal issues and maintains a resume bank for members.

The "Of Counsel" Agreement: A Guide for Law Firm and Practitioner, American Bar Association, 1991, $59.95, with sample agreements. Order from ABA, Attn: Publication Orders, P.O. Box 10892, Chicago, IL 60610–0892; (800) 285–2221, or e-mail abasvcctr@attmail.com

Guide to Small Firm Employment, NALP, 1992, $3.50. Addresses advantages and disadvantages of small firm employment, methods and resources for the job search, and resumes, cover letters, and interviews for small firm employment. Order from National Association for Law Placement, 1666 Connecticut Avenue, N.W., Suite 325, Washington, DC 20009; (202) 667–1666, www.nalp.org

Guide to Law Specialties, NALP, 1996. Presents summaries of various practice areas, preparation required for the field, and types of employers practicing in the area. Order from National Association for Law Placement, 1666 Connecticut Avenue, N.W., Suite 325, Washington, DC 20009; (202) 667–1666, www. nalp.org

Attorney Jobs: National & Federal Legal Employment Report, published by Federal Reports, 1010 Vermont Avenue, N.W., Suite 408, Washington, DC 20005; (800) 296–9611. Each monthly issue contains 500 to 600 current public/private sector jobs. Fee is $45 for 3 months.

The Lawyer's Guide to the Internet, G. Burgess Allison, ABA, 1995. Order from the ABA, Attn: Publication Orders, P.O. Box 10892, Chicago, IL 60610–0892; (800) 285–2221, or e-mail abasvcctr@attmail.com

The Lawyer's Guide to Creating Web Pages, Kenneth Johnson, ABA, 1997. Order from the ABA, Attn: Publication Orders, P.O. Box 10892, Chicago, IL 60610–0892; (800) 285–2221, or e-mail abasvcctr@attmail.com

Counsel Connect (www.counsel.com) is an on-line subscription service that offers CLE courses, discussions groups, a virtual library, and a way to meet with other lawyers nationwide.

West's Legal Directory (www.wld.com) has information on lawyers across the United States, if they subscribe to the service.

Parker Directory of California Attorneys, updated annually, lists lawyers and law firms by name and practice area, as well as federal and state government offices. Call (800) 521–8110 for information.

There are national associations of lawyers in most specialty practice areas, such as sports, transportation, elder law, bonds, family issues, trial, computers, immigration, etc.

Check out the several online matchmaking services for law-

yers. For example, see www.emplawyernet.com, www.attorneys
atwork.com., and www.lawmatch.com.

• Solo, Small, Firm and Small Town Practice

Going out on your own or starting a new firm with several
other lawyers can seem like a formidable task, but for those
individuals who desire self-sufficiency and want to choose their
own cases, clients, and lifestyle, it is a viable alternative. Just keep
in mind that a solo or small law firm is a small business, and
typically half your time will be taken up by the issues of running
and marketing a practice. Additionally, practicing law combined
with running a small business often takes more hours than working as an employee for someone else. Furthermore, there's no
regular paycheck . . . but the business *is* yours.

To avoid the sense of isolation that solo practice can create,
it may be wise to rent space in an existing law office—perhaps
by exchanging some of your research or court appearance time
for free or reduced-rent office space—or share space with other
solo practitioners. These methods also cut down on costs if they
provide access to a library, conference room, and amenities that
a new solo cannot usually afford.

Another productive technique for choosing space is to set up
your office in collaboration with the type of business in which
you would like to specialize, such as in the offices of an accountant, labor union, or insurance brokerage, where you could possibly obtain client referrals. But if you do decide to work out of
your home, you could arrange to rent space as needed for meetings and depositions from a legal colleague or a space provider
such as Headquarters Company, which has meeting rooms, copi-
ers, and receptionists.

Many attorneys are electing to join small firms or start their
own practices in rural communities, for quality of life reasons or
to be a big fish in a small pond. As the only attorney—or one
of just a few—in a small community, a practitioner often can gain
a sense of relationship with clients, a sense of directly affecting a
case, and a stature that is often more difficult to achieve in a big
city. And for those of you who desire to have a general practice,

rather than specializing in one narrow field, small towns are fertile hunting grounds.

RESOURCES

Flying Solo: A Survival Guide for the Solo Lawyer, edited by Joel P. Bennett, ABA, updated 1994, $59.95. Lots of good information on opening and running a one-person shop. Order from Publication Orders, P.O. Box 10892, Chicago, IL 60610–0892; call (800) 285–2221, or send an e-mail to abasvcctr@attmail.com.

The American Bar Association has a Law Practice Management Section, which publishes a magazine entitled *Law Practice Management,* and a General Practice Section, with a magazine entitled *The Compleat Lawyer.* Call (312) 988–5619 for LPM membership information and (312) 988–5648 for GP membership information. The ABA also has a Solo and Small Firm Committee, and the *American Bar Association Journal* has a monthly column about solo and small practice issues.

Most state and some large bar associations have solo and small firm practice sections. These bar associations also generally have both a law practice management section and a general practice section (members tend to be solo or small practitioners). The sections usually sponsor yearly programs or panels on starting, maintaining, and marketing a practice. Some also have mentorship programs. If you are opening your own practice, joining a small firm, or contemplating doing so, be sure to use these sections for networking and gaining information.

Guide to Small Firm Employment, NALP, 1992, $3.50. Addresses advantages and disadvantages of small firm employment, methods and resources for the job search, and resumes, cover letters, and interviews for small firm employment. Order from National Association for Law Placement, 1666 Connecticut Avenue, N.W., Suite 325, Washington, DC 20009; (202) 667–1666, www.nalp.org.

Experience is a magazine for "older lawyers" put out by the Senior Lawyers Division of the American Bar Association. Contact the Senior Lawyers Division at (312) 988–5582, or order the magazine from ABA, Attn: Publication Orders, P.O. Box 10892, Chicago, IL 60610–0892; (800) 285–2221, or e-mail abasvcctr@attmail.com.

Look in any law library card catalog for solo practice or law firm/practice management books and guides. Also ask the librarian for recommendations, as there are numerous books. Additionally, you can locate information and discussion groups for solo practitioners on the Internet.

Informative Books

How to Get and Keep Good Clients, Jay Foonberg, 2nd edition, National Academy of Law, Ethics, & Management, 1990.

Hillman on Lawyer Mobility: The Law and Ethics of Partner Withdrawals and Law Firm Breakups, Robert Hillman, 2nd edition, Little Brown & Co., 1998.

The Rainmaking Machine: Marketing, Planning, Strategies, and Management for Law Firms With 1996 Supplement, Phyllis Weiss Haserot, Shepard's, 1989.

Opening a Law Office, California Young Lawyers Association, $25. Not specific to California, so this publication is useful to anyone, anywhere. Order from CYLA, State Bar of California, 555 Franklin Street, San Francisco, CA 94102; (415) 561–8200.

Following is a sample of publications from the American Bar Association. Call or write the ABA, Attn: Publication Orders, P.O. Box 10892, Chicago, IL 60610–0892; (800) 285–2221, or e-mail abasvcctr@attmail.com

- *Marketing Success Stories: Personal Interviews With 66 Rainmakers,* Hollis Hatfield Weishav, 1997.
- *How to Start and Build a Law Practice,* Jay Foonberg, 3rd edition, 1991.
- *Action Steps to Marketing Success: How to Implement Your Marketing Program,* Robert Denney and Carol Scott James, 1991.
- *Running A Law Practice on a Shoestring,* Theda Snyder, 1997.
- *Planning the Small Law Office Library,* edited by Catherine Pennington, 1994.

- *Practical Systems: Tips for Organizing Your Law Office,* Charles Coulter, 1991.
- *Win-Win Billing Strategies: Alternatives that Satisfy Your Clients and You,* edited by Richard Reed, 1992.
- *Getting Started* (forming partnerships and setting up firms), R. Williams, 1996.
- *Do-It-Yourself Public Relations: A Success Guide for Lawyers,* David Gumpert, 1995.

ARTICLES

"Main Street U.S.A.: An Inside Look at Small Town Law," Steven Keeva, *ABA Journal,* October 1992.

"The Great Escape: The Joys and Woes of Resort Town Practice," Joel Kaplan, *ABA Journal,* August 1993.

"Welcome to Paradise, Now Get Out," B. J. Palermo, *California Lawyer,* February 1993. The pros and cons of small town law practice.

• Part-Time, Contract, and Flexible Work Schedules

The acceptance of alternative work schedules for lawyers has grown dramatically in the last few years. While these alternatives are not universally accepted, a growing number of law firms have part-time policies that allow for some or all of the following: a reduced work week, telecommuting, job-sharing, flextime, and contract lawyering. See chapter 4 for more detail about these alternative work schedules. If you are interested in a flexible work schedule, contact your local bar association for its policy on part-time issues and see if it has a list of local firms that adhere to that policy. If your bar association doesn't have such a policy, contact the American Bar Association for its model policy and then help your local bar to institute and publicize one!

Some state codes or regulations (e.g., California State Government Code Section 19996.19 et seq. and regulations in Title 2 of California Regulations, Article 19, Section 599.830) require that state employees be allowed a reduced work week, either by

hours or days. In California, once the employee requests a reduced work schedule, the burden shifts to the department to
show that the employee's change of schedule will have an adverse
effect. A similar policy is in effect for federal employees through
the Federal Employees Part-Time Career Employment Act of
1978, activated in 1980.

CONTRACT ATTORNEY PLACEMENT SERVICES

Placement agencies are located in many of the larger cities and
often place attorneys throughout the state, or sometimes even
nationally. Look in your telephone book yellow pages under
Employment—Temporary. Keep in mind that the agencies will
add a fee, payable by the employing law firm, of from 20 percent
to 100 percent per hour on top of the hourly fee you receive
from the agency. Therefore, the $50 per hour you receive can
easily become a cost of $70 to $100 per hour to the law firm.
For that reason, cultivating your own contract legal work can
often secure you a better hourly fee, as well as more personal
and continuing client relationships. See chapter 4 for a more
detailed discussion of this issue.

RESOURCES

Association of Part-Time Professionals, 7700 Leesburg Pike, Suite
216, Falls Church, VA 22043; (703) 734–7975. A national
nonprofit group that promotes adjusted work schedules for
professionals. They publish "Working Options," a bimonthly
newsletter. Membership for individuals is $45.
How to Work As a Contract Lawyer, Hindi Greenberg, Lawyer's
in Transition[SM], 1998. A comprehensive audio tape covering
all you need to know to develop clients and work as a contract
lawyer including marketing, pricing, and malpractice issues.
Order from Lawyers in Transition[SM], P.O. Box 31026, San
Francisco, CA 94131–0026; (415) 285–5143.
Breaking Out of 9 to 5: How to Redesign Your Job to Fit You, Maria

Laqueur and Donna Dickerson, Peterson's Guides, 1994. At bookstores or order from Peterson's Guides at (800) 338–3282.

Breaking Traditions: Work Alternatives for Lawyers, ABA, 1993, $79.95. Essays on alternatives to traditional law practice and law firms; chapter 20 is on contract lawyering. Order from ABA, Attn: Publication Orders, P.O. Box 10892, Chicago, IL 60610–0892; (800) 285–2221, or e-mail abasvcctr@attmail. com. Also available at law school career services offices.

New Ways to Work is a nonprofit organization working nationally to promote alternative work-time options. They publish a newsletter, "Work Times," which covers issues relating to alternative work time, and they have numerous other publications. New Ways to Work published *Negotiating Time: New Scheduling Options in the Legal Profession,* Feiden and Marks, 1986, and *The Job Sharing Handbook,* Olmstad and Smith, 1996. They also make available *Creating a Flexible Workplace: How to Select and Manage Alternative Work Options,* Olmstad and Smith, 2nd edition, AMACOM Press (American Management Association), 1994. Contact them at 785 Market Street, Suite 950, San Francisco, CA 94103; (415) 995–9860; their Internet address is http://www.nww.org.

The Complete Guide to Contract Lawyering: What Every Lawyer and Law Firm Needs to Know About Temporary Legal Services, Deborah L. Arron and Deborah Guyol, Niche Press, 1995. Covers whether you should work as a contract lawyer and how to do it.

Lawyers and Balanced Lives: A Guide to Drafting and Implementing Workplace Policies for Lawyers, ABA, 1990, $44.95. A discussion of alternative work schedules and parental leave, with sample policies for law firms. Order from ABA, Attn: Publication Orders, P.O. Box 10892, Chicago, IL 60610–0892; (800) 285–2221, or e-mail abasvcctr@attmail.com.

Changing Jobs, The 2nd Edition, edited by Heidi McNeil, ABA Press, 1994, $59.95. A practical guide for successful job searches and long-term career planning; it includes chapters contributed by experts in career planning and lawyer placement. Also has articles focusing on job change within law (such as chapter 31, entitled "Part-time, Temporary and Contract Employment") or related fields. Can be ordered from ABA,

Attn: Publication Orders, P.O. Box 10892, Chicago, IL 60610–0892; (800) 285–2221, or e-mail abasvcctr@attmail.com.

Home Sweet Office: The Ultimate Out-of-Office Experience: Working Your Company Job from Home, Jeff Meade, Peterson's Guides, 1993. Covers the basics of "how to" telecommute.

Telecommuter's Handbook: How to Earn a Living Without Going to the Office, Debra Schepp and Brad Schepp, 2nd edition, McGraw Hill, 1995.

In many states, there are appellate projects that select lawyers to handle criminal appeals on a paid but freelance basis. In some programs, if you are a young attorney or one without a lot of in-point experience, you could be paired with a more experienced practitioner. Check with your local federal or state appeals court.

The Three–Career Couple: Mastering the Art of Juggling Work, Home and Family, Marcia Byalick and Linda Saslow, Peterson's Guides, 1993. Call Peterson's Guides at (800) 338–3282.

ARTICLES OF INTEREST

Bay, "Life, Law, and the Pursuit of Balance," 20 *Barrister* 4, Winter 1994.

Clarke, "Getting Flexible About Work Schedules," 13 *American Lawyer* 34, Apr 1991.

Friedman, "Temping Can Keep Wolves from the Door While Opening It Up," *National Law Journal,* Aug 1993.

Ginzberg, "Lawyer for Hire: You Too Can Practice Law As An Independent," *California Lawyer,* Mar 1991.

Hansen, "Another Possibility in a Tight Job Market: Temporary Lawyer," *American Bar Assn. Journal,* Mar 1995.

Kushner, "Job Sharing: An Alternative to a Traditional Law Practice," 11 *Legal Economics* 24, Nov–Dec 1985.

McGarry, "Have J.D., Will Travel: Contract Lawyering is the Day Job of the '90's," *California Lawyer,* Jul 1992.

• International Law and Business, or a Change of Geographic Location

International law is both a style of practice and a specialized practice area. Some people use language skills or multicultural backgrounds or experiences to advantage when prospecting for international work experiences. However, international law work often emanates from the same U.S. office as the firm's other legal practice areas—the only difference is that the clients may have international interests or be from another country. So you may end up writing contracts for an Italian company while sitting in your office in Peoria. Although there may be some work-related international travel involved, that usually doesn't happen immediately for a new hire, but only after the new associate gains a year or two of experience. This is generally true whether you work as a lawyer or on the business side of the company.

A successful technique for obtaining work in the international field is to obtain a job with a U.S. company that does international business, then volunteer for as many projects as possible related to international issues. Demonstrate your flexibility and interest in multicultural issues. Foreign language capability might be an asset, but is not necessarily required for lawyers; however, if you wish to move to the business side, cultivating a relevant foreign language can be a plus, especially if you intend to focus your work in one country or area.

Hint: If you really want to be hired as a non-lawyer by a U.S. multinational or a foreign company, get a job oversees teaching English as a second language (ESL). Many people have parlayed that job into a position within a multinational company in training, organization development, or personnel.

If you want to move within the United States, check for announcements of job openings in the state and local bar association publications in the locales that interest you. If copies are not available in your local law libraries, subscribe by mail. Check your local law school career services offices; they often have employment listings for jobs nationwide. Contact also the career services offices at the law schools in the locality where you want to move. Subscribe to the legal and business newspapers in the new locale in order to familiarize yourself with local issues and gain access to local job listings.

Resources

Directory of Opportunities in International Law, 9th edition, John Bassett Moore Society of International Law. Available for $20 from John Bassett Moore Society, University of Virginia School of Law, Charlottesville, VA 22901; (804) 924–3087. Contains lists of U.S. and international law firms, government jobs, and relevant educational programs.

"International Lawyer's Newsletter," Kluwer Law International, 675 Massachusetts Avenue, Cambridge, MA 02139; (617) 354–0140. Fee is $132.50 per year for 6 issues. Mainly substantive articles on international law, but also posts international job listings and lists international placement agencies.

Careers in International Law, 2nd edition, ABA Press, 1993, $19.99. Available by contacting ABA, Attn: Publication Orders, P.O. Box 10892, Chicago, IL 60610–0892; (800) 285–2221, or e-mail abasvcctr@attmail.com. Put out by the ABA Section on International Law and Practice.

"International Employment Hotline," edited by Will Cantrell, $39 per year for 12 issues of job listings (not many law jobs). Available through the New Careers Center in Boulder, Colorado; (800) 634–9024.

International Jobs, Eric Kocher, 5th edition, Addison Wesley, 1998. Careers in law, nonprofits, business, publishing, government, and schools—where they are, how to get them.

"Attorney's Guide to State Bar Admission Requirements." Lists each state's requirement. $17.95 from Federal Reports, 1010 Vermont Avenue, N.W., Suite 408, Washington, DC 20005; (800) 296–9611.

"Federal Jobs Digest," a biweekly list of government jobs in the United States and internationally. Fee is 3 months for $34, 6 months for $59. Available from Breakthrough Publications, (800) 824–5000.

Ulrich's International Periodicals Directory, R.R. Bowker. Updated annually. Listings of newsletters and other periodicals published by international organizations and companies.

World Trade Centers Association's *World Business Directory 1998,* Gale Research, 1997. Too expensive to buy, so peruse it at a public library or call (800) 877–GALE. Four volumes listing international companies, products/services, locations, etc.

Encyclopedia of Associations: International Organizations, Gale Research, updated annually. Two volumes. Too expensive to buy, so peruse at a public library or call (800) 877–GALE. The definitive book for locating relevant international associations for networking purposes.

Guide to Careers in World Affairs, 3rd edition, put out by the Foreign Policy Association, 470 Park Avenue South, 2nd floor, New York, NY 10016; (212) 764–4050 or (800) 477–5836. Describes qualifications required and application procedures for over 250 organizations involved in international business, law, journalism, nonprofits, etc.

American Bar Association, Section of International Law and Practice, 740–15th Street, N.W., 10th Floor, Washington, DC 20005; (202) 662–1660, www.abanet.org/intlaw/. Has publications, a newsletter, a quarterly journal called "The International Lawyer," and sponsors programs on international business law and policy.

Craighead's International Business, Travel, and Relocation Guide to 81 Countries, updated every two years, Gale Research. Too expensive to buy, so peruse it at a public library or call (800) 877–GALE.

Gale Research publishes the following very expensive but very useful books, available at most public libraries:
- *Major and Medium Companies of Europe*
- *Major Companies of the Arab World*
- *Major Companies of the Far East and Australasia*

Federation of International Trade Associations, 1851 Alexander Bell Drive, Reston, VA 20191; (703) 620–1588, www.fita.com. Umbrella organization of 300 North American trade associations.

World Affairs Organizations in Northern California: A Guide to the Field, edited by Chris Carlisle, World Without War Publications, 1995.

Uniworld Business Publications, Inc., at 257 Central Park West, New York, NY 10024; (212) 496–0735, has available a number of directories useful for international job hunting, such as *Directory of American Firms Operating in Foreign Countries,* 14th edition, and *Directory of Foreign Firms Operating in the United States,* 9th edition, plus regional and individual country editions, listing companies within those geopolitical breakdowns. Best to use at a public library.

• Legal Clinics and Pre-Paid Legal Services Offices

These are a number of positions available at legal clinics:

- managing attorney (of one or several offices)
- staff attorney
- telephone intake (either screening callers for legal needs or answering legal questions by telephone)
- interviewer
- founder
- owner

Legal clinics and legal services offices generally service large groups of individuals in limited matters such as family, personal injury, landlord–tenant, bankruptcy, and sometimes, criminal law. Some of the legal services offices have contracts with companies, hospitals, or labor unions to provide services at a set fee to the employees of each (often called prepaid legal services programs). Some of the services handle legal questions only by telephone, then refer out any matters that cannot be answered with less than an hour of research and a half hour telephone appointment. Each prepaid legal services and legal clinic firm sets up its own arrangement, so if you are interviewing, you need to carefully question what your responsibilities and liabilities will be.

RESOURCES

Who's Who in Prepaid Legal Services, American Prepaid Legal Services Institute (affiliated with the American Bar Association),

541 N. Fairbanks Court, Chicago, IL 60611; (312) 988–5751. Annual national membership directory of prepaid legal services plans is $37.50 for members, $75 for nonmembers.

Jacoby & Meyers, 100 California Street, Suite 700, San Francisco, CA 94111; (415) 399–8951. Locations also in Sacramento and New York, (800) 975–3425.

• Corporations and Business

Possible positions include:

- general counsel
- associate general counsel
- staff attorney
- department legal advisor, especially in tax, real estate, labor relations, contracts, public information, and acquisitions
- in-house insurance defense (can work either in an insurance company handling defense of insurance claims against a client of the insurance company or in a non-insurance employer handling self-insured claims against the employer)
- bank trust officer (handles trust legal issues and perhaps manages and invests the trust portfolio)
- litigation manager (manages inside and/or outside litigation attorneys)

Corporate counsel are gaining in responsibility, stature, and salary. In fact, in-house counsel usually hire and supervise the lawyers from the law firms who do the corporation's outside legal work (and who often secretly wish they were working in the corporation rather than the law firm).

Many lawyers regard working in a corporation as an attractive alternative to a stressful private practice—especially litigators who feel like they are spread too thin in both subject matter and time. They see the corporation (whether wrongly or rightly) as an environment where everyone pulls together for the common good of the employer, and as a friendly alternative to the extreme competition of private practice, where everyone is constantly competing, even against their own law firm partners.

Some of the benefits of working in-house are that: 1) many companies don't require the billing of time; 2) most companies consult their in-house lawyers for preventive legal purposes, rather than solely for remedies after a liability is incurred (if the company is particularly proactive in taking preventive steps, the attorneys might be utilized to counsel and train company employees and departments in measures appropriate to prevent future legal complications); 3) in-house lawyers are sometimes involved in management decisions and policy making; 4) there are no rainmaking/marketing requirements; and 5) the role played by an in-house lawyer, especially general counsel, can often be as broad as desired, and is not defined solely as the coordinator of outside law firms or the drafter of contracts.

However, there are possible detriments to in-house work: 1) management sometimes has a problem accepting relevant business advice, as opposed to legal advice, from a lawyer, since business-people often view lawyers as deal-breakers rather than deal-makers; 2) generally, the pay for in-house attorneys (other than general counsel) is not as high as that earned by lawyers with the same number of practice years who work in the largest law firms—although it is probably comparable to earnings in most other firms; 3) most complex litigation, specialty work, and big cases are still sent to outside counsel.

In a 1990 study about general counsel, cited in *California Lawyer* magazine, the mean age for that top position was 45.75 years; 89 percent were male; and the mean salary was $166,190. However, the number of women and the mean salary have increased in the past several years, while the age of general counsel has lowered somewhat. The study indicated that only half of all general counsel positions were filled from existing staff lawyers; the rest were recruited from outside the company, usually from law firms or other corporations in the same or a similar industry. Over half of all general counsel had previous international experience. As for all in-house lawyers, about three-quarters came from private practice, often from a firm that did not represent the company.

The study indicated, in descending order of preference, the previous experience of lawyers who were the most attractive candidates for the average company; general corporate, litigation, government/regulatory affairs, securities/antitrust, real estate, finance, labor, patent/copyright/licensing, environmental, ERISA/ pensions, tax. Of course, if a company is involved mainly in a specialty, such as technology, the previous experience of an aspiring in-house lawyer would have to be weighted toward that specialty in order to qualify him or her as an attractive candidate.

The general counsel of a company is the legal decision maker, on the second tier below the chief financial officer in terms of salary and benefits. This person might also have an executive or board of directors position, and in a smaller company might be involved in the business decisions; often, in the larger companies, there is a strict division of duties between the legal and business departments. In fact, in only a small percentage of cases does someone from the legal department move to the business side of a company.

The associate general or managing counsel is usually a liaison between the general counsel and the staff attorneys, and is on the lowest rung of executives. Staff attorneys are just that—staff, most often without special perks such as stock options or other executive benefits. They might handle specific practice areas (such as environmental, intellectual property, or contracts), or they might be generalists, depending upon the needs of the employer.

If you are interested in learning about in-house counsel work and which companies are hiring, a good resource is the in-house section (usually within the business or corporate law sections) of your state or local bar association. By attending these meetings, you will meet real-life corporate counsel, who will either reinforce your desire to work in-house or give you a much needed reality check about the negatives associated with their job.

RESOURCES

Many state and local bar associations have sections or committees on in-house counsel, often within their Business Law Sections.
Directory of Corporate Counsel, updated annually, Aspen Law & Business, $449 plus handling and postage; CD-ROM for $620. Information on corporate law departments, structure, and

background on 30,000 lawyers who work for 6,200 companies. Call (800) 447–1717 to order, or find it in law libraries.
American Corporate Counsel Association, 1025 Connecticut Avenue, N.W., Suite 200, Washington, DC 20036; (202)
293–4103; www.acca.com. To become a member, you must
be employed in a corporate law department. Has regional
chapters; check your area. Publishes a quarterly newsletter of
in-house information and has a resume bank for in-house
counsel positions. If you aren't qualified for membership, find
out if any of your in-house friends are, so you can check out
the newsletter.
*Lawyers Register International by Specialties and Fields of Law, Includ-
ing a Directory of Corporate Counsel,* 15th edition, Lawyers Register Publications, 1997, $329. Inquire whether your law
library has this.

• Government

OPPORTUNITIES IN THE FEDERAL JURISDICTION

These are a number of positions open in the federal jurisdiction. A partial list includes:

- judge
- research attorney (central staff or for a specific judge)
- U.S. Attorney's office
- federal public defender's office (some appellate work)
- U.S. bankruptcy trustee (appointed to take over businesses)
- federal magistrate (hears cases pertaining to federal government issues, such as crimes committed on federal land)
- administrative law judge in an agency or department (generally handles internal complaints and labor disputes)
- judge advocate general office, military active or reserve
- staff attorney in agencies such as EEOC, GSA, U.S. Marshall's Service, FTC, SSA, SEC, Department of Labor, Bureau of Alcohol, Tobacco and Firearms, Health & Human
  Services, DEA, Department of Education, Federal Mediation

and Conciliation Service, FHA, FCC, FBI, EPA, FDA, GAO, INS, IRS, HUD, ICC, NLRB, CIA

Although there are as many styles of lawyering and areas of inquiry within the government as there are in private firms, most agencies handle matters only within their purview. That specialization fits the needs of those lawyers who do not want to be generalists. Lawyers often move into government agencies after developing a specialty in a law firm for several years (although others leave a government agency, parlaying their acquired specialty into an offer from a law firm). The absence of competition for partnership—although there may be competition for promotion—lessens the stress within many agencies. Additionally, most government offices do not require lawyers to keep time records, a great relief to many. However, a downside to the reduction in stress is that there is usually a reduction in income, as compared to law firm salaries. Seniority and increased responsibility can raise earnings, although income will generally remain well below the income of most law firm partners.

Government work often provides job security and good benefits—health, dental, retirement. Public agencies also are generally more receptive than the private sector to putting women and minority workers in positions of responsibility. Additionally, older attorneys and solo practitioners may find that a public agency will look at their record with a less jaundiced eye; when considering an experienced practitioner, law firms almost always require either a book of business (client roster) or a specialized educational and/or practice background, neither necessarily required by a public agency.

To find out about job openings, call the federal, state, county, or city personnel offices, or pay a visit to those offices to view recent job postings (both law and other professional positions). Also contact the personnel departments for the agencies in which you are interested—individual agencies don't always list their openings with the main personnel office.

RESOURCES

Federal Information Center. Phone (800) 688– 9889 nationwide
for job information and how to apply for a particular type of
position within the federal government. Keep trying, as numbers are often busy. Also contact individual agencies, because
they often hire independently. National office of U.S. Jobs by
Phone is in Georgia at (912) 757–3000.

The government's U.S. Office of Personnel Management (OPM)
has a telephone system called Career America Connection
(CAC), available 24 hours a day. The Federal Job Opportunities Board is available for data access by computer and
modem—dial (912) 757–3100, or use the Internet via telnet
at FJOB.MAIL.OPM.GOV. It also has a website at www.
usajobs.opm.gov/ that allows searches by job category. Call
(912) 757–3090, then ask for Factsheet EI-42, which lists
CACs in various metropolitan areas, as well as locations for
Employment Information Computer Kiosks, featuring touch
screens to access employment information.

Now Hiring: Government Jobs for Lawyers, ABA Press, 1997,
$19.95. Order from ABA, Attn: Publication Orders, P.O. Box
10892, Chicago, IL 60610–0892; (800) 285–2221, or e-mail
abasvcctr@attmail.com. This book has a directory of agencies,
as well as hiring policies and other pertinent information.

Federal Careers for Attorneys, $21.95. Sets out hiring procedures,
work goals of each office, gives addresses of recruiting offices.
Contact Federal Reports, Inc., 1010 Vermont Avenue, N.W.,
Suite 408, Washington, DC 20005; (800) 296–9611.

Attorney Jobs: National & Federal Legal Employment Report. A
monthly listing of available attorney, court, and law-related
professional positions with the federal government and other
public and private employers in Washington, D.C., the United
States, and abroad. Subscription rates are $45 for 3 months,
$75 for 6 months. Available through Federal Reports, Inc.,
1010 Vermont Avenue, N.W., Suite 408, Washington, DC
20005; (800) 296–9611.

FedWorld is a website specifically directed to government information databases. It has a site within it that lists federal jobs,

at www.fedworld.gov/jobs/jobsearch.html. An even better site is The Federal Jobs Digest at www.jobsfed.com/fedjob4.html.

Federal and State Judicial Clerkship Directory, updated annually and published by National Association for Law Placement (NALP), 1666 Connecticut Avenue, N.W., Suite 325, Washington, DC 20009; (202) 667–1666, www.nalp.org. Costs $100 or is available at most law school career services offices. Lists positions and criteria for federal and state court clerkships nationwide.

"The Lawyers' Job Bulletin Board," a monthly job placement newsletter for attorneys interested in federal practice. Newsletter is free for members, $30/year for nonmembers. Federal Bar Association, 1815 "H" Street, N.W., Suite 408, Washington, DC 20006–3697; (202) 638–0252.

Army Civilian Attorney Recruiting Program; (703) 695–1353. Employees remain civilians while employed by the army.

Navy Civilian Attorney Recruiting Program; (703) 602–2701. Employees remain civilians while employed by the navy, concentrating their practice on environmental, utility, contract, and general practice issues.

Environmental Protection Agency; (202) 260–2090. Many regional offices have recorded listings of job openings. Check with the office in your region.

Army JAG (Judge Advocate General) Corps, JAG Recruiting Service, 901 N. Stuart Street, Suite 700, Arlington, VA 22203; (800) 336–3315. This is the recruiting and office for Army attorneys.

Air Force JAG (703) 614–5941; Marine JAG (703) 614–1242; Navy JAG (901) 874–4084.

"Federal Jobs Digest," a biweekly list of government jobs (not necessarily law) in the United States and internationally. Fee is 3 months for $34, 6 months for $59. Breakthrough Publications. Call (800) 824–5000.

"The Third Branch," newsletter of the federal court, with occasional listing of judicial and magistrate positions. Free from the Administrative Office of the U.S. Courts, 1 Columbus Circle, N.E., Room 7–400, Washington, DC 20544; (202) 273–1120.

Judicial Fellows Programs. One-year paid federal fellowships for experienced lawyers. Contact Administrative Director, Judicial

Fellows Program, Room 5, Supreme Court of the United States, Washington, DC 20543; (202) 479–3374.

The ALJ Handbook: An Insider's Guide to Becoming a Federal Administrative Law Judge, 3rd edition, 1997, $49.95. Available through Federal Reports, Inc., 1010 Vermont Avenue, N.W., Suite 408, Washington, DC 20005; (800) 296–9611.

The Directory of Federal Jobs and Employers, Ronald Krannich and Caryl Krannich, Impact Publications, 1996. Identifies major hiring agencies, contacts, and programs in the legislative and judicial branches of government, although not necessarily law jobs.

"What Lawyers Earn," *National Law Journal.* An annual compilation of legal salaries in law firms, corporations, law schools, government, and public interest organizations.

American Association of Public Welfare Attorneys, 810 First Street, N.E., Suite 500, Washington, DC 20002; (202) 682–0100. Members are employed by public welfare agencies, attorney general and public defender offices, etc.

The U.S. Department of Justice puts out an annual directory with descriptions of the numerous agencies and professional jobs within those agencies. The department can be reached at 950 Pennsylvania Avenue, N.W., Washington, DC 20530–0001 or at its website at www.usdoj.gov/, which has information on legal jobs at the department.

OPPORTUNITIES IN STATE, COUNTY, AND CITY JURISDICTIONS

There are also a number of positions available in state, county, and city jurisdictions. A partial list includes:

- judge
- deputy or attorney general/deputy or district attorney
- administrative law judge (hears and rules on matters under the purview of the department to which she or he is assigned)
- counsel to sheriff's office/law enforcement legal advisor
- county counsel/legal advisor (in larger counties, this is a full-time job, in smaller, it can be farmed out to a law firm)

- board of supervisors legal advisor
- commission head (e.g., airport commission, park commission, port commission, etc.—often appointed by the mayor of the city, although in some cities, commission heads are elected)
- hearing officer (often juvenile, traffic claims, or smaller disputes at the direction of the presiding judge)
- research attorney (central staff or assigned to one judge)
- legislative analyst (analyzes, drafts, interprets legislation)
- deputy or state public defender (emphasis on appeals)/deputy or county public defender
- court commissioner (often assigned by the presiding judge to handle probate, law and motion or other procedural matters)
- deputy or city attorney (handles matters that run the gamut from municipal to environmental to tort to contract. Larger cities have full-time attorneys, smaller ones may farm the work out to a private law firm)
- rent control hearing officer
- probate referee (handles probate matters other than trial)
- Staff attorney for agencies such as Alcohol and Beverage Control, Banking, Public Utilities Commission, Consumer Affairs, Corporations, Board of Equalization, Franchise Tax Board, Health Department, Department of Insurance, Secretary of State, Department of Real Estate, Equal Employment and Housing Bureau, etc.

RESOURCES

Call the personnel office in your state, county, or city for current job listings. And also call the particular agency, department, or office in which you have an interest because many times an agency, department, or office hires independently of the centralized personnel office for the state, county, or city and does not list its openings with those personnel offices.

Parker Directory of California Attorneys, updated annually, lists public defender and district attorney offices, as well as other federal and state government offices in California. Call (800) 521–8110 to order.

Directory of State and Local Government Resources, NALP, 1993. Lists multi-state resources, as well as state-by-state bibliographies of resources. Order from National Association for Law Placement, 1666 Connecticut Avenue, N.W. Suite 325, Washington, 20009; (202) 667–1666, www.nalp.org.

Jobs Available: A Listing of Employment Opportunities in the Public Sector, $28 for 26 issues—an issue mailed every 2 weeks. Lists a wide range of professional positions in the Western states, in management, law, finance, human resources, etc. Call (209) 571–2120.

• Legal Aid/Legal Services

Possible positions within the arenas of legal aid or legal services include:

- director
- staff attorney
- intake worker
- investigator

Lawyers in these jobs generally handle either indigent criminal defense or civil matters for clients who fall below a basic income standard. The majority of civil issues are in the landlord-tenant, family, and breach of contract areas, with some offices handling agricultural and migrant labor, mining, immigration, or other specialized issues.

RESOURCES

Program Directory, free. Legal Services Corporation, 750 First Street, N.E., 10th floor, Washington, DC 20002-4250; (202) 336-8800. Addresses of legal aid societies nationwide.

The Directory of Legal Aid and Defender Offices in the United States, updated biannually. Contact National Legal Aid & Defender

Association, 1625 "K" Street N.W., 8th floor, Washington, DC 20006; (202) 452–0620. Also has a newsletter called "The Cornerstone."

Directory of California and Nevada Legal Services Programs, Western Center on Law & Poverty, 3701 Wilshire Blvd., Suite 208, Los Angeles, CA 90010; (213) 487–7211.

Check the program directory from the Legal Services Corporation, listed above, your phone directory, or call your state or local bar association's volunteer program for a list of agencies and organizations.

• Public Interest and Volunteer Lawyers

Possible positions include:

- directing or supervising attorney
- staff attorney
- staff researcher
- lobbyist (working for a nonprofit organization to monitor and shepherd appropriate legislation)
- legislative analyst/legislative writer
- policy and planning attorney (more of an emphasis is now put on these positions, since many courts are not as receptive to lawsuits by public interest firms or organizations, creating the need for input by these entities before an item becomes law, rather than after)

RESOURCES

If there is a special topic that particularly interests you, it probably has a nonprofit group that lobbies, monitors, volunteers, or strives to create interest in it. For example, if you are interested in children's legal issues, the National Center for Youth Law (114 Sansome Street, Suite 900, San Francisco, CA 94104; (415) 543–3307) is an activist organization on behalf of kids' legal issues. If you can't find an organization that focuses on

your area of interest, contact either your local bar association
or your state's office that regulates nonprofits (in California,
that would be the Charitable Trust Division of the Attorney
General's Office) to obtain a list and to get information about
the various organizations.

Human Rights Organizations and Periodicals Directory, 9th edition,
Meiklejohn Civil Liberties Institute (P.O. Box 673, Berkeley,
CA 94701—0673; (510) 848–0599), lists organizations, federal
agencies, and periodicals, along with internships.

Public Interest Employment Service: Job Alert!, available from Public
Interest Clearinghouse, 100 McAllister Street, San Francisco,
CA 94102; (415) 255–1714, www.pic.org. A bimonthly listing
of public interest jobs around the West for lawyers, administrators, and others. The clearinghouse also publishes "Public Interest, Private Practice," a directory of progressive firms in
Northern California that do public interest work. The clearinghouse is connected with public interest organizations in the
West; call them to find out if there are similar organizations
in your state.

ACCESS: Networking in the Public Interest, 1001 Connecticut
Avenue, N.W., Suite 838, Washington, DC 20036; (202)
785–4233, www.communityjobs.org, is a national non-profit
resource center on employment and careers in the non-profit
sector. It publishes "Community Jobs: The National Employment Newspaper for the Nonprofit Sector," with national listings of mostly non-profit sector jobs and relevant articles.

Volunteer Lawyers for the Arts, 1 East 53rd Street, 6th floor,
New York, NY 10022; (212) 319–2910. This is a good resource for meeting other lawyers in entertainment and media
law, along with artists. Call for roster of affiliated groups nationwide—for instance, in Atlanta, Seattle, Chicago, San Francisco, etc.

California Lawyers for the Arts, Fort Mason Center, Bldg. C,
Room 255, San Francisco, CA 94123; (415) 775–7200. Also
at 1212 Broadway, Suite 834, Oakland, CA 94612; (510)
444–6351; at 926 "J" Street, Suite 811, Sacramento, CA
95814; (916) 442–6210. Also at 1641–18th Street, Santa Mon-
ica, CA 90404; (310) 998–5590. Legal, dispute resolution, educational, and resource services for artists, performers, and

writers by volunteer attorneys. This is a good resource for meeting other lawyers working with artists, media, and entertainment people. Web address is www.sirius.com/~c/a.

Career Resource Guide. Available for $10 from the National Association for Public Interest Law (NAPIL), 2120 "L" Street, N.W., Washington, DC 20037; (202) 466–3686. Lists all resources for public interest placement within the United States. They also administer a postgraduate fellowship program that puts no cap on years of prior practice experience; in fact, they encourage very experienced attorneys to propose a project in tandem with a nonprofit so that NAPIL can fund the first year.

United Way Social Services Directory. Lists numerous agencies and organizations dealing with public and individual needs. United Way also has a telephone number in each major city for resource referrals.

An annual public interest job fair is held in San Francisco in late February or early March each year. It is student-oriented, but it does provide opportunity even for experienced practitioners to meet with representatives of public interest organizations throughout the West. Contact the Public Interest Clearinghouse, (415) 255–1714, www.pic.org.

Public Interest Job Search Guide, $15 for students, $35 for attorneys. Harvard Law School's handbook, for law students and practitioners, on how and where to find public interest work and fellowships. An annual publication about public interest positions, with listings of employers and fellowships across the country. Contact the Public Interest Advising Office, Harvard Law School, Pound 328, Cambridge, MA 02138; (617) 495–3108.

Directory of Pro Bono Programs, ABA, updated annually, $20. This directory lists over 800 programs in a state-by-state format. Order from the ABA, Attn: Publication Orders, P.O. Box 10892, Chicago, IL 60610–0892; (800) 285–2221, or e-mail abasvcctr@attmail.com.

Environmental Law Careers Directory. Available for $10 from the *Ecology Law Quarterly,* Attn: Careers Directory, 493 Diamond Hall, University of California, Berkeley, CA 94720; (510) 642-0457 or order from U.C. Press at (510) 642-9129. Lists law firms, as well as nonprofit and government agencies that provide opportunities for the environmental lawyer. An environmental law careers conference is held each fall at Boalt Hall Law School at U.C. Berkeley, with information on careers in private and public interest firms. Contact the programs director at the *Ecology Law Quarterly*.

Most state and local bar associations have volunteer programs, or they can introduce you to public interest organizations that can use your services.

Public Service Careers Resource Guide 1998–99, Yale Law School Career Development Office, 1998. Information on public service jobs in law firms and government agencies. Call (203) 432–1676 to order.

Good Works: A Guide to Careers in Social Change, Donna Colvin and Ralph Nader, 5th edition, Barricade Books, 1994. Includes over 800 organizations in a variety of public interest areas.

Lawful Pursuit: Careers in Public Interest Law, Ronald W. Fox, ABA, 1995, $19.95. Order from ABA, Attn: Publication Orders, P.O. Box 10892, Chicago, IL 60610–0892; (800) 285–2221, or e-mail abasvcctr@attmail.com.

• Courts

Possible positions in federal, state, county, or city jurisdictions (trial or appellate level) include:

- law clerk (even some of the county courts have clerks)
- central research staff (handling writs, appeals, habeas petitions)
- magistrate/commissioner (see comment in section on government)
- pro-tem (in some courts, these are volunteer positions, in others they are paid by the day)
- judge
- small claims advisor (to assist claimants with forms, legal concerns and procedures)
- hearing officer (see comment in section on government)
- O-R, bail or pre-trial diversion project attorney (this position is usually used to investigate and recommend "own

recognizance" or bail release, as well as do pretrial diversion investigations and recommendations)

- state judicial council staff or director (many states have a council used to monitor and work on issues associated with the judiciary)
- Commission on Judicial Performance staff attorney or director (legal advisor to the commission that investigates and disciplines errant judges)

Not all research attorneys for courts are new law school graduates; many of these attorneys have a number of practice years before entering court employment. I know of an attorney who had practiced for fifteen years before being hired to do research for an appellate court judge. Most courts, from state trial level to the U.S. Supreme Court, have career attorneys who handle necessary legal research and writing. Some work as central staff, working on research matters in general, such as writs, appeals, and habeas petitions. Others work for an individual judge, assisting in the research and writing of opinions specifically assigned to their judge.

RESOURCES

California Courts Directory & Fee Schedule, published annually by the California Association of Court Clerks. Complete list of all federal, state, and county courts in California, including names and addresses of courts and clerks. Send $15 plus $3 shipping and handling to the California Association of Court Clerks, P.O. Box 38, San Leandro, CA 94577–0138; (510) 553–0401. Many states have comparable publications.

Parker Directory of California Attorneys, updated annually. It contains names and addresses of all California judges, commissioners, and court administrators. Call (800) 521–8110 to order.

Federal and State Judicial Clerkship Directory, updated annually and published by National Association for Law Placement (NALP), 1666 Connecticut Avenue, N.W., Suite 325, Washington, DC 20009; (202) 667–1666, www.nalp.org. Fee is $100, or available at most law school career services offices. Lists positions and criteria for federal and state court clerkships nationwide.

"The Third Branch," newsletter of the federal court, with occasional listing of judicial and magistrate positions. Free from the Administrative Office of the U.S. Courts, 1 Columbus Circle, N.E., Room 7–400, Washington, DC 20544; (202) 273–1120.

Judicial Fellows Programs. One-year paid federal fellowships for lawyers. Contact Administrative Director, Judicial Fellows Program, Room 5, Supreme Court of the United States, Washington, DC 20543; (202) 479–3374.

"What Lawyers Earn," *National Law Journal.* An annual compilation of legal salaries in law firms, corporations, law schools, judgeships, and public interest organizations.

• Labor Unions

Possible positions include:

- general counsel
- associate counsel

RESOURCES

AFL-CIO Lawyers Coordinating Committee Subscription List, 815 16th Street, N.W., Room 807, Washington, DC 20006; (202) 637–5214. A state-by-state listing of counsel for the AFL-CIO. However, to obtain a subscription, you must meet membership criteria, which include the requisite amount of labor law experience. If you don't meet the criteria, but want to see the list, locate a colleague who fits the criteria and would get you a copy.

• School Districts

Possible positions include:

- general counsel
- staff attorney

RESOURCES

Lawyers work within most school systems, on the elementary, secondary, and college level. Contact your local unified or rural school district's personnel office, or personnel offices at colleges or universities or specialty schools (for instance, law or business schools). Don't overlook some private schools and colleges, which might have in-house attorneys.

National Association of College & University Attorneys, One Dupont Circle, N.W., Suite 620, Washington, DC 20036; (202) 833–8390. Has a position registry, which lists job openings twice a month and costs $60 per year for members, $65 for nonmembers.

Counsel of School Attorneys of the National School Boards Association, 1680 Duke Street, Alexandria, VA 22314; (703) 838–6711. Membership consists mainly of private attorneys who represent school districts. They publish a newsletter and journal.

"School Law as an Evolving Legal Specialty," *Student Lawyer* magazine, American Bar Association, September 1991.

• Law Schools

Possible positions in law schools include:

- tenure-track professor
- instructor (can be full-time, but not on tenure, perhaps because of lack of scholarly publication)
- lecturer (often teaches only one or two courses in a specialty, or is visiting)

- adjunct (part-time or visiting, teaching a specialty course)
- director of law center
- director or supervising attorney of clinical education program (either head of all clinical programs or in charge of a particular program, such as trial practice, poverty law clinic, etc.)

There are many career-track and non-career-track positions at law schools, as indicated above. Although tenured teaching jobs in law schools are not easy to get—there is great competition for the limited slots that open each year—they are more easily obtainable by beginning attorneys who aspire to academia, experienced attorneys who have an in-depth specialty area, or others who have an impressive scholarly publication portfolio. Teaching at most professional schools involves one-third time in the classroom, one-third time researching and publishing, and the last third involved in faculty committees.

One tactic for obtaining a full-time teaching job is to start out slow—teach a course on legal research and writing or one adjunct class. This will allow you to get to know the dean and some faculty members, enhancing your chance for permanent employment.

RESOURCES

Placement Bulletin, $59 per year or $14 per issue, published about six times a year by the Association of American Law Schools, 1201 Connecticut Avenue, N.W., Suite 800, Washington, DC 20036–2605; (202) 296–8851. Lists faculty, deanships, administrative, and visitorship positions for American and international law schools.

"What Lawyers Earn," *National Law Journal.* An annual compilation of legal salaries in law firms, corporations, law schools, judgeships, and public interest organizations.

Once a year there is a national law school "hiring fair" where potential new faculty are screened. It is a good networking opportunity and a chance to find out about various law schools. Inquire at your local law school to find out where it will be held, since it is in a different city each year.

Check your state bar association for listings of local law schools.

• Bar Associations

Possible positions include:

- disciplinary proceedings coordinator or prosecutor
- state bar court judge (hears and rules on discipline cases)
- general counsel (handles the legal issues of the bar association)
- staff counsel
- special project coordinator (e.g., publications on legal issues for the general population, Law Day)
- continuing legal education staff attorney (monitors and enforces legal education for bar members)
- volunteer legal services project director (recruits attorneys for pro bono projects)
- director of lawyer referral service
- legal ethics hotline telephone responder (for those bar associations that have a special number to call with ethics questions, this position provides someone to answer the questions)

RESOURCES

American Bar Association Red Book Directory, $14.95, updated annually. Listings of ABA and affiliated local bar association employees and officers. Order from ABA, Attn: Publication Orders, P.O. Box 10892, Chicago, IL 60610–0892; (800) 285–2221, or e-mail abasvcctr@attmail.com.

National Organization of Bar Counsel holds semi-annual meetings and is comprised of counsel to state bar associations. Contact Teresa Boyd, Administrative Assistant, Office of Bar Counsel, 515 Fifth Street, N.W., Room 127, Washington, DC 20001; (202) 638–1501.

Call your state bar association for a list of local bar associations.

• A Note on the Use of Headhunters

Once you have targeted an area of interest within the law, it is sometimes possible to work successfully with an executive search consultant. Headhunters, as they are commonly known, are paid by an employer and therefore are looking for an applicant whose experience exactly matches the job profile requested by their customer. That profile generally targets associates from larger, well-known business and corporate law firms who have one to six years experience (law firms don't generally pay to obtain first-year associates, since these new lawyers don't yet have experience to offer) and who either previously worked at prestigious law firms or have outstanding academic records; in addition, they're looking for associates or partners with certain "hot" specialties or an existing client base.

Most legal and executive headhunters are not interested in working with individuals desiring to cross over into fields outside law, as a crossover person usually does not fit the job search parameters given them by the employer. Because of this, headhunters do not attempt to place lawyers in non-law jobs.

Also, since headhunters are compensated only if they successfully place an applicant, they generally aren't willing to conduct a job search on your behalf—that is, to work for you, or attempt to fit you into a job. (And they are compensated *well,* as they usually receive a fee from the employer of 25 to 30 percent of the first year's salary of whomever they place.)

If you fit the general profile set out above, and are looking for a more suitable job within the legal profession—perhaps moving from one law firm to another or from a law firm to a corporation—contacting a headhunter could be helpful. Occasionally, even if you do not fit the general profile, your unique skills or large client base may be in demand. If so, contacting a few headhunters could be worth a *small* investment of time.

Moreover, since headhunters do wish to develop goodwill, and since they are good information resources, use them to assist in your research. After all, they hope that your best friend might fit the search they are currently doing for a law firm.

RESOURCES

National Association of Legal Search Consultants, 355 Lexington Avenue, 17th Floor, New York, NY 10017; (888) 256–2732. Call them to get a directory of headhunters in your area.

American Lawyer magazine annually publishes a national directory of legal recruiters in the January issue.

The National Law Journal also publishes a directory.

Either look in your telephone book under Executive Recruiters or call one or two of the large law firms in town to ask which recruiters they use.

The Directory of Executive Recruiters, 27th edition, Kennedy Publications, 1997. A directory of law and nonlaw recruiters.

The New Career Makers: America's Top Executive Recruiters, John Sibbald, HarperBusiness, 1994.

Job Seekers Guide to Executive Recruiters, Christopher Hunt and Scott Scanlon, John Wiley & Sons, 1997.

CHAPTER SEVEN

Options Related to the Law

*It's a funny thing about life, if you refuse to accept
anything but the best, you very often get it.*
—SOMERSET MAUGHAM

The positions discussed in this chapter are considered law-
related either because they are in a legal environment, or because
the skills required by the job make a legal background very useful. But, although a legal background is helpful and lawyers often
are hired in these positions, most do not require an active license
to practice. Thus, if you have not taken the bar, have not passed
it, are on inactive status, or even if you have been disbarred,
these options are obtainable because of the skills and knowledge
you have gained through your legal training.

If you are just finishing law school or have little practice experience, your legal training will often interest employers who do
business with law firms because it has given you a certain way
of thinking, communicating, and analyzing that can be useful to
them. These employers realize that many practicing lawyers,

when buying computers, working with management consultants, analyzing legal research needs, or hiring numerous other services, feel more comfortable doing business with individuals trained as lawyers. A law graduate, even one who has never practiced law, is thought to better understand the legal world, its language, and lifestyle and, therefore, is more able to understand the practicing lawyer's needs than someone who has not studied or worked in the field.

Unfortunately, if you are far beyond entry level in the legal field, it often is difficult to move between law firms. As discussed previously, law is one of the very few fields in which increased experience increasingly limits your practice choices and ability to change firms unless you have a large "book of business" (client roster) or an esoteric practice area that is in demand (see discussion of this issue in chapter 6 under Law Firms). However, you will find that many non-law employers actively seek to hire experienced individuals with a legal background because they appreciate that you can communicate effectively with their lawyer-clients and other professionals.

In the lists of positions enumerated in this chapter, not one position has been made up—each has been filled by a former lawyer. And these are only a sample of the variety of positions that exist and are created each year. If you don't find one you like, create your own!

RESOURCES

Lawyers in Transition^{SM} Newsletter, published quarterly, contains articles about various career paths in, related to, and outside of law, as well as interviews with lawyer career changers. Fee is $20 per year for four issues from Lawyers in Transition^{SM}, P.O. Box 31026, San Francisco, CA 94131; (415) 285–5143.

Beyond L.A. Law: Break the Traditional "Lawyer" Mold, edited by Janet Smith, Harcourt Brace, 1997. Profiles of 47 lawyers who are working in diverse jobs in and out of law. Very interesting and motivational.

J.D. Preferred: Legal Careers Alternative Notebook, $75 plus postage and handling from Federal Reports, Inc., 1010 Vermont Avenue, N.W., Suite 408, Washington, DC 20005; (800) 296–9611. It lists general career information and options, but concentrates on options within the areas of ethics, international trade, media, technology transfer, insurance/risk management, ADR, and academic administration.

Nonlegal Careers for Lawyers: In the Private Sector, 3rd edition, Gary Munneke and William Henslee, ABA Press, 1994. Available through ABA, Attn: Publication Orders, P.O. Box 10892, Chicago, IL 60610–0892; (800) 285–2221, or e-mail abasvcctr @attmail.com. Also available at many law school career services offices.

Turning Points: New Paths and Second Careers for Lawyers, Senior Lawyers Division of the ABA, 1994, $49.95. A guide to career opportunities for new or retiring lawyers. Can be ordered from ABA, Attn: Publication Orders, P.O. Box 10892, Chicago, IL 60610–0892; (800) 285–2221, or e-mail abasvcctr@attmail.com.

Alternative Careers for Lawyers, Hillary Mantis, Princeton Review, 1997. Addresses career evaluation and alternatives from her perspective as director of a law school career services office.

Judgment Reversed: Alternative Careers for Lawyers, Jeffrey Strausser, Barrons Educational Series, 1997. Addresses how lawyers can move into several alternative careers within the business sector.

What Can You Do With A Law Degree?: A Lawyer's Guide to Career Alternatives Inside, Outside and Around the Law, Deborah Arron, 3rd edition, Niche Press, 1997. Thoroughly covers career assessment, options, and resources.

• Law Firms

Nonlaw positions which lawyers have held in law firms include:

- client services manager
- director of professional development (in-house training for the law firm's lawyers, by arranging a member lawyer to teach a course, or negotiating and arranging with an outside vendor to present a program)
- director of training (for clerical/paralegal personnel)

- firm manager (often involved in decisions affecting every facet of firm operation, including hiring new associates, budgets, marketing, etc.)
- in-house communications (writes firm newsletter or informational newsletters sent to clients of various practice areas)
- office administrator (in charge of support staff functions and logistics)
- personnel director (hires and manages support staff)
- public relations manager
- marketing director
- recruiting administrator (recruits/interviews lawyers)
- business development director
- practice management director
- paralegal (some firms won't hire lawyers to work as paralegals, believing that the lawyer will leave as soon as a law job is offered elsewhere)
- librarian (generally need a Master's in Library Science, at least for the larger firms)

RESOURCES

Association of Legal Administrators, 175 E. Hawthorn Parkway, Suite 325, Vernon Hills, IL 60061–1428; (847) 816–1212, www.alanet.org. Members are law firm managers and personnel directors of law firms.

"Spotlight on Change," *Lawyers in Transition*sm *Newsletter,* January–March 1991, p. 6. Profile of woman who evolved from associate position to marketing director of large law firm. Copy of newsletter available from LIT for $5.

In-House Training Resource Guide, 1993 (a bit dated), National Association for Law Placement, 1666 Connecticut Avenue, N.W., Suite 325, Washington, DC 20009; (202) 667–1666. Descriptions of the various training programs within firms, a list of nonprofit organizations that provide services and products to support that training, and a bibliography of references.

Legal Marketing Association, 401 N. Michigan Avenue, Chicago, IL 60611; (312) 245–1592 www.lma.org/. Has newsletter and provides education and information programs for marketers

within, and those who market to, law firms. Also has job
listings for marketing positions in law firms.

American Association of Law Libraries, 53 W. Jackson Blvd.,
Suite 940, Chicago, IL 60604; (312) 939–4764, www.aala.net.
org, has a newsletter with job announcements and a 24-hour
Career Hotline at (312) 939–7877.

Contact the American Bar Association; (800) 285–2221, or your
state or local bar for a list of organizations that provide training
for lawyers and hire instructors and course designers.

• Bar Associations

Positions lawyers have held include:

- director (head of all bar activities and relationships)
- assistant director
- administrator (in charge of staff)
- bar foundation director (directs the fund-raising arm)
- human resources director (in charge of personnel)
- community relations liaison
- publications director

RESOURCES

Contact your state and local bar associations to see what positions
they have available or what openings they anticipate in the
near future.

National Association of Bar Executives, c/o ABA Division of
Bar Services, 541 N. Fairbanks Court, Chicago, IL 60611;
(312) 988–5360. Members are professional staff of state and
local bar associations.

"Directory of Bar Associations." Listings of ABA-affiliated bar associations nationwide. Available for $95 from ABA, Attn: Publica-
tion Orders, P.O. Box 10892, Chicago, IL 60610–0892; (800)
285–2221, or e-mail abasvcctr@attmail.com or at many law
libraries.

See information about bar associations under that heading in chapter 6, at page 179.

• Business

Positions lawyers have held in business include:

- affirmative action officer
- pension operations for insurance company
- bank trust officer (managing the trust portfolio for either individual clients or for the bank itself)
- commercial loan administrator
- contract compliance administrator (either reviewing contracts and insuring compliance through telephone relations, or by on-site and public relations visits to vendors/contract sites)
- contract specialist (similar to above, but expert in the analysis and interpretration of contracts)
- director, employee/labor relations (usually a division within the human resources department)
- director, human resources department
- estate planning/sales with insurance company or financial planning organization
- ethics officer (insures compliance of company, university, hospital, or government agency with "mission" of organization and with community standards)
- manager, employee benefits (usually a division within the human resources department)
- manager, community relations (responsible for generating goodwill for organization, through distribution of charitable donations or involvement with community programs)
- ombudsman (see page 199 for more information)
- policy and legislative analyst
- prepaid legal plan administrator (monitors prepaid legal plan that may be provided to employees as a "perk")
- risk management advisor for insurance company, corporation, government agency, university or hospital (assesses risk

of action to be undertaken, insures for it, and minimizes liability if incurred)

RESOURCES

Legal Careers in Business, vol. 3, edited by Penny J. Parker, National Association for Law Placement, 1984. Out of print but available at some law school career services offices.

American Association of Attorney-CPAs, headquartered at 24196 Alicia Parkway, Suite K, Mission Viejo, CA 92691; (714) 768–0336.

Encyclopedia of Associations, Gale Research, at most public libraries. Look up information about the associations in your area of interest, such as human resources management or contract compliance.

Risk management organizations include:

- Society for Risk Analysis, 1313 Dolly Madison Blvd., Suite 402, McLean, VA 22101; (703) 790–1745, www.sra.org. An international organization with members in law, academia, government, and industry.
- Risk and Insurance Management Society, Inc., 655 Third Avenue, 2nd floor, New York, NY 10017; (212) 286–9292, www.rims.org. A nonprofit organization drawing members from the industrial, nonprofit, public, and service sectors.
- Most states have a statewide risk management association, with membership from the public and private sector. Check your local phone directory or the *Encyclopedia of Associations* at the public library.
- University Risk Management and Insurance Association, 2 Wisconsin Circle, Suite 1040, Chevy Chase, MD 20815; (301) 718–9711, www.urmia.org. Members work in risk management, insurance, and employee benefits.

National Contract Management Association, 1912 Woodford Road, Vienna, VA 22182; (703) 448–9231, www.ncmahq.org. Has regional chapters. Publishes *Contract Management,* a monthly magazine on contract management developments. Fee for 1 year is $75.

Ethikos, a bimonthly forum for ethics officers examining business ethics issues. Fee is $145 per year. Ethikos, Inc., 154 E. Boston Post Road, Mamaroneck, NY 10543; (914) 381–7475.

Human Resources Departments are the old "personnel office." HR departments usually handle employee relations, employee-employer relations, employee benefits, disability issues, and training of new employees. If the company is of any size, the HR department might be divided into sub-offices to handle various specialities within a field, such as an employee-employer relations sub-office that focuses on EEOC and Americans with Disabilities Act issues.

Opportunities in Human Resource Management Careers, William Traynor and J. Steven McKenzie, VGM Career Horizons, 1994.

Judgment Reversed: Alternative Careers for Lawyers, Jeffrey Strausser, Barron's Educational Series, 1997. Addresses how lawyers can move into several alternative careers within the business sector.

See other resources under "Business" in chapter 8, on page 226.

• Politics/Government

Positions lawyers have held include:

- campaign manager
- campaign finance director
- city/county clerk
- court administrator
- director of commission or agency (sometimes appointed, sometimes elected, may receive small stipend or, in some communities, large payments)
- elected official
- ethics officer
- foreign service officer
- land use examiner
- legislation and policy analyst
- lobbyist
- ombudsman (see page 199 for more information)
- political fund-raiser

- risk manager (see page 188 and 191 for more information)
- speechwriter
- special project administrator (e.g., media coverage for a political campaign or database installation within a government office)
- staff support in a political campaign

RESOURCES

Federal Information Center. Phone (800) 688–9889 nationwide for job information and how to apply for a particular type of position (not only legal) within the federal government. Keep trying, as numbers are often busy. Also contact individual agencies, because they often hire independently. National office of U.S. Jobs by Phone is in Georgia at (912) 757–3000.

Federal Law-Related Careers Directory: A Guide to Over 150 Law-Related Careers, edited by Richard Hermann, 3rd edition, 1994. Alternative legal careers within the federal government. Sets out the hiring procedures of offices that require a legal background for employment in non-law jobs, and gives addresses of recruiting offices. Available for $24.95 from Federal Reports, Inc., 1010 Vermont Avenue, N.W., Suite 408, Washington, DC 20005; (800) 296–9611.

The Directory of Federal Jobs and Employers, Ronald Krannich and Caryl Krannich, Impact Publications, 1996. Identifies major hiring agencies, contacts, and programs in the legislative and judicial branches of government.

American League of Lobbyists, P.O. Box 30005, Alexandria, VA 22310; (703) 960-3011, www.alldc.org.

Several helpful websites listing government jobs are: Federal Jobs Digest (www.jobsfed.com/fedjob4.html) is an excellent site; FedWorld Federal Jobs Search (www.fedworld.gov/job/jobsearch.html) is an official U.S. government site; and Office of Personnel Management (www.usajobs.opm.gov) is another official site.

Federal Career Opportunities, $39 for 3 months, $77 for 6 months. Federal government job listings from Federal Research Services, Inc., 370 Maple Avenue West, Suite 5, Vienna, VA 22183; (703) 281–0200.

Risk management organizations include:

- Society for Risk Analysis, 1313 Dolly Madison Blvd., Suite 402, McLean, VA 22101; (703) 790–1745, www.sra.org. An international organization with members in law, academia, government, and industry.
- Risk and Insurance Management Society, Inc., 655 Third Avenue, 2nd floor, New York, NY 10017; (212) 286–9292, www.rims.org. A nonprofit organization drawing members from the industrial, nonprofit, public, and service sectors.
- Public Risk Management Association, 1815 N. Ft. Myer Drive, Suite 1020, Arlington, VA 22209; (703) 528–7701, www.prmacentral.org. Members work in the public sector. Publishes "State of the Profession" survey, $35 for members, $50 for nonmembers.

Council on Governmental Ethics Laws, Center for Governmental Studies, 10951 West Pico Blvd., Suite 120, Los Angeles, CA 90064; (310) 470–6590. Members have responsibilities in government ethics, campaign finance, lobbying laws, and elections. Most states have government ethics offices/officers.

The Complete Guide to Public Employment, Ronald Krannich and Caryl Rae Krannich, 3rd edition, Impact Publications, 1994.

Federal Jobs in Law Enforcement, John W. Warner, Macmillan 1992. Some enforcement agencies prefer applicants with a J.D.

Job Seekers Guide to California State Government, Myrlys Hollis, Columbia Publishers, $14.95. Order from Columbia Publishers; (415) 668–9561. This book has listings "for all 128" state departments, information about how to find out about and prepare for state interviews, and how to get promoted from within.

Jobs Available: A Listing of Employment Opportunities in the Public Sector, $28 for 26 issues—an issue mailed every 2 weeks. Lists a wide range of professional positions, in the Western states, in management, law, finance, human resources, etc. Call (209) 571–2120.

See information in the section on Government in chapter 6, beginning on page 164.

• Education Systems/Continuing Education Providers

Positions lawyers have held include:

- director of alumni relations at a law school (often involves fund-raising)
- business law professor at a graduate school of business
- dean of student affairs at a law school (often also teaches one or two courses)
- instructor in a court reporter program
- instructor in a legal assistant program
- instructor of continuing education for real estate salespeople
- instructor for community college law-related courses (e.g., business law, "Your Legal Rights," copyright law for artists and writers, etc.)
- instructor, course designer, or coordinator for either a for-profit or not-for-profit continuing legal education business
- instructor for bar association–sponsored CLE programs
- law librarian
- law school dean
- law school career services office director
- ombudsman (see page 199 for more information)
- risk manager (see page 188 and 191 for more information)

RESOURCES

Academy of Legal Studies in Business is an organization of over 1,000 J.D.s who teach law-related subjects in institutions other than law schools—for instance, in business schools. Publishes a newsletter and has a small free placement service for members. Contact Professor Daniel Herron, c/o Department of Finance, School of Business Administration, 120 Upham Hall, Miami University, Oxford, OH 45056; (800) 831–2903.

National Association for Law Placement (NALP), 1666 Connect-icut Avenue, N.W., Suite 325, Washington, DC 20009; (202) 667–1666, www.nalp.org. An association with membership consisting of law school career services directors, in-house law firm and corporate legal recruiters, some headhunters, and interested others.

University Risk Management and Insurance Association, 2 Wisconsin Circle Suite 1040, Chevy Chase, MD 20815; (301) 718–9711, www.urmia.org. Members work in risk management, insurance, and employee benefits.

American Association of Law Libraries, 53 W. Jackson Blvd., Suite 940, Chicago, IL 60604; (312) 939–4764. The association has a magazine, *AALL Spectrum,* with job announcements and a 24-hour Career Hotline at (312) 939–7877. Job listings are also on their website at www.aallnet.org.

Association for Continuing Legal Education, Attn: Donna Passons, P.O. Box 4646, Austin, TX 78765; (512) 453–4340. Members are continuing legal education providers; this association provides education for its own members.

Here is a sampling of some continuing legal education providers—there are many, many more nationwide (you can teach through them, manage them, or market for them):

- ALI/ABA, 4025 Chestnut St., Philadelphia, PA 19104; (800) CLE-NEWS, www.ali-aba.org.
- Practicing Law Institute, 810 Seventh Avenue, New York, NY 10019; (212) 824–5700, www.pli.edu.
- The Rutter Group, 15760 Ventura Blvd., Suite 630, Encino, CA 91436; (800) 747–3161, www.rutter.com.
- California Continuing Education of the Bar (CEB), 2300 Shattuck Avenue, Berkeley, CA 94704; (510) 642–3974, www.ceb.ucop.edu.
- National Practice Institute, 701 Fourth Avenue South, Suite 1710, Minneapolis, MN 55415; (800) 328–4444, www.npilaw.com.
- The Professional Education Group, Inc., 12401 Minnetonka Blvd., Minnetonka, MN 55305; (800) 229–2531.

• Labor Unions

Possible positions in labor unions include:

- administrator/manager
- labor negotiator
- ombudsman (see page 199 for more information)
- union representative

RESOURCES

Encyclopedia of Associations, section on Labor Unions, Associations
and Federations. Available at public libraries or contact Gale
Research, (800) 877–GALE.

• Mediation, Arbitration, and Ombudsman

Possible employers include:

- labor unions
- university, hospital, prison, media, government and corporate ombudsman programs
- court systems
- government agencies
- panels such as American Arbitration Association
- private practice
- affiliation with a not-for-profit group
- community dispute resolution boards in various cities

Alternative Dispute Resolution (ADR) is the encompassing
title for arbitration, mediation, and other dispute-resolving techniques. There are major differences between the processes. An
arbitrator acts as a hearing officer, taking evidence, hearing witnesses, and eventually issuing a ruling in favor of one party or
another. An arbitrator needn't be a lawyer—just a thoughtful and
careful listener, generally with some background in the subject
matter of the specific arbitration.

Similarily, a mediator doesn't have to be a lawyer. In fact, many lawyers make terrible mediators because they aren't able to discard their advocate's persona, and a mediator must remain neutral to be effective. The minute a mediator is perceived to take one side or the other, she or he loses all credibility and usually stymies any further progress. This is because a mediator, unlike an arbitrator, takes neither side, but functions as a neutral facilitator to enable and assist the parties in presenting information relevant to their issues. The mediator may take each party aside and point out the inadequacies of an asserted position, but never issues a judgment or ruling. Instead, the parties themselves, aided by the mediator, develop their own settlement terms and subsequently have them reviewed by their respective attorneys.

Mediation is a growing field on both the East and West Coasts. In the Heartland, it is developing a bit more slowly, but it should become a potent practice in the future. In a number of jurisdictions, the courts are beginning to require that litigants be apprised of the availability of ADR and what it is, before they can file a lawsuit; more and more disputes are being handled by ADR because of its quicker and less expensive resolution. However, in many areas of the country, the majority of mediators are volunteering their time in order to gain experience and are making only a partial living from mediation.

If you are interested in ADR, join the mediation section of your local and state bar associations, the relevant local mediation associations, and gain experience through vounteering before you take an expensive training program, both to see if you like working as a mediator and to research whether supporting yourself as a mediator is a viable option in your town or city.

RESOURCES

American Bar Association Section on Dispute Resolution, 740–15th Street, N.W., Washington, DC 20005–1009; (202) 662–1680, www.abanet.org/dispute/. The website is an excellent starting point to link to numerous dispute resolution sites of other ADR organizations and resources. Published *1993 Dispute Resolution Directory,* setting out mediation, conciliation, and arbitration programs alphabetically, as well as state by state; also includes international dispute resolution programs. Fee is $60 plus postage and handling, although it's somewhat out of date. The ABA also has standing committees on dispute resolution within its Business Law and Family Law Sections. Contact the ABA at (312) 988–5000 or (800) 285–2221.

American Arbitration Association. Maintains a panel of arbitration and mediation attorneys for referral; requires at least ten years current experience, mainly in construction, securities, computers, or commercial law to be a panel member. Main office is at 140 W. 51st Street, New York, NY 10020–1203; (212) 484–4000, www.adr.org/. Over 37 offices in cities nationwide. It publishes the *Dispute Resolution Journal,* a quarterly magazine with ADR articles, for $50 per year.

Federal Mediation and Conciliation Service, 2100 "K" Street, N.W., Washington, DC 20427; (202) 606–8100 www.fmcs. gov/. District offices nationwide. Mediates federal labor disputes.

Better Business Bureaus use volunteer arbitrators/mediators and offer ADR training. Main office is at 4200 Wilson Blvd., Suite 800, Arlington, VA 22203; (703) 276–0100, with offices nationwide. Website is www.bbb.org. Volunteering with the BBB is a good way to get experience.

National Association of Securities Dealers, Office of Dispute Resolution, 125 Broad Street, 36th floor, New York, NY 10004; (212) 480–4881, www.nasd.com. Offers training, then has volunteers arbitrate disputes between customers and member brokerage firms.

J.A.M.S./Endispute. Corporate office at 1920 Main Street, Suite 300, Irvine, CA 92714–7229; (949) 224–1810, www.jams-endispute.com, with branch offices nationwide. J.A.M.S previously hired only retired judges, but merged with Endispute (an East Coast ADR company that had previously merged with Bates-Edwards, a San Francisco–based attorney mediation service), and now utilizes judges, lawyers, and knowledgeable others to conduct ADR proceedings, often in large cases.

Check your state's Department of Consumer Affairs to see if they have a dispute resolution office.

Many counties nationwide have professional mediation programs in their court systems—for instance, Los Angeles Superior Courts' Conciliation Service.

CPR Institute for Dispute Resolution, 366 Madison Avenue, New York, NY 10017; (212) 949–6490. An international nonprofit organization that encourages the integration of ADR into law practice. Has publications and training. Members are general counsel, law firm lawyers, academicians, etc.

American Health Lawyers Association, 1120 Connecticut Avenue, N.W., Suite 950, Washington, DC 20036; (202) 833–1100. Provides ADR for health care disputes.

Citizenship and Law-Related Education Center, 9738 Lincoln Village Drive, Sacramento, CA 95827; (916) 228–2322. A nonprofit organization with services that include the implementation of school-based conflict resolution programs, plus student, parent, and staff training.

Many state and local bar associations sponsor mediation training and provide opportunities for volunteering. Many have mediation sections for networking and education purposes.

Society for Professionals in Dispute Resolution (SPIDR), 1621 Connecticut Avenue, N.W., Suite 400, Washington, DC 20009; (202) 265–1927, www.spidr.org/. This is a prominent international organization of mediators, with regional chapters, whose members come from both the public and private sector. Publishes a newsletter and is an ADR clearinghouse, in addition to sponsoring educational programs and writing summaries of other organizations' programs. SPIDR also has a Job Line with recorded ADR job listings—call (202) 783–7277 for information on the Job Line.

National Institute for Dispute Resolution, 1726 "M" Street, N.W., Suite 500, Washington, DC 20036; (202) 466–4764, www.nidr.org/. Publishes *Dispute Resolution Resource Directory* and other publications to promote ADR in and out of law.

ConflictNet is a fee-based on-line gateway for ADR information. Contact Institute for Global Communications at (415) 561–6100. For a free look, log on at www.igc.org then click on ConflictNet.

Mediation, Jay Folberg, Jossey-Bass, 1984. Contact Jossey-Bass at (415) 433-1767.

Mediation Quarterly, $56 per year, published by Jossey-Bass, San Francisco; (415) 433–1767.

Finding Common Ground: A Field Guide to Mediation, Barbara Ashley Phillips, Hells Canyon Publishing, 1996. How and when to mediate—about the inner workings of mediation by an experienced mediator.

Martindale-Hubbell Dispute Resolution Directory, updated annually. State by state listings of professionals involved in ADR. Available at most law libraries.

For other relevant books, log on to www.amazon.com on the web, then enter the search word "mediation."

ADR CENTERS

Many medium and large communities across the country have set up community dispute resolution centers, which hear disputes between neighbors, community groups, small businesses, and school kids. Many of these centers provide some training in ADR, requiring a minimum volunteer commitment in return. These are excellent places to try your hand at mediation—see if you like it before spending money on training programs or committing a lot of time.

MEDIATION TRAINING PROGRAMS

Numerous training programs offer courses state and nationwide. Many bar associations offer fairly good programs, and CLE programs increasingly provide mediation classes. Non–bar association training programs usually address the issues of marketing and client development—concerns not always covered in bar association or law school ADR training programs. There are now hundreds of trainers and programs all over the country, some good and some not so good, since many people are discovering that they can make more money teaching mediation than doing mediation. Interview a prospective trainer very carefully, before you pay your registration fee, and inquire into her or his credentials.

Plus, ask for referrals to several people who previously took the training to make sure they thought it was worthwhile.

Ombudsman

Ombudsman is a position that has been available in Europe for some years but is just gaining recognition in the United States. An ombudsman is "one skilled in dealing with reported complaints to help achieve equitable settlements" and usually works as an employee within an organization in the media, corrections, universities, hospitals, corporations, government, or another field to help settle internal disputes before the disputes become public, embarrassing, and expensive. Employees can confidentially speak to the ombudsman about difficulties with another employee or supervisor, and the ombudsman will arrange a confidential mediation between the parties. Whistle-blowers also can confidentially report to the ombudsman. Here are several of the organizations that have formed and are growing to support those working as ombudsmen, as well as to encourage the development of the ombudsman concept:

- University and College Ombudsman Association, c/o Ella Wheaton, Director, Campus Ombudsperson, University of California at Berkeley, 2539 Channing Way, Berkeley, CA 94720; (510) 642–7823.
- The Ombudsman Association, c/o Carole Trocchio, 5521 Greenville Avenue, #104–265, Dallas, TX 75206; (214) 553–0043, www.igc.org/toa. Members work in business, government, nursing homes, hospitals, etc.
- Organization of News Ombudsmen, c/o Arthur Nauman, Executive Secretary, 6307 Surfside Way, Sacramento, CA 95831; (916) 391–1314.
- United States Ombudsman Association, c/o Patricia Seleen, Ombudman for Corrections, 1885 University Avenue W., Suite 395, St. Paul, MN 55104; (612) 643–3656.

• Law Enforcement

Positions lawyers have held in law enforcement include:

- CIA agent
- court bailiff
- criminal investigator
- FBI agent
- juvenile justice director
- ombudsman (see page 199 for more information)
- police administration
- police officer
- probation officer
- sheriff
- special agent with the Department of Justice in customs, narcotics, U.S. Marshall service, border patrol, Secret Service

RESOURCES

Check with the appropriate government agency for job listings and descriptions.

100 Best Careers in Crime Fighting: Law Enforcement, Criminal Justice, Private Security, and Cyberspace Crime Detection, Mary Price Lee, Richard Lee, and Carol Dilks, MacMillan, 1998.

The U.S. Department of Justice puts out an annual directory with descriptions of agencies and professional jobs within those agencies. The department can be reached at 950 Pennsylvania Avenue, N.W., Washington, DC 20530–0001 or at its website at www.usdoj.gov/.

Opportunities in Law Enforcement and Criminal Justice, James Stinchcomb, VGM Career Horizons, 1996.

• Legal Publishers, Research Firms, and Legal Writing

Positions lawyers have held within these fields include:

- editor
- managing editor
- research and writing
- reporter
- product development manager
- computer-aided legal research trainer (e.g., Westlaw)
- computer-aided legal research sales or service representative
- continuing legal education program designer
- continuing legal education program panelist
- CD-ROM sales or service representative
- law book sales

The upside to working for a legal publisher is that there isn't a competition for partnership or requirement to produce new business, nor is there a need to bill time or work zillions of hours. The downside is that the salary is often quite low, even when compared to small-law-firm pay. Additionally, there has recently been a massive consolidation in the legal publishing field, with several major players gobbling up all of the small publishers. This has caused the elimination of many research jobs, creating a surfeit of experienced researchers and editors looking for work. However, many publishers have regional offices, which hire local lawyers full-time or they hire freelance writers, even from across the country, who submit their work by fax and modum instead of visiting the office. Check with publishers that produce publications in your area of specialty or interest.

Resources

Many organizations, bar associations, trade associations, and law firms publish newsletters, which they hire staff or freelancers to write.

Law and Legal Information Directory. Gale Research. Lists legal and

law-related publishers. Available at public libraries or call
(800) 877–GALE.

Legal Newsletters in Print, Infosources Publishing, updated annually, $90. Over 2,000 legal, legislative, and regulatory newslet-
ters. You can reach Infosources Publishing at 140 Norma
Road, Teaneck, NJ 07666; (201) 836–7072.

Index to Legal Periodicals, H.W. Wilson Company. Available at
law libraries. Listing of legal publications.

American Bar Association, 750 N. Lake Shore Drive, Chicago,
IL 60611; (800) 285–2221, www.abanet.org. The ABA publishes hundreds of publications, both informative and scholarly.

Aspen Law & Business, 1185 Avenue of the Americas, 37th floor,
New York, NY 10036; (212) 597–0200, www.aspenpub.com.
Publishes the *Directory of Corporate Counsel,* among other
legal publications. Acquired Prentice-Hall Law & Business
publications.

BNA (Bureau of National Affairs, Inc.) has over 200 resources
in print, CD, and on-line, including *U.S. Law Week, Toxics
Law Reporter, Family Law Reporter, Criminal Law Reporter*
1231–25th Street, N.W., Washington, DC 20037; (800)
372–1033, www.bna.com.

CEB (California Continuing Education of the Bar), 2300 Shattuck Avenue, Berkeley, CA 94704; (510) 642–3974,
www.ceb.ucup.edu. Provides both continuing education
courses and numerous practice books, tapes, and videos.

CSC Legal, 2730 Gateway Oaks Drive, Suite 100, Sacramento,
CA 95833; (800) 222–2122. Does information and document
searches and corporate filings.

CCH, Incorporated, 2700 Lake Cook Rd., Riverwoods, IL
60015; (847) 267–7000, www.cch.com, administrative office.
(There are offices in various other states also.) They specialize
in tax and business-related publications, and software.

Lexis-Nexis (computer-aided legal research), owned by Reed
Elsevier, P.O. Box 933, Dayton, OH 45401; (800) 253–5624,
www.lexis-nexis.com. Also has sales and training offices in
various major cities around the country.

Martindale-Hubbell (Reed Elsevier is parent company), 121
Chanlon Road, New Providence, NJ 07974; (908) 464–6800.

Matthew Bender & Co. (Reed Elsevier is parent company), 2

Park Avenue, New York, NY 10016; (800) 252–9257, www.bender.com. West Coast office at 201 Mission Street, 26th floor, San Francisco, CA 94105–1831; (415) 908–3200.

Nolo Press (the self-help legal book publisher, staffed by "reformed lawyers"), 950 Parker Street, Berkeley, CA 94710; (510) 549–1976.

Quo Jure Corporation, 1663 Mission Street, Mezzanine Level, San Francisco, CA 94103; (415) 553–4000 or (800) 843–0660. Provides contract (hourly) legal research and writing to lawyers by lawyers nationwide.

The Rutter Group, 15760 Ventura Blvd., Suite 630, Encino, CA 91436; (818) 990–3260 or (800) 747-3161. Sponsors continuing education courses and publishes practice guides.

Shepard's (Reed Elsevier is parent company), 555 Middle Creek Parkway, Colorado Springs, CO 80921; (719) 488–3000, www.shepards.com./Research and cite-/.

West Group, 610 Opperman Drive, Eagen, MN 55123; (800) 328–9352, www.westgroup.com, was formed when West Publishing and Thomson Legal Publishing merged in 1996. Call West Group in St. Paul to get information about how to contact its subsidiaries, since they continue in a state of flux. A sample of West Group's subsidiaries, whose names have or will all be changed to West Group, include the following (though there are at least several more):

- West Group (formerly Bancroft-Whitney), 50 California Street, 19th floor (P.O. Box 7005), San Francisco, CA 94111; (800) 762–5272.
- Barclay's, 50 California Street, 19th floor, San Francisco, CA 94111-4624; (800) 888–3600.
- West Group (formerly Clark Boardman Callaghan), 375 Hudson Street, New York, NY 10014; (800) 422–2101. Branches in Rochester, NY; (800) 327–2665, and Deerfield, IL; (800) 323–8067.
- RIA Group (Research Institute of America), 90 Fifth Avenue, New York, NY 10011; (212) 645–4800.
- RIA Group (formerly Warren, Gorham & Lamont), 395 Hudson, 4th floor, New York, NY 10014; (212) 367–6300.
- Westlaw, computer-aided legal research subsidiary, almost exclusively hires law graduates as sales and account represen-

tatives. They have offices in Boston, Atlanta, Chicago, Dallas, Washington, DC, Denver, Houston, Kansas City, Los Angeles, Miami, Minneapolis, New Orleans, New York City, Philadelphia, Phoenix, St. Louis, Salt Lake City, San Francisco, and Seattle.

• Writing/Editing

Positions lawyers have held include:

- editor of legal magazine
- editor of legal newspaper
- editor, writer, owner or publisher of a legal newsletter, reporting on developments in specific areas of law
- freelance writer for legal magazine, newspaper, or newsletter
- reporter for legal magazine, legal newspaper, or law section of general interest newspaper
- writer or editor for an on-line legal news service

RESOURCES

Gale Directory of Publications and Broadcast Media, Gale Research, updated annually. Comprehensive nationwide listings of newspapers, journals, magazines, newsletters, radio, TV, and cable. Very expensive, so peruse at public libraries or call (800) 877–GALE.

Newsletters in Print, Gale Research, updated annually. A costly but excellent guide to assorted free and membership publications issued by businesses, government agencies, associations, etc. Available at public libraries or call (800) 877–GALE.

Index to Legal Periodicals, H.W. Wilson Company. Available at law libraries. A listing of legal publications.

Many organizations, bar associations, trade associations, and law firms publish newsletters, which they hire staff or freelancers to write.

Law and Legal Information Directory. Gale Research. Lists legal and law-related publishers. Very costly, so use at a public library or call (800) 877–GALE.

Legal Newsletters in Print, edited by Arlene Eis, Infosources Publishing, updated annually, $90. Over 2,000 legal, legislative, and regulatory newsletters. You can reach Infosources Publishing at 140 Norma Road, Teaneck, NJ 07666; (201) 836–7072.

Magazines: Most state and some local bar associations, as well as independent legal publishers, publish a monthly magazine, such as *ABA Journal, ABA Student Lawyer, American Lawyer, Ohio Lawyer, California Bar Journal.*

Oxbridge Directory of Newsletters, Oxbridge Communications, Inc., updated annually. Current edition is $645. Over 20,000 newsletters, including legal newsletters. Contact Oxbridge Communications, Inc. at 150 Fifth Avenue, Suite 302, New York, NY 10011; (212) 741–0231, www.mediafinder.com.

Newspapers and newsmagazines, both local and national, for example the *Los Angeles Daily Journal, National Law Journal, San Francisco Recorder.* Check the legal newspaper in your area.

• Providing Products and Services to Law Firms and Lawyers

Many lawyers go to work for companies or start companies that provide products and services to other lawyers. Review any edition of the *ABA Journal, American Lawyer, National Law Journal,* or other local or national legal publications; they're available at most law libraries. Look for display advertisements by companies that provide products or services to law firms and lawyers, both for ideas as to "what's hot," if you wish to develop your own product or service, and for leads to expanding companies that might hire you. If you find a company with a product or service that you like, spend some time thinking about what you have to offer that company in terms of skills or knowledge, then develop a proposal setting out what you can do for the company and why you should be hired. Many career changers obtain jobs by creating and developing a niche for themselves that a company hadn't even considered until the career changer's proposal pointed out the problem and how to solve it. Following are some products and services lawyers have provided.

Products include:
- advertisements in legal newspapers and magazines
- computer hardware/software
- computer systems
- corporate kits
- legal forms
- law books and directories
- office machines
- office supplies
- printing
- telephone systems and equipment

Services include:
- accounting/bookkeeping
- case management support (computer or skilled staff support)
- career and life planning for lawyers
- computer-generated accident reconstruction
- corporate communications, such as a newsletter for law firms
- deposition, hearing, other testimonial videotaping
- exhibit preparation and design
- headhunting
- investigator, criminal or civil
- legal research
- legal writing courses
- machine sales and service
- malpractice, office liability, disability, life, and health insurance coverage brokering
- messenger and document filing service
- paralegal services—document organization, indexing, and retrieval
- public relations
- temporary/contract attorney placement
- trial presentation skills courses
- valuations and appraisals

RESOURCES

California Lawyer magazine, *California Law Business* (published every other Monday and inserted within the San Francisco and Los Angeles *Daily Journal*), and the *California Bar Journal* all feature articles with listings of new legal products and services that are often marketed nationally by companies located inside and outside of California. Check your legal paper for similar articles.

Law Practice Management, published by the Law Practice Management Section of the American Bar Association, has articles on developments in services and products used by lawyers. The magazine is sent free to section members. If you are not a member, order from ABA, Attn: Publication Orders, P.O. Box 10892, Chicago, IL 60610–0892; (800) 285–2221, or e-mail abasvcctr@attmail.com.

Legal Marketing Association (LMA), 401 N. Michigan Avenue, Chicago, IL 60611; (312) 245–1592, www.lma.org/. Has newsletter and provides education and information programs for marketers within, and those who market to, law firms. Also has job listings for marketing and related positions in law firms and with legal vendors.

• Consulting to Law Firms and Lawyers

Lawyers have set themselves up as consultants in the following areas of expertise:

- business valuations
- communication with clients and juries
- computer usage: consulting on systems purchase and training clerical and professional staff in making full use of the systems
- employee selection, both professional and staff
- expert witness on lawyer standard of care or legal ethics
- jury selection research and information
- law firm management
- law firm growth, development, mergers and acquisitions
- lawyer training: providing advice by the hour, day-long pro-

grams focusing on a particular skill, and long-term design
and execution of training courses
- legal education
- marketing and promotion, including graphic design
- office design
- pension and profit-sharing plans
- stress/relaxation
- wardrobe and personal appearance, especially for jury
  presentations

RESOURCES

Review any edition of the *ABA Journal, American Lawyer, California Lawyer,* or other local or national legal publications to
observe trends and developments to help you determine
your niche.

Legal Marketing Association (LMA), 401 N. Michigan Avenue,
Chicago, IL 60611; (312) 245–1592 www.lma.org/. Has
newsletter and provides education and information programs
for marketers within, and those who market to, law firms.
Also has job listings for marketing and related positions in law
firms and with legal vendors.

The Professional Advisor, edited by Bernard Hale Zick, Academy
of Professional Consultants and Advisors. Each issue has information and business development ideas of interest to consultants generally, not just those in the legal field. Subscription
is $120 for one year. Order from Bernard Hale Zick at P.O.
Box 6432, Kingwood, TX 73325; (281) 360–4719.

Log on to the web at www.amazon.com, then enter the word
"consulting" in the search box—you will be overwhelmed by
the many good books on this topic.

The Consultant's Calling: Bringing Who You Are to What You Do,
Geoffrey Bellman, Jossey-Bass, 1992. Contact Jossey-Bass at
(415) 433–1767.

Law Practice Management, published by the Law Practice Management Section of the American Bar Association, has articles by
consultants on new or growing consulting possibilities. The
magazine is sent free to section members. If you are not a

member, order from ABA, Attn: Publication Orders, P.O. Box 10892, Chicago, IL 60610–0892; (800) 285–2221, or e-mail abasvcctr@attmail.com.

Consultants & Consulting Organizations Directory, Gale Research. Published annually. Very expensive, so peruse at a public library or call (800) 877–GALE.

Contact Paul Franklin at The National Training Center in Portland, Oregon at (503) 650–3091 for a free catalog of consulting resources.

How to Succeed as an Independent Consultant, Herman Holtz, 3rd edition, John Wiley & Sons, 1993. Covers marketing, client retention, finances, and IRS issues, pricing and more.

Marketing Your Consulting or Professional Services, David Karlson, Crisp Publications, 1988. Tells how to define your market and objectives, build a marketing plan, evaluate competition, identify your uniqueness, and promote yourself.

How to Develop and Promote Successful Seminars and Workshops, Howard Shenson, John Wiley & Sons, 1990. Before he died prematurely, Shenson was the guru of consultants and seminar presenters. This is the definitive guide to creating and marketing programs, either as an end in themselves or as a vehicle to market your other services and products.

Flawless Consulting: A Guide to Getting Your Expertise Used, Peter Block, Pfeiffer & Co, 1981. As current and useful today as when it was first published—highly evaluated by other consultants.

The Contract and Fee-Setting Guide for Consultants and Professionals, Howard Shenson, John Wiley & Sons, 1989. A complete and effective guide to running a consulting business. Continues to be one of the top books on this topic.

CHAPTER EIGHT

─────◆─────

Options Outside of the Law

When one door closes another door opens,
but we so often look so long and so regretfully upon the
closed door that we do not see the ones which open for us.
—ALEXANDER GRAHAM BELL

While there aren't any definitive studies that indicate which jobs outside of law are most satisfying or successful for a lawyer-career changer, there certainly are numerous individual lawyers who have found them. For example, every one of the jobs listed in this chapter has been filled by a lawyer—the jobs aren't made up. Lawyers are generally bright and, by virtue of their intense but broad legal education and experience, are well trained to handle a variety of tasks and situations. This diversity of experience and skills allows them to realistically pursue many alternative career objectives.

However, for many positions outside of law, specific—as opposed to general—legal training and experience are neither necessary nor even assets. In fact, you might have to overcome objections to your being a lawyer with exposure only to "legal-think." Based on sterotypes of your presumed limited perspective, it may be asserted that you don't know anything about (fill in the blank) *the business of business,* or *education,* or *real estate sales,* and on and on. The stereotype is that as a lawyer you have a narrow perspective, looking only at the legal issues of a topic, or that you are "a deal-breaker rather than a deal-maker." For example, when I worked as an in-house lawyer, I constantly heard this refrain from the CEO: "Don't show me why I *can't* do something, show me how I *can* do it"—even when there was no legal way to proceed.

Of course, as discussed in chapter 5, if you assess your skills in a way that will allow you to clearly explain them to a potential employer, you will have much less problem overcoming the lawyer stereotypes, for you will then be able to describe the experience you bring to a job, rather than naming the (perhaps) irrelevant and often incomprehensible legal tasks you have performed.

Be sure to remind a potential employer that you bring additional and useful skills to the workplace—not only the ones you identified through your self-assessment but also those a trained attorney develops. You can be a "two-for-the-price-of-one" employee, who has the skills a particular job requires as well as the ability to understand legal terminology, analyze information, and use reason to find solutions. You also have learned and developed persuasion and counseling techniques that are useful in many marketplaces.

When contemplating the big step of changing careers completely, your main considerations should be your ability, interest, and desire to pursue and undertake the work required, in a field which you value and enjoy. Your new work may build on your previous experience. It may pay you as much or more than you now earn. However, sometimes it means stepping back for a bit in earnings, prestige, and control while you take the time to develop expertise in a new area. You might even have to start at the bottom. One of my clients decided he wanted to turn his gardening avocation into a career. He first thought that all he had to do was to "hang out his garden shears," until he learned that in order to get the best jobs he would have to apprentice for a few years to more fully learn the business and make good connections. So he supported himself with some contract legal work while he learned his trade, working as a gardener for a few years, and today owns a gardening service employing five people. It may be a lot of work to start from basics, but how exciting to watch yourself climb back up, and enjoy the process! As a speaker at a Lawyers in Transition[SM] program said, when discussing her career change into the nonprofit sector, "I question my decision to leave law occasionally when I look at my paycheck, but never when I look at my life."

• Famous Career Changers

Following is a list of career changers, all whom were trained as lawyers and then went on to acquire fame in some other field. For many of them, their legal background did not directly benefit their later work. However, it is likely that their legal training did contribute to some of the skills, such as discipline and perseverence, that they utilized to achieve their goals.

Franz Kafka (*writer*)
Rene Descartes (*philosopher/ mathematician*)
Francis Scott Key (*composer*)
Scott Turow (*author*)
Terry Louise Fisher (*co-creater of LA Law*)
Paul Robeson (*actor/singer/ civil rights activist*)
Geraldo Rivera (*broadcast journalist*)
Richard Thalheimer (*president/The Sharper Image*)
Noah Webster (*lexicographer*)
John Wesley Hardin (*outlaw/ murderer*)
Mahatma Gandhi (*Indian political/spiritual leader*)

Tony LaRussa (*former Oakland A's manager*)
Henry Fielding (*author*)
Vladimir Ilyich Lenin (*Communist leader*)
Mortimer Zuckerman (*owner of U.S. News & World Report*)
Erle Stanley Gardner (*creator of Perry Mason*)
Sir Thomas More (*English statesman/saint*)
Pat Haden (*former LA Rams quarterback*)
Charlie Rose (*broadcast journalist*)
Rossano Brazzi (*actor*)
Washington Irving (*author*)

Howard Cosell (*sportscaster*)
Hoagy Carmichael (*songwriter*)
Edgar Lee Masters (*poet/novelist*)
Wassily Kandinsky (*painter*)
Peter Tchaikovsky (*composer*)
Fred Graham (*CBS TV reporter*)
Fidel Castro (*politician*)

Otto Preminger (*film director*)
Madalyn Murray O'Hair (*reformer*)
Ralph Nader (*consumer advocate*)
Jules Verne (*author*)
Archibald MacLeish (*poet*)
Studs Terkel (*oral historian*)

• Top Fields and Jobs for the Future

According to the U.S. Bureau of Labor Statistics, some of the fields that are estimated to grow by more than 20 percent over the next ten years are:

- professional fields, such as accounting
- computer industry, both hardware and software, and anything to do with this industry—writing and design, sales, marketing, technical support, manufacturing, service
- geriatric, motivation, and stress counseling and advice
- teaching, especially in adult education
- marketing and sales
- business, health, retail, educational, and social services
- expert-systems development, such as in technical support and personnel systems

Some of the specific jobs that are projected to show greatly increased growth in the next ten years are:
- nursery and greenhouse managers
- detectives
- corrections officers
- speech language pathologists and audiologists
- special education teachers
- physical scientists (excluding chemists, geologists, geophysicists, oceanographers, and meteorologists)
- paralegals
- computer-related jobs such as systems analysts, computer en-

gineers, network engineers, training, consulting, technical support, and computer-related graphic arts, with positions such as page designer and webmaster

RESOURCES

Lawyers in Transition^{SM} *Newsletter,* published quarterly by Lawyers in Transition^{SM}, P.O. Box 31026, San Francisco, CA 94131; (415) 285–5143. Subscription is $20 a year. Has articles about alternative options in and out of law, profiles of career changers, career counseling advice, and book reviews.

Beyond L.A. Law: Break the Traditional "Lawyer" Mold, edited by Janet Smith, Harcourt Brace, 1997. Profiles of 47 lawyers who are working in diverse jobs in and out of law. Very interesting and motivational.

The Road Not Taken, Kathleen Grant and Wendy Werner, National Association for Law Placement (1666 Connecticut Avenue, N.W., Suite 325, Washington, DC 20009; (202) 667–1666, www.nalp.org/) 1991, $20. Reference and workbook on exploring alternative careers, with a section directed to career counselors and the balance to job seekers.

Running from the Law: Why Good Lawyers Are Getting Out of the Legal Profession, Deborah L. Arron, Ten Speed Press, 1991. Out of print but probably available at law school career services offices. Contains profiles of lawyers who have changed careers.

Life After Law: Second Careers for Lawyers, Mary Ann Altman, The Wayne Smith Co., 1992. Call (202) 484–5620 to order.

Careers for Sports Nuts & Other Athletic Types, William Heitzman, VGM Career Horizons, 1997.

Outdoor Careers: Exploring Occupations in Outdoor Fields, Ellen Shenk, Stackpole Books, 1992. Available from bookstores or call Stackpole at (800) 732–3669.

Experience, a magazine for "older lawyers" put out by the Senior Lawyers Division of the American Bar Association, has a partial focus on what avenues other than law a mature practitioner can pursue, using legal skills as a foundation. Contact the Senior Lawyers Division at (312) 988-5583, or order the magazine from ABA, Attn: Publication Orders, P.O. Box 10892, Chicago, IL 60610–0892; (800) 285–2221, or e-mail abasvcctr@attmail.com.

Environmental Career Guide, Nicholas Basta, John Wiley & Sons, 1991.

The New Complete Guide to Environmental Careers: The Environmental Careers Organization, John Cook, Kevin Doyle, and Bill Sharp, 2nd edition, Island Press, 1993.

Green at Work: Finding a Business Career that Works for the Environment. Susan Cohen, Island Press, 1995. Focuses on business careers that work for the environment, including management, marketing, and development. Includes a corporate directory.

The Student Conservation Association isn't just for students. It helps people gain experience to begin or advance their conservation careers. Contact them at SCA, P.O. Box 550, Charlestown, NH 03603; (603) 543–1700, www.sca-inc.org. The SCA has regional offices in Seattle, Denver, Oakland, and Newark.

Flying High in Travel: A Complete Guide to Careers in the Travel Industry, Karen Rubin, John Wiley & Sons, 1992.

Jobs in Paradise: The Definitive Guide to Exotic Jobs Everywhere, Jeffrey Maltzman, Harper & Perennial, 1993. Written by a lawyer, with about 200,000 jobs worldwide.

100 Jobs in Social Change, Harley Jebens, MacMillan, 1997.

National Job Bank, Bob Adams Publications. Information on job categories and backgrounds sought by 10,000 U.S. companies. Bob Adams, Inc. also publishes a paperback Jobs Bank Series for various regions of the country (i.e., *Boston Job Bank*), which have employer profiles, names of relevant associations, and listings of industry publications.

"The National Ad Search," (800) 992–2832. Comprised of 96 plus pages of employer advertising for positions from entry to executive level in 56 fields. Also check out their website at www.nationaladsearch.com.

International Jobs, Eric Kocher, 5th edition, Addison-Wesley, 1998. Careers in law, nonprofits, business, publishing, government, and schools—where they are, how to get them.

"International Employment Hotline," edited by Will Cantrell,

$39 per year for 12 issues of job listings. Available through the New Careers Center at (800) 634–9024.

America's Top 300 Jobs: A Complete Career Handbook, J. Michael Farr, 6th edition, Jist Works, 1998.

"Affirmative Action Register," 8356 Olive Blvd., St. Louis, MO 63132; (800) 537–0655. Job listings by employers with equal employment policies for handicapped, female, or minority employees. Fee is $15/year for 12 issues, $8 for 6 issues.

Opportunities in Library and Information Science Careers, Kathleen De La Pena McCook and Margaret Myers, VGM Career Horizons, 1996.

McFadden American Financial Directory, published by Thomson Financial Publishing, $435. Lists names and phone numbers of top decision makers in the financial industry, including banks, savings institutions, credit unions, holding companies, and financial services firms nationwide. Available in public libraries or order at (800) 321–3373.

Job Hunter's Sourcebook, 3rd edition, Gale Research, 1996. Describes major resources in 155 occupations, including directories and associations.

"JobSmart" is an extensive web site that catalogs useful job hunting sites. Its Salary Information section alone registers 50,000 hits a day. Access it at www.jobsmart.org.

Career Opportunities in Travel and Tourism, John K. Hawks, Facts on File, 1995.

Career Success with Pets, Kim Barber, Howell Book House, 1996.

The Off-the-Beaten-Path Job Book, Sandra Gurvis, Citadel Press, 1995. Information on unusual and enjoyable work.

American Society of Appraisers, P.O. Box 17265, Washington, DC 20041; (800) ASA–VALU, www.appraisers.org. A nonprofit organization that teaches, tests, and certifies appraisers in all disciplines, including business, real estate, probate, collectables, etc.

"The Inc. 500," provided by Inc. Magazine, lists the 500 fastest-growing companies in the United States based on percentage of growth of revenue over a 5-year period. The list can be browsed by name, state, or industry and has links to each company's home page when available. Log on at www.inc.com/500/.

America's Top Office, Management, and Sales Jobs, J. Michael Farr, 4th edition, Jist Works, 1998.

How to Be an Importer and Pay for Your World Travel, Mary Green and Stanley Gillmar, Ten Speed Press, 1993.

Career Web contains the *Wall Street Journal's National Employment Weekly* job listings at www.cweb.com.

America's Job Bank, an on-line listing of job openings run by the Department of Labor and 1,800 state employment services offices can be accessed at www.ajb.dni.us.

Survival Jobs: 154 Ways to Make Money While Pursuing Your Dreams, Deborah Jacobson, Bantam, 1998. Jobs, on and off the beaten path, to keep food on your table while pursuing less lucrative dreams.

Research Centers' Directory, published by Gale Research. Lists think tanks that are funded by government money. *Research Services Directory: A One–Step Guide to Commercial Research Activity,* also from Gale Research, lists for-profit, private think tanks. If you go to www.amazon.com on the net, then enter the words "research centers," you will find numerous books listed for various research specialties. Many directories, journals, and newsletters are published by specific industries or professional organizations. They, as well as business magazines, can add to your knowledge of occupations and potential employers. They can usually be found in the reference or business section at the main public library in each larger city, and they are useful for general research about various fields, to find information about specific companies or industries and, sometimes, even to find specific contact names. See Part III—especially chapter 9—of this book for effective ways to use these publications. Note that numerous helpful directories are published by Gale Research, but if you want to use them, you'll probably prefer going to the public library since most Gale directories cost in the $300-$500 range.

Business Information Sources, edited by L. M. Daniels, University of California Press. A guide to finding facts about business and industries through published sources. It includes bibliographies of works on specific companies, organizations, and individuals, forcign and domestic economic trends and statistics, and business management.

County Manufacturers Guide. A comprehensive listing of county manufacturers by product and industrial involvement. Includes company address, size, sales market, gross annual sales, founding date, and key names.

Directory of (your state name) Manufacturers. An extensive list of firms by company title, product(s) manufactured, and location. Includes company address, size, sales market, and key names.

Human Services Inventory. Comprehensive listing of community service organizations. Arranged in functional categories with miscellaneous information as to services provided.

Encyclopedia of Business Information Sources, Gale Research. A comprehensive guide to business information resources, such as books, websites, and directories.

International Trade Directory of Contacts, Sources, Services, Hilary House Publishing. Lists firms and their services or products as well as agencies engaged in exporting and importing. Cross-referenced system, alphabetically, by product, or by foreign country. Includes address, phone number, and key names.

The Career Guide 1997: Dun's Employment Opportunities Directory, Dun & Bradstreet, Inc. Lists U.S. companies with over 1,000 employees and company information, hiring practices, and contacts.

Directory of American Firms Operating in Foreign Countries, Uniworld Business Publications. Lists U.S. corporations and the foreign firms they control. Includes CEOs, foreign officers, products or services, countries of operation, addresses of subsidiaries, branches, and home offices.

Directory of Corporate Affiliations, National Register Publishing Co. Section one lists parent companies, giving their domestic and foreign divisions, subsidiaries, affiliates, top management, telephone number, address, state of incorporation, number of employees, line of business, and approximate dollar amount of sales. Section two lists the corporate "children" with their addresses, approximate sales, number of employees, and chief operating officers.

Directories in Print, Gale Research. Published annually. Describes approximately 10,000 business and industrial directories, professional and scientific rosters, biographical dictionaries, directory databases, directory issues and periodicals, and other lists and guides. Indexed by title and subject.

Oxbridge Directory of Newsletters, updated annually. Current edition is $645. Oxbridge Communications, Inc., 150 Fifth Avenue, Suite 302, New York, NY 10011; (212) 741–0231, www.mediafinder.com. Lists over 20,000 newsletters.

World Business Directory, 1998, published jointly by World Trade Centers Association and Gale Research.

F & S Index of Corporations and Industries, Predicasts, Inc. Weekly, with cumulatives. Guide to articles about U.S. companies in more than 750 publications. Separate indexes list the company by name and by Standard Industry Classification. Information given includes product names, brief abstract of the article, publication name and address, date of publication, and page number.

F & S Index International and *F & S Index Europe.* Companion guides to above, with similar information about foreign companies. Indexed by company name, SIC code, and country.

Guide to American Directories, B. Klein Publications, 1998. Published every two to three years. Contains details about more than 6,000 directories, including some foreign publications. Industrial, professional, and mercantile directories are listed.

National Directory of Women-Owned Business Firms and *National Directory of Minority-Owned Business Firms,* Business Research Services, 4201 Connecticut Avenue, N.W., Suite 610, Washington, DC 20008; (202) 364–6473.

Dun & Bradstreet Million Dollar Directory, Dun & Bradstreet, Inc. Lists firms with net worth over $1 million. Arranged alphabetically and by location. Entries include address, phone number, size, sales, products, key names.

Thomas Register of American Manufacturers, Thomas Publishing Co. Annual. First seven volumes list manufacturers alphabetically by city and state. Remainder consist of company catalogs. Includes estimates of total tangible assets, subsidiaries, affiliates, and cable address.

Moody's Industrial Manual, Moody's Investor Services, Inc. Annual. Covers companies trading on New York, American, and regional stock exchanges. Gives capital structure, stock and bond descriptions, Moody's rating, interest or dividends, brief history of the company, management, product or service, principal plants or properties, comparative financial information over last seven years, financial and operating data, assets and liabilities.

Wall Street Journal Index, Dow Jones Books. Monthly with annual cumulatives. Subject index to *WSJ* articles. Divided into corporate news and general news sections. Gives brief abstract of article and date, page and column on which it appeared.

Encyclopedia of Associations, Gale Research. Published annually. Three volumes, arranged by topic, naming national associations, including name and address, number of members, number of employees, CEO, description of organization's activities, publications, dates of regular conventions and meetings, then lists the same associations organized geographically, with an index of CEOs.

Encyclopedia of Associations: International Organizations, Gale Research, updated annually. Lists of international associations, with relevant membership information.

Brands and Their Companies, Gale Research. Shows which manufacturer makes which trade name product. Gives trade name, describes product, names manufacturer or importer or distributor. Focuses on consumer products.

U.S. Industrial Directory, United States Industrial. Annual. Lists 40,000 industrial suppliers, 20,000 products classifications, and 45,000 trade names. Mentions size of staff, brochures, or catalogs.

Dun & Bradstreet Reference Book, Dun & Bradstreet, Inc. Complete geographical listings of companies, organized by state, giving name of town or city, county and population, names of officers, approximate holdings of banks in town, business name and SIC code, company's financial rating.

Dun's Regional Business Directory, Dun & Bradstreet, Inc. Similar to the *Reference Book* directly above, but only for each region.

Standard & Poor's Register of Corporations, Directors and Executives, Standard & Poor's. Annual. Lists 37,000 corporations, giving names, addresses and telephone numbers, titles, and functions of about 39,000 officers, accounting firm, primary banks, law firm, SIC codes, annual sales, number of employees, and background on corporate executives.

Standard & Poor's Corporation Descriptions, Standard & Poor's. Updated every other week. Lists more than 6,300 largest companies, giving background, plant locations, subsidiaries, securities, annual earnings and expenditures, number of employees, name of auditor.

Standard & Poor's Industry Surveys, Standard & Poor's. Examines prospects for a particular industry. Analysis of trends and problems presented in historical perspective. Major segments of industry are highlighted. Comparative analysis of companies.

Standard Directory of Advertisers, National Register Publishing Co. There are two annual versions, one classified by product, the other by geography. Lists companies doing national or regional advertising, their products and services. Identifies roughly 80,000 executives, with their titles, plus agencies handling advertising, media used, and amounts spent.

Dictionary of Occupational Titles, U.S. Department of Labor. Describes more than 12,000 jobs, with information about the industries in which they are found.

The following are just a sampling of helpful websites—they post job openings, career information, and links to other sites. There are many more, but these should keep you busy for a while.

- America's Career Infonet (www.acinet.org) has links to state information.
- America's Job Bank (www.ajb.dni.us/) is run by the Department of Labor and 1,800 state employment services offices.
- Hoover's Online (www.hoovers.com) is a guide to information about companies, officers, products, etc.
- Yahoo has lists of professional organizations (www.yahoo.com/Economy/organizations/Professional) and general career and job information, with links to other sites (www.yahoo.com/Business/Employment/Jobs/).
- The Riley Guide (www.jobtrak.com/jobguide/) is an extensive and very useful gateway site, with excellent links to other sites.
- William and Mary's guide to job resources by region or geographic location (www.wm.edu/csrv/career/stualum/jregion.html) has links to many other job services.
- CareerMosaic (www.careermosaic.com) is a voluminous,

general purpose career site, including job listings and lists
of associations.

- Online Career Center (www.occ.com) is a big, general job site
sponsored by a nonprofit association of large corporations.
- E-Span (www.espan.com/) is a general job site with an
e-mail feature; it will forward jobs to you that match your
profile.
- The Monster Board (www.monster.com/) is just that—
overwhelming amounts of career information.
- Careerpath (www.careerpath.com) is a free compilation of
job ads in the *Boston Globe, N.Y. Times, L.A. Times, Chicago
Tribune, San Jose Mercury News,* and the *Washington Post.*
- Richard Bolles of *What Color is Your Parachute?* fame lists his
favorite job search links, courtesy of the *Washington Post*, at
(www.washingtonpost.com/parachute).

• Communications

Although lawyers pursue many avenues of endeavor, a great
number seem to transfer their writing, investigative, problem
solving, and organizational skills into the various communications
fields, such as creative writing, journalism, technical writing,
public relations, or publishing. Many lawyers are good with
words, whether written or spoken, and desire to continue to
make their living working with language and how it influences
and impacts upon people.

Positions which lawyers have held in communications include:

- agent for athletes or actors/actresses
- author of children's books
- author of book on exotic jobs
- corporate communications company president
- director of contracting for corporation
- freelance magazine article writer
- freelance newspaper reporter or "stringer"
- freelance writer of nonfiction articles and corporate pieces
- humor columnist/consultant on "lightening up" speeches
- marketing manager for software company

- newspaper or magazine reporter
- newspaper columnist
- editor at Nolo Press, publisher of legal self-help books
- producer of the *People's Court* and other TV programs
- public relations/account exec managing client's P.R. projects
- novelist
- publisher or editor of environmental issues newsletter
- publisher or editor of specialty journals
- publisher of magazines
- publisher of newspapers
- screenplay writer
- scriptwriter for *L.A. Law*
- radio/TV news reporter
- technical writer
- video producer for commercial advertising and training pieces
- writer or editor for an on–line magazine

RESOURCES

International Association of Business Communicators (IABC), One Hallidie Plaza, Suite 600, San Francisco, CA 94102; (415) 433–3400 or (800) 776–4222, www.iabc.com. International job listings in communications field, with emphasis on public relations, writing, and editing. Publishes magazines, books, and a bibliography of communications-related books. Chapters located all over the country and world—call San Francisco headquarters for the phone number of your local chapter.

Newspaper's Career Directory: A Practical, One-Stop Guide to Getting a Job in Newspaper Publishing, 4th edition, Gale Research, 1993.

Gale Directory of Publications and Broadcast Media, Gale Research. Nationwide listings of newspapers, journals, magazines, newsletters, radio, TV, and cable. Available at public libraries or call (800) 877–GALE.

Author's Guild, 330 W. 42nd Street, 29th floor, New York, NY 10036; (212) 563–5904, www.authorsguild.org. Members are either published writers or those with a contract already signed; however, attorneys can be associate members, since the Guild deals with a lot of the legal issues surrounding writing and publishing.

Career Opportunities for Writers, Rosemary Guiley, 3rd edition, Facts on File, 1995.

Career Opportunities in Advertising and Public Relations, Shelly Field, Facts on File Publications, revised, 1997.

How to Start and Run a Writing and Editing Business, Herman Holtz, John Wiley & Sons, 1992.

The Tech Writing Game: A Comprehensive Guide for Aspiring Technical Writers, Janet Van Wicklen, Facts on File, 1992.

The Career Novelist: A Literary Agent Offers Strategies for Success, Donald Maass, Heinemann, 1996.

Writer's Market, Writers Digest Books, published annually. The "writer's bible," it lists all print media for publishing your articles, with contacts, requirements, and rates paid. Current edition is $27.99. Available in most public libraries and bookstores.

Careers for Bookworms & Other Literary Types, Marjorie Eberts and Margaret Gisler, 2nd edition, VGM Career Horizons, 1995.

1998 Guide to Literary Agents: 500 Agents Who Sell What You Write, Writer's Digest Books, 1998.

Starting & Running a Successful Newsletter or Magazine, Cheryl Woodward, Nolo Press, 1997. Written by the founder of *PC Magazine, PC World, Macworld,* and *Publish.*

Oxbridge Directory of Newsletters, updated annually. Current edition is $645.

Oxbridge Communications, Inc., 150 Fifth Avenue, Suite 302, New York, NY 10011; (212) 741–0231. Lists over 20,000 newsletters.

National Writers Union, 113 University Place, 6th floor, New York, NY 10003; (212) 254–0279. E-mail: nwu@nwu.org. Advocates for freelance writers, with legal counsel, programs, and newsletter. Sponsors group health insurance.

International Literary Marketplace, R.R. Bowker. Updated annually. Publishing industry information and resources.

Broadcasting & Cable Yearbook, R.R. Bowker. Updated annually. Resources and lists of companies.

Public Relations Society of America, 33 Irving Place, 3rd floor, New York, NY 10003; (212) 995–2230, www.prsa.org. Publishes a monthly newspaper and a quarterly magazine. Has regional chapters.

Infocom Group, 5900 Hollis Street, Suite R-2, Emeryville, CA 94608; (800) 959–1059, www.infocomgroup.com. Sponsors conferences on how to better use media contacts in various areas, such as business media or lifestyle media. Publishes bimonthly listings of public relations jobs and news in a Western and Eastern edition, a lifestyle edition entitled *Lifestyle Media-Relations Reporter*, listing contacts in the lifestyle media (health care, fitness, travel, food, culture, entertaining) and how to successfully pitch proposals to them ($349 for a year), and a business version of the lifestyle edition, entitled *The Bulldog Reporter*, which covers PR and the news media for communications professionals ($349 for a year). Publishes *PR Pitch Book*, a directory of print, broadcast, and TV media nationwide ($425).

PR Business Wire, 44 Montgomery Street, 39th floor, San Francisco, CA 94104; (415) 986–4423. Free monthly nationwide public relations job listings—send four stamped, self-addressed envelopes and one resume, and they'll send you the listings.

This Business of Television, Howard Blumental and Oliver Goodenough, 2nd edition, Watson-Guptill Publications, 1998. A practical guide to the TV/video industries for producers, directors, writers, performers, agents, and executives.

Television and Cable Factbook, updated annually, Warren Publishing, Inc., 2115 Ward Court, N.W., Washington, DC 20037; (202) 872–9200. Describes commercial and non-commercial TV and cable networks and stations.

Job Listings by Capital Cities/ABC. Weekly listing of national media positions in public corporations, broadcasting, and networks. Available at many American Broadcasting Corporation offices.

Creative Screenwriters Group is a national organization that will direct you to a current local group or help you set up your own. Send them your name, address, and telephone number, along with a description of your writing interests and a self-addressed, stamped envelope to 518 Ninth Street, N.E., Suite 308, Washington, DC 20002.

Everyone's Guide to Successful Publications, Elizabeth Adler,

Peachpit Press. Out of print, but worth looking for in a used bookstore. Nuts-and-bolts information about planning, writing, and designing desktop publishing, then printing and distributing publications, from newsletters to manuals.

Society for Technical Communications, 901 N. Stuart Street, Suite 904, Arlington, VA 22203; (703) 522–4114. Members are writers and editors working in the technical communications field. The society publishes a magazine and has regional chapters.

Magazines about publishing include: *Publisher's Weekly* and *Small Press*.

How to Develop and Promote Successful Seminars and Workshops, Howard Shenson, John Wiley & Sons, 1990. This is the definitive guide to creating and marketing programs, by the guru of seminar presenters.

National Speaker's Association, 1500 S. Priest Drive, Tempe, AZ 85281; (602) 968–2552. Local chapters across the country. Membership consists of aspiring and professional speakers, who make either a part or their entire living giving talks at seminars, conventions, or lunch meetings, and consulting with companies on their field of expertise.

Speak & Grow Rich, Dottie Walters and Lily Walters. Prentice Hall, revised, 1997. A nuts-and-bolts book on how to develop a business as a professional speaker. Dottie Walters also runs Walters International Speaker's Bureau (P.O. Box 1120, Glendora, CA 91740; (626) 335–8069), acting as agent for experienced professional speakers. They also publish *Sharing Ideas* newsmagazine.

• Business

Positions which lawyers have held in business include:

- agent for athletes/entertainers
- actuary
- adjuster in claims department of insurance company
- bank vice president
- business appraiser
- baseball team manager

- CEO of a movie studio
- commercial pilot
- computer programmer
- computer software designer
- corporate marketing
- director of public relations
- errors and ommissions examiner
- equal opportunity officer
- event management
- facilities manager
- field education director
- financial plans sales director
- financial products sales
- headhunter for engineers (has a J.D./engineer background)
- human resources manager
- independent insurance adjuster
- institutional sales
- insurance broker
- insurance brokerage owner
- international trade analyst
- investment banking
- leasing contract administrator for financial institution
- manager of a printing company
- managing director of multinational company
- mergers and acquisitions specialist
- MIS director (in charge of computer systems)
- newswriter and producer for network television affiliate
- pension and profit sharing analyst
- private merchant banker
- professional athlete
- public affairs producer for television station
- regulation analyst at bank
- stockbroker
- telecommunications director
- venture capitalist
- VP, corporate administration, development, or research
- VP, business affairs, network television
- VP, job-placement firm

I have been asked many times if obtaining an M.B.A. degree would be helpful in securing a job in business. As with so many questions, my answer is, It depends . . . It depends on whether you want to get into top management, whether you have any significant business experience, whether you are looking for a job with a large, established company or a small business or an entrepreneurial start-up. I would recommend the degree if you want to enter the top management echelon, if you don't have much prior business involvement (either through your legal clients or on your own), or if you want to work for a large company. The degree will give you management tools and theories, and it will help you focus on a functional area of interest, such as finance, marketing, or operations. However, most small companies and start-ups are less impressed with the M.B.A. credential and more impressed with your general skills and experience and how those apply to the business at hand. But if you do go for an advanced degree of any sort, try to attend the best program you can afford and have access to, since employers often rate your training by where you obtained it. The unfortunate reality is that an M.B.A. from an unknown school is not worth very much in the world of big business.

RESOURCES

Encyclopedia of Associations, Gale Research. Look up associations in your areas of interest, such as American Management Association, National Association of Life Underwriters, etc.

National Association of Professional Insurance Agents, 400 N. Washington Street, Alexandria, VA 22314; (703) 836–9340, www.pianet.com. Chapters in most states.

County Manufacturers Guide. A comprehensive listing of county manufacturers by product and industrial involvement. Includes company address, size, sales market, gross annual sales, founding date, and key names.

Directory of (your state's name) Manufacturers. An extensive list of firms by company title, product(s) manufactured, and location. Includes company address, size, sales market, key names.

Financial Yellow Book: Who's Who at Leading U.S. Financial Institutions, Monitor Publishing.

American Banker, (800) 221–1809. A daily trade publication with classified ads. Listings are not extensive, but they are usually at the executive level, in public relations, law, marketing, and finance, within the banking field.

International Trade Council, 3114 Circle Hill Road, Alexandria, VA 22305; (703) 548–1234, www.itctrade.com. An association of businesses involved in import and export.

National Foreign Trade Council, 1270 Avenue of the Americas, Suite 206, New York, NY 10020; (212) 399–7128. Members are importers, exporters, manufacturers, and banks.

Opportunities in Human Resource Management Careers, William Traynor and J. Steven McKenzie, VGM Career Horizons, 1994.

American Society of Appraisers, P.O. Box 17265, Washington, DC 20041; (800) ASA–VALU, www.appraisers.org. A nonprofit organization that teaches, tests, and certifies appraisers in all disciplines, including business. Contact them for a free copy of "Information on the Appraisal Profession."

A website for people looking for jobs in human resources and training and development—check it out at www.tcm.com/hr–careers/career.

American Marketing Association, 250 S. Wacker Drive, Suite 200, Chicago, IL 60606; (312) 648–0536, www.ama.org.

National Directory of Women-Owned Business Firms and *National Directory of Minority-Owned Business Firms,* Business Research Services, 4201 Connecticut Avenue, N.W., Suite 610, Washington, DC 20008; (202) 364–6473.

Sales and Marketing Executives International, 5500 Interstate N. Parkway, Suite 545, Atlanta, GA 30328; (770) 661-8500, www.smei.org.

High Tech Careers magazine. Job listings and articles on job hunting strategy and business trends in the high tech field in an Arizona or an Eastern or Western edition. (408) 970–8800.

Federation of International Trade Associations, 1851 Alexander Bell Drive, Suite 400, Reston, VA 20191; (703) 620–1588, www.fita.org. The umbrella organization for 300 plus U.S. trade associations.

Association of Environmental Professionals, c/o Stefan/George Associates, 1333–36th Street, Sacramento, CA 95816; (916) 737–2371. A California statewide organization with local chapters. Check for similar organizations in your state.

National Association of Women Business Owners, 1100 Wayne Avenue, Suite 8, Silver Springs, MD 20910; (301) 608-2590, www.nawbo.org. Regional chapters have education and networking meetings.

Your local Chamber of Commerce is an excellent networking venue—attend its meetings and become active on its committees in order to meet contacts and hear about potential job openings. Offer to arrange or chair a program as a way to get your name known.

The Insider's Guide to the Top 20 Careers in Business and Management, edited by Tom Fischgrund, McGraw-Hill, 1993.

International Trade Directory of Contacts, Sources, Services, Hilary House Publishing. Lists firms and their services or products, as well as agencies engaged in exporting and importing. Cross-referenced system, alphabetically, by product, or by foreign country. Includes address, phone number, and key names.

American Society of CLU & ChFC (270 S. Bryn Mawr Avenue, Bryn Mawr, PA 19010; (888) 243–2258, www.asclu.org) is a national organization of insurance and financial service professionals.

Dun & Bradstreet Million Dollar Directory, Dun & Bradstreet, Inc. Lists firms with net worth over $1 million. Arranged alphabetically and by location. Entries include address, phone number, size, sales, products, key names.

Dun & Bradstreet Reference Book, Dun & Bradstreet, Inc. Complete geographical listing of companies, organized by state, giving name of town or city, county and population, names of officers, approximate holdings of banks in town, business name and SIC code, company's financial rating.

Dun's Regional Business Directory, Dun & Bradstreet, Inc. Similar to the *Reference Book* directly above, but only for each region.

Peterson's Hidden Job Market: 2,000 High Growth Companies That Are Hiring, updated annually. Peterson's Guides; (800) 338–3282 or at a bookstore.

Poor's Directory of Corporations and *Moody's Industrial Manual.* List organizations that have securities sold to the public. Provide comprehensive descriptions of the businesses, their operations, subsidiaries, financial situation, and officers.

Moody's Bank and Financial Manual, Moody's Investors Service. Annual. Volume 1 covers banks, trust companies, savings & loans, and federal credit agencies. Volume 2 covers insurance companies, finance companies, real estate and investment companies. Includes summaries of stock and debt issue, outstanding amounts, historical prices, earnings and dividends, type of business done, cost of money borrowed or lent, seven-year statistics such as net income, balance sheet, breakdown of domestic vs. foreign earnings, Moody's ratings, management names and titles.

Guide to American Directories, B. Klein Publications, 1998. Published every two to three years. Contains details about more than 6,000 directories, including some foreign publications. Industrial, professional, and mercantile directories are listed.

Career Guide: Dun's Employment Opportunities Directory. Lists U.S. companies with over 1,000 employees and company information, hiring practices, and contacts.

The Wall Street Journal (www.wsj.com). National business information, special reports, and job listings. Its publication, *National Business Employment Weekly* (www.nbew.com), has ads for jobs nationwide. Call (800) JOB–HUNT.

Look through *Inc., Business Week,* and other magazines dealing with business issues.

Read the business publications published in the community you want to work in—look for specific companies, ideas for jobs, business trends, names of major players in the community. Write an article for publication as a way to get your name known.

• Real Estate

Positions which lawyers have held in real estate include:

- commercial real estate sales
- condominium development

- facilities, management and procurement
- head of real estate subsidiary of major corporation
- independent commercial real estate developer
- independent residential real estate developer
- property management
- real estate appraisal
- real estate syndication strategist/planner
- residential real estate agent
- residential real estate broker
- residential remodel contractor
- shopping center developer
- Victorian residence restoration

RESOURCES

Check with local community colleges for courses in real estate sales, renovation, and management. Remember, in some states, if you are a licensed attorney, you can immediately take the broker's exam without having to either serve an apprenticeship as an agent or take the otherwise required preliminary course work.

"Dealing for Dollars," *California Lawyer,* August 1990, page 41. An article about the many "dirt" lawyers who themselves become real estate developers.

American Society of Appraisers, P.O. Box 17265, Washington, DC 20041; (800) ASA–VALU, www.appraisers.org. A nonprofit organization that teaches, tests, and certifies appraisers in all disciplines, including real estate. Contact them for a free copy of "Information on the Appraisal Profession."

National Association of Realtors, 430 North Michigan Avenue, Chicago, IL 60611; (312) 329–8200, www.realtors.com.

• Entrepreneurial

Many lawyers decide they want to be their own boss, with success as well as failure attributable directly to their own efforts.

Here is just a sample of numerous entrepreneurial endeavors that former attorneys have started and successfully operated.

RETAIL

- maps to on-location production sites in Hollywood
- nightclub owner
- restaurant owner/operator
- cookie shop owner
- erotic playtoys shop owner and producer of workshops on erotica
- antique dealer
- import-export business

MANUFACTURING

- sofabed manufacturer and sales
- ceramic Christmas tree ornaments manufacturer
- jewelry designer and manufacturer
- winemaker
- doormat manufacturer

WHOLESALING

- paper goods broker
- imported specialty items
- pet toys

SERVICE

- owner of luxury bed-and-breakfast inn
- professional convention and meeting speaker
- chef
- adventure travel leader
- channeler

- horse trainer
- massage therapist
- underwater diver-planner
- owner of $3 per minute legal advice by telephone business
- prepaid legal plan promoter
- bicycle tour organizer and leader
- concert promoter
- consultant to businesses on cost, quality, and effective use of legal services
- founder of seminar company that teaches law to non-lawyers
- historical walking tours leader
- intellectual property protection and licensing consultant
- landscape gardener/landscape architect
- mountain trek company using llamas
- small business consultant
- social matchmaker
- scuba dive shop owner
- video production
- yacht party company owners
- small hotel owner/manager
- teaching financial planning seminars to lay people
- the "Noodge Lady," who gets things done for people who are unable to resolve a business or bureaucratic problem

If some of these business ventures sound interesting, but you are not sure whether working on your own, without salary and employer-paid benefits, is for you, take a course or two on starting a small business. Most community colleges offer free or low-cost courses on how to start your own business, as do local Chambers of Commerce. Or attend a lecture on becoming an entrepreneur, at your local Chamber of Commerce or nonprofit career center. For a reality check, be sure to talk to a lot of small business owners so you can hear the entire panoply of likes and dislikes about working alone and having the ultimate responsibility for your livelihood.

If you decide you are ready to take the risk (a high percentage of small businesses never make it past their second year), the next step is to obtain as much information as you can. Whether you are trying to decide what area of interest to explore or you already have a firm idea of the entrepreneurial endeavor you wish to pursue, it is important to be involved in relevant networking groups, both for support and for ideas. If you haven't yet crystalized your idea but definitely know you want to start your own business, attend meetings of entrepreneurship groups and "pick some brains." If you already know what you want to do, join relevant associations—it's a waste of time to reinvent the wheel, and those individuals already doing work similar to yours often can give you great tips to try and things to avoid. Once your business is off the ground, be sure to continue with networking meetings so that you keep current and relevant, and obtain feedback for your new ideas. Additionally, consulting for a few hours with a good small business advisor may give you the direction you need.

RESOURCES

"Franchise and Business Opportunities Monthly," a twice-a-month feature in *The Wall Street Journal National Business Employment Weekly.*" Call (800) JOB–HUNT or log on at www.nbew.com.

Relevant magazines: *Entrepreneur, Success, New Business Opportunities, Small Business Opportunities.*

Entrepreneur magazine has a collection of on-line business-related resources called Small Business Square. Access it at www.entrepreneurmag.com.

Export Hotline—a 24-hour news update phone service on trade and export-related issues. Call (800) USA–XPORT.

For import-export, the business section of your main library most likely has information on trade, products, foreign markets, export-import regulations, and statistics.

How to Succeed in Exporting and Doing Business Internationally, Eric Sletten, John Wiley & Sons, 1994.

Building an Import/Export Business, Kenneth Weiss, 2nd edition, John Wiley & Sons, 1998.

Federation of International Trade Associations, 1851 Alexander Bell Drive, Suite 400, Reston, VA 20191; (703) 620–1588, www.fita.org. The umbrella organization for 300 plus U.S. trade associations.

International Trade Administration of the Department of Commerce has offices in various U.S. cities. Assists businesses with international trade. Holds seminars on international trade and import/export issues.

The American Home Business Association sponsors a website (www.HomeBusiness.com) that connects small businesspeople to numerous resources, including insurance benefits, professional services, publications, and discount buying programs. Call them at (800) 664–2422.

Service Corps of Retired Executives (SCORE). A non-profit organization that offers free one-on-one business counseling and workshops on all facets of business (i.e., business plans, marketing, accounting systems, etc.) by experienced volunteer businesspeople, in conjunction with the Small Business Administration. Offices nationwide in more than 750 locales. To find out where your local SCORE office is, call your regional SBA office. Highly recommended as an informative, helpful, unbiased, and cost-effective resource.

The Small Business Administration (www.sba.gov) has over 100 free and low-cost publications (most under $4) on all aspects of starting and running a small business. It also sponsors workshops. The SBA has local Small Business Development Centers to provide counseling and training to business owners. It also has an answer desk, which has information on small business issues. Call (800) 827–5722 for information. The answer desk has a bulletin board, which can be accessed via computer at (800) 697–4636.

National Federation of Independent Business, with 600,000 members, is the largest small business advocacy organization in the United States. Call them at (202) 554–9000, www.nfibonline.com.

The Whole Work Catalog contains descriptions of numerous books on every facet of running, starting up, or selecting a small business, especially a home-based business; you can order any of the books from the catalog. To receive a free catalog, contact The New Careers Center, 1515 23rd Street, P.O. Box 339, Boulder, CO 80306; (800) 634–9024.

Business@Home (www.gohome.com) is an on-line magazine with news and advice for all aspects of running a small business.

Jobs in Paradise: The Definitive Guide to Exotic Jobs Everywhere, Jeffrey Maltzman, Harper & Perennial, 1993. Written by a lawyer, with about 200,000 jobs and small businesses worldwide.

The America Institute for Small Business publishes books, videos, software, and educational materials on every aspect of running your own business, including the two-volume *How to Set Up Your Own Small Business,* by Max Fallek, 1997; (800) 328–2906, www.aisbofmn.com.

The Nonprofit Entrepreneur: Creating Ventures to Earn Income, edited by Edward Skloot, Foundation Center, 1988. Contact the Foundation Center at 79 Fifth Avenue, New York, NY 10003–3076; (800) 424–9836.

Yahoo Small Business Informant (www.yahoo.com/Business/ Small_Business_Information/) links to numerous small business websites.

Directory of Federal and State Business Assistance: A Guide for New and Growing Companies, U.S. Department of Commerce. Available at U.S. Government Printing Office bookstores (usually in the main federal building).

101 Internet Businesses You Can Start from Home: Plus a Beginner's Guide to Starting a Business Online, Ron E. Gielgun, Actium Publishing, 1997.

Outdoor Careers: Exploring Occupations in Outdoor Fields, Ellen Shenk, Stackpole Books, 1992. Available from bookstores or call Stackpole at (800) 732–3669.

The National Restaurant Association offers a self-help kit to prospective new restauranteurs for $12. The kit covers information on location, menu, costs, revenues, suppliers, etc. Contact them at 1200–17th Street, N.W., Washington, DC 20036; (202) 331–5960.

Working Solo (www.workingsolo.com) is an excellent website for finding more than 1,200 business resources.

The following is a partial list of books from John Wiley & Sons Publishing (a number of other publishers also have "How To" books) suggesting various interesting fields of endeavor:

- *How to Make Money in Mail-Order,* L. Perry Wilbur, 1990.
- *How to Develop and Promote Successful Seminars and Workshops,* Howard Shenson, 1990.
- *Catering Like a Pro,* Francine Halvorsen, 1994.
- *How to Open & Run a Successful Restaurant,* Christopher Egerton-Thomas, 2nd edition, 1994.
- *How to Succeed as an Independent Consultant,* Herman Holtz, 3rd edition, 1993.
- *How to Start and Run a Writing and Editing Business,* Herman Holtz, 1992.
- *Starting On a Shoestring: Building a Business Without a Bankroll,* Arnold Goldstein, 3rd edition, 1995.
- *How to Succeed With Your Own Construction Business,* Stephen Diller and Janelle Diller, Craftsman Book Co, 1991.

Here is information on running a bed-and-breakfast:
- The Professional Association of Innkeepers International, P.O. Box 90710, Santa Barbara, CA 93190; (805) 569–1853.
- David Caples, of Lodging Resources at 998 S. Fletcher Avenue, Amelia Island, FL 32034; (800) 772–3359 for innkeeping seminars and private consultations.
- *So—You Want to Be an Innkeeper: The Definitive Guide to Operating a Successful Bed-and-Breakfast or Country Inn,* edited by Mary E. Davis, 3rd edition, Chronicle Books, 1996.
- *How to Open and Operate a Bed & Breakfast,* Jan Stankus, 5th edition, Globe Pequot Press, 1997.

The Home–Based Business Bookstore (www.advgroup.com/books/books.htm) provides on-line access to home-based business oriented books, with links to other sites.

Working From Home, Paul Edwards and Sarah Edwards, 4th edition, Putnam Publishing, 1994.

Small Time Operator: How to Start Your Own Business, Bernard Kamoroff, 22nd edition, Bell Springs, 1997. One of the best books on how to start your own business.

Marketing Without Advertising, Salli Rasberry and Michael Phillips, 2nd edition, Nolo Press 1997.

Starting Your New Business: A Guide for Entrepreneurs, Charles L. Martin, Crisp Publications, 1995.

Growing A Business, Paul Hawken, Fireside, 1988. Still a great book, with a more humane viewpoint than many business books.

Running A One–Person Business, Claude Whitmyer and Salli Rasberry, 2nd edition, Ten Speed Press, 1994.

The Best Home Businesses for the 90's, Paul and Sarah Edwards, 2nd edition, J.P. Tarcher, 1995.

Getting Business to Come to You, Paul Edwards, Sarah Edwards, and Laura Douglas, 2nd edition, Putnam Publishing Group, 1998.

Secrets of Self-Employment: Surviving and Thriving on the Ups and Downs of Being Your Own Boss, Sarah Edwards and Paul Edwards, Putnam, 1996.

If you are on the Internet, most of the online services offer access to numerous small business resources. Here are just a few services:

- CompuServe: access to business databases and research sources. Has a Working From Home Forum and the Entrepreneur's Forum to provide information on tax laws and allow you to converse with fellow small/home office professionals. Call (800) 848–8990.
- America OnLine: hosts the Microsoft Small Business Center, which carries business advice and real-time seminars. You can also hook up with the SBA and the U.S. Chamber of Commerce. Call (800) 827–6364.
- Dow Jones News/Retrieval: you can search hundreds of business magazines and journals, although rates exceed $2 per minute. Call (800) 522–3567.

• Foundations and Not-For-Profit Organizations

Positions which lawyers have held include:

- community liaison
- director of development (fund–raising)
- director of historical society
- director of private family charitable foundation

- director of humane society
- endowment department (handles charitable giving)
- executive director
- freelance development/fund-raising assistant
- humane society ethicist
- lobbyist
- planned giving director
- public relations director

RESOURCES

Foundation Center, 79 Fifth Avenue, New York, NY
   10003–3076; (800) 424–9836, www.fdncenter.org. A national
   nonprofit clearinghouse for information on grants and foundations. Publishes the following books:
- *Foundation Directory,* annually updated list of over 6,000 U.S.
   foundations, $185.
- *Corporate Foundations Profile,* annual, $155. Describes
   foundations.
- *Careers for Dreamers and Doers: A Guide to Management Jobs
   in the Nonprofit Sector,* Lilly Cohen and Dennis Young,
   1989. $24.95.
- *The Nonprofit Entrepreneur: Creating Ventures to Earn Income,*
   edited by Edward Skloot, 1988, $19.95.
*Community Jobs: The National Employment Newspaper for the Non-
   Profit Sector.* Monthly listings of nonprofit job openings, relevant articles and resource lists. Contact ACCESS, 1001 Connecticut Avenue, Suite 838, Washington, DC 20036; (202)
   785–4233, www.communityjobs.com.
American Society of Association Executives, 1575 "I" Street,
   N.W., Washington, DC 20005; (202) 626–2723, www.
   asaenet.org. Members are the directors and assistant directors
   of foundations and other nonprofit organizations.
Earth Work magazine, for and about people who work to protect
   the land and environment. It lists paid positions from entry
   level to CEO. Published monthly by the Student Conservation
   Association. Order from SCA, CR Dept., P.O. Box 550,

Charlestown, NH 03603–1828; (603) 543–1700, at www.sca-inc.org. They also produced *Earthwork: Resource Guide to Nationwide Green Jobs,* published by HarperCollins.

Human Services Inventory. Comprehensive listing of human services organizations. Available at public libraries.

Good Works: A Guide to Careers in Social Change, Donna Colvin and Ralph Nadar, 5th edition, Barricade Books, 1994. Lists law and non-law jobs in over 800 organizations in a variety of public interest areas.

The Institute for Nonprofit Organization Management at the University of San Francisco offers a credentialed program. Call (415) 422–6867 for information. There are other schools around the country that offer similar coursework.

National Society of Fundraising Executives, 1101 King Street, Suite 700, Alexandria, VA 22314; (800) 666–FUND, www.nsfre.org. Has a newsletter with national job listings, but you should also call local chapters for local job listings.

Chronicle of Philanthropy, P.O. Box 1989, Marion, OH 43306–2089, (800) 728-2803, website at philanthropy.com. A biweekly journal covering issues in the nonprofit sector.

Managing a Nonprofit Organization, Thomas Wolf, Prentice Hall, 1990.

A Legal Guide to Starting and Managing a Nonprofit Organization, 2nd edition, Bruce Hopkins, John Wiley & Sons, 1993.

United Way usually has local directories of nonprofit organizations in each office's respective area.

Also check the resources listed on pages 171–74 under "Public Interest and Volunteer Lawyers" in chapter 6 for publications and organizations that list both law and non-law opportunities with nonprofits.

Most sizeable communities have libraries with information on nonprofits and foundations, funding sources, grant writing, and the like—for instance, San Francisco's Foundation Center Library. Additionally, some communities have centers that provide programs and publications on non-profit management—for example, the Southern California Center for Non-Profit Management in Los Angeles.

• Teaching and Training

Positions lawyers have held in these fields include:

- college professor
- community college teacher
- elementary school teacher
- facilitator of personal growth or transformational seminars
- high school teacher
- member of an educational think tank
- New Age seminar facilitator
- professor at a specialized school, such as an art academy
- employee trainer
- workshop trainer
- organization development specialist

RESOURCES

The Chronicle of Higher Education, P.O. Box 1955, Marion, OH 43306–2055; (800) 728-2803, chronicle.com. A weekly publication with extensive listings of education-related positions. Fee is $75 for one year, $40.50 for 6 months.

Independent Educational Services, 1101 King Street, Alexandria, VA 22314; (800) 257–5102 or (703) 548–9700. A not-for-profit teacher placement service.

Education Week, 6935 Arlington Road, Suite 100, Bethesda, MD 20814; (301) 280-3100, www.edweek.org. Has articles, events, books, and job listings of interest to teachers. Fee is $69.94 for 43 issues per year.

American Society for Training and Development, Box 1443, 1640 King Street, Alexandria, VA 22313–2043; (703) 683–8100, www.astd.org. Local chapters nationwide, some with newsletters that have job listings and education/networking meetings. Membership consists of individuals working as employees or consultants in training and/or organization development in business, nonprofit, government, or education.

This is a website for people looking for work in training and development—check it out at www.tcm.com/hr–careers/career.

• Counseling

Positions lawyers have held include:

- career counselor
- corporate counseling with a master's degree in applied behavioral science
- experimental psychology and cognitive science with a Ph.D.
- outplacement counselor (for fired or laid-off workers)
- psychological counseling with a master's degree in psychology
- psychological counseling with a Ph.D. in psychology
- MFCC (marriage, family, and child counseling degree)
- therapy group leader
- MSW (master in social work)

RESOURCES

National Board for Certified Career Counselors, 3-D Terrace Way, Greensboro, NC 27403; (336) 547–0607, www.nbcc. org. Maintains a registry, requirements, and testing for certified career counselors.

International Association of Career Management Professionals, c/o Janet Saunder, P.O. Box 1484, Pacifica, CA 94044; (650) 359–6911, www.iacm.org. Members are involved in outplacement and career counseling in the United States and other countries. Produces bimonthly publication called the *Highlighter.*

American Counseling Association, 5999 Stevenson Avenue, Alexandria, VA 22304; (703) 823–9800, www.counseling.org. Members are career counselors, psychologists, therapists, etc.

American Psychological Association, 750 First Street, N.E., Washington, D.C. 20002; (202) 336-5500, www.apa.org has chapters in various cities.

Most states have a board that regulates MFCC (marriage, family, and child counseling), MSW (master in social work), and other licenses and has written licensing requirements.

• Creative Pursuits

Pursuits lawyers have engaged in include:

- actor/actress
- art exhibit creator (for galleries, office spaces, building lobbies, special events)
- artist's representative
- ballet dancer
- fashion model
- gallery owner
- graphic artist
- jazz dancer
- manager of band
- museum curator
- musician
- painter
- photographer
- sculptor
- theatrical producer or director

If you feel your creative nature isn't exercised in your law practice and you have a talent you would like to further develop and make a living at, give yourself some room to explore. Take courses at your local community college or art, dance, or music school. Try it out before you leap, to make sure you can make a living doing what you love. If you don't think you can fully support yourself by your creative skills alone, consider combining them with work that does bring in a reliable income, like contract legal work or a part-time salaried job, whether in or out of law.

Or look at possibilities for using your interest in creative endeavors in less conventional ways, like the lawyer who loved sculpting and the multidimensional aspects of his art. He put together a business setting up art-related displays (of Art Deco juke boxes, opera costumes, assemblage sculpture) in the lobbies of office buildings. He had to design the displays and arrange them within the lobby space, as well as negotiate for the use of the art pieces, secure insurance, research and write appropriate placard information for each piece, obtain display materials, manually assemble the display, and arrange for publicity for the showing—an excellent combination of both his legal and creative abilities, with some manual dexterity thrown in for good measure.

Resources

ArtSearch, published by Theater Communication Group, 355 Lexington Avenue, New York, NY 10017; (212) 697–5230. A national listing of performing arts positions, including arts training, internships, and fellowships. Fee is $54 per year for 23 issues, also available through an e-mail subscription for $10 extra. Available at some public libraries.

Artist's & Graphic Designer's Market (Cox), *Photographer's Market* (Lane), and *Songwriter's Market* (Horton) for Writers Digest Books. The books are updated annually and tell how and where to sell your work.

The Artists' Survival Manual, Toby Judith Klayman and Cobbett Steinberg, Toby Judith Klayman Publishing, 1996. How to market your work.

FYI is a newsletter (suggested "donation" is $18) listing arts-related grant opportunities and requirements, primarily in New York, available from the New York Foundation for the Arts, 155 Sixth Avenue, 14th floor, New York, NY 10013; (212) 366–6900, or at public libraries.

Careers for Culture Lovers and Other Artsy Types, Marjorie Eberts and Margaret Gisler, VGM Career Horizons, 1992.

Creative Screenwriters Group is a national organization that will direct you to a current local group or help you set up your own. Send your name, address, and telephone number, along with a description of your writing interests, and a self-addressed, stamped envelope to them at 518 Ninth Street, N.E., Suite 308, Washington, DC 20002.

All You Need to Know About the Music Business, Donald S. Passman, Simon & Schuster, updated, 1997. Covers advisors (managers, lawyers, agents), recording deals, publishing (copyright, contracts, and royalties), tours, merchandising, and movies.

The Commercial Theater Institute, New York, 250 West 57th Street, Suite 1818, NY 10107 holds 3-day educational seminars for beginning theatrical producers, as well as 14-week programs for more experienced producers. Good educational and networking opportunity. Call (212) 586–1109.

Relevant magazines for stage actors, producers, and directors are *American Theater, Theater Week,* and *Variety,* as well as the *New York Times* for its theater reviews (and on Fridays, its section on who's doing what, where).

Survival Jobs: 154 Ways to Make Money While Pursuing Your Dreams, Deborah Jacobson, Bantam, 1998.

Career Opportunities in the Music Industry, Shelly Field, 3rd edition, Facts on File, 1996.

Career Opportunities in Theater and the Performing Arts, Shelly Field, Facts on File, 1995.

Career Opportunities in Art, Susan Haubenstock and David Joselit, Facts on File, 1995.

Careers in Photography, Art Evans, Photo Data Research, 1992.

Careers in the Visual Arts, Dee Ito, Watson–Guptil Publications, 1993.

100 Best Careers in Entertainment, Shelly Field, Arco Publishing, 1995.

PART THREE

HOW TO FIND THE JOB YOU WANT

The future is not something we enter.
The future is something we create.
—LEONARD I. SWEET

If you are like most people, you want to work at a job that gives you satisfaction, some enjoyment, a feeling of accomplishment, and adequate remuneration. Desirable jobs exist—they really do—but some just take more work to discover or obtain than others. Particularly for career changers, the job development process is often more involved than just picking up the phone and making a few calls.

Yet I receive numerous calls from lawyers who want to know, "Do you have the name of a headhunter who places lawyers in the [fill in the blank] field outside of law?" Upon inquiry, I find out that most callers were hoping for an affirmative response so that they could make one phone call, go on one interview, and be placed next week in a new, wonderful job. These callers are looking for the panacea that will allow them to bypass the effort that they all know, deep down, is going to be necessary in order to find a new job or career. I find myself in the reality-check role of reminding them that it probably ain't gonna be that easy!

Possibly one or two people will have a serendipitous experience. They will run into an old friend who, upon seeing the lawyer, will exult that the timing couldn't be better, because the friend's company was just now looking to hire someone with exactly the lawyer's skills and background, and of course, the lawyer could have the job at an excellent salary with fabulous benefits. Although it would be wonderful if the process were that easy, the reality is that for most job and career changers, many hours are spent on networking, informational interviewing, drafting and sending out cover letters and resumes, and then interviewing for actual jobs before they obtain a new position in a satisfying field. As Beverly Sills, the opera superstar, once said, "There are no shortcuts to anyplace worth going."

My mom used to tell me when I was young, "If you're going to do something, you might as well concentrate on it and do it well, do it fully, and be done with it." Although in those days she most often was referring to cleaning my room, I believe that exhortation applies equally to a job search. If you really do want to change jobs or careers, rather than just sending out a resume to the occasional ad that tickles your fancy and making a networking call once a week or so, you must reprioritize your list of everyday activities and move job hunting up near the top. You must devote the same amount of time to a job search as you would to planning a long exotic vacation or putting together a large surprise party for your best friend. Somehow we all find time to do these fun activities, but clients always tell me that they are so busy at work that they don't have time to look for another job. Yet if I query them, they will eventually admit that they have a tennis game every Saturday at noon, or take French lessons on Wednesdays at 5:00, or meet with a friend for breakfast every Monday.

If job change is important to you, it needs to become a top priority until you achieve your goal. One way to keep on track is to calendar job hunt–related activities. Make appointments with yourself for telephone or informational interviewing time—for instance, Tuesdays from 3:00 to 5:00 P.M. and Thursdays from 9:00 to 11:00 A.M. You need to provide time during normal business hours for phone calls and interviewing—most of your contacts probably aren't going to be willing to talk or meet with you at 7:00 A.M. or 6:00 P.M.—so you may just have to fit them in during the day and then work later or on weekends. But do schedule your time. After all, you keep your appointments with your clients, and for now, your job hunt is your most important client.

Once you've identified some interesting job possibilities, the chapters in this section will cover some of the techniques for getting you to where you want to go. Since less than 20 percent of available jobs are advertised, one of the biggest mistakes a job changer—and particularly a career changer—can make is to focus all efforts on want ads. Another mistake is to send out hundreds of unsolicited resumes. According to Richard Bolles, author of *What Color Is Your Parachute?,* only one job is offered for every 1,470 resumes sent out, so it is important to be highly selective when sending resumes.

Bolles's research likewise indicates that only a very small percentage of jobs are obtained on the Internet, unless you are looking for work in the computer industry. However, as the Internet's uses expand, more job hunting will be done online. (See chapter 2, starting at page 38, for some online job hunt resources.) In fact, if you type in the word "job," you will be overwhelmed with more than two million job-related sites! There are even a number of on-line "matchmaking" services specifically for lawyers and law employers if you are inclined to take a job very similar to what you currently have, and if your work history and education credentials are top notch; for example, see www.emplawyernet.com or www.attorneysatwork.com.

Other sources for job leads are:

1. The career services office of your law school for law jobs.
2. Job listings in trade and professional magazines, newspapers, and other publications—be sure to also read the news stories in these publications to detect employment growth areas and

new business activity that may be relevant to your career focus.

3. Consulting firms that work with various industries or organizations on a contract basis.

4. Employment agencies and temporary agencies, which match a candidate with a job opening, either permanent or temporary. The fee should always be paid by the employer. In most cases, the agency is seeking an employee for a job the agency has been hired by an employer to fill.

While some people actually do find jobs through the want ads or from an unsolicited contact, there is an extremely large "hidden market" of both legal and non-legal jobs not advertised in print, but instead publicized through word of mouth among friends and employees of the prospective employer. Many unadvertised jobs are filled by, or created for, friends of friends. The majority of high-level management and executive jobs, as well as some senior associate and law partner positions, are recruited this way. Therefore, you must tap into that "hidden market" by developing your contacts, through networking and informational interviewing. This will allow you to spend your time on, and target your resume to, jobs that you know have hiring potential.

RESOURCES

Jobs for Lawyers: Effective Techniques for Getting Hired in Today's Marketplace, Hillary Mantis and Kathleen Brady, Impact Publications, 1996. Includes the job search process, including networking, resumes, and interviewing.

Guerilla Tactics for Getting the Legal Job of Your Dreams, Kimm Walton, Harcourt Brace, 1997. Step-by-step job hunt advice, directed primarily to newer lawyers.

CHAPTER NINE

Ask the Experts: Networking and Informational Interviewing

The person who gets hired is not necessarily the one who can do that job best but the one who knows the most about how to get hired.

—RICHARD BOLLES

• Networking

You call your friend Joan to find out about a vegetarian restaurant she recently recommended. Joan gives you the name of a friend of hers who knows a lot about the vegetarian restaurants in town. That friend gives you numbers of several eateries, which you then call to get information. Whether you realize it or not, you are networking.

251

We all network to obtain information and answers relevant to whatever questions we currently have. Somehow most people don't feel uncomfortable with this type of "brain-picking," but when it comes to asking about job-related information, the same people freeze up. Lawyers in the job hunt process often remind me of the stereotypical male driver. Unwilling to stop and ask for help or directions, he is willing instead to wander around unproductively, even aimlessly, hoping to eventually find the right locale, when a simple, well-placed question could probably put him right on target.

Even though the word "networking" has developed a negative connotation for many people, conjuring up an image of a glad-handing "user," most people enhance their careers and businesses by utilizing effective contacts. Basically, networking consists of asking other people for information and connections; it isn't "using" others, since most people are happy to share information. Often, they fully understand that it may be their turn, the next time, to be on the questioning end of an inquiry. Although they may not be currently looking for a new job, most people know that it's only a matter of time before they want to or have to change jobs, and if they're now in your network, you are also in theirs. So always remember to reciprocate—it makes good business sense and, for those of you who feel like you are imposing on people when you ask for information, it allows you to pay off your debt.

Networking has always been an effective way to get a new job and is especially useful for individuals who are looking for jobs in career fields unrelated to the one in which they now work. If your resume doesn't fit the job description of the work you would like to do, it is very important to develop networking contacts in the new field. These contacts, the information they give you, and anyone they introduce you to will allow you much more access to opportunities than your unsolicited, mismatched resume.

Before you can productively network, it is important to have an idea of what job or area of work you are interested in pursuing. You don't have to make a commitment to just one job yet—there is nothing wrong with checking into various areas of interest—but you should have several possibilities in mind. While most people are quite willing to answer questions about a field, they don't want to waste their time with someone who calls and says, "I don't know what I want, so can you give me some ideas?"

How do you develop networking contacts? Once you have a few specific areas of interest, you are ready to cultivate contacts. Whether you stay in law or want to move outside the profession, the following points should be helpful:

Make a list of people you know. Don't think about how helpful each person would be. Ranking the names from "most helpful" to "least helpful" is the second step, after you write down as many names as possible. Your list should consist of family, old and new friends, former and new neighbors, people from your gym/church/hiking group/political club, other volunteers and staff at community groups with which you are involved, your doctor/dentist/baker/accountant/plumber/banker/local merchant/clergyperson/real estate broker/insurance agent, previous job supervisors, teachers and professors, parents in your child's little league group/car pool/swim group, etc. etc. Even if you don't think some of these people would be helpful, you never know who on that list might have a cousin or a friend who would be an excellent contact for you. Take, for example, Elisha, who was introduced by her masseuse to another massage client whose company was thinking about setting up internal dispute resolution trainings—Elisha's field of interest. Most of us have no idea about the other facets of the lives of the people we come into contact with, or how those other facets may materialize into information useful for us. Everyone has circles of friends, and you want to tap into your friends' circles. Your list should particularly include everyone who owes you any favors.

Make a list of vendors in the industry you're pursuing. Vendors often know which companies are growing, hiring, have happy employees. To find relevant vendors, check the ads in the journals that are published by or marketed to your targeted industry.

Make a list of your college and law school classmates. Even if you went to school outside of your present town, those old school contacts may have moved into your area. Call your law school alumni office and get the alumni roster—you might find that an old chum or acquaintance is now general counsel at a company where you want to practice law or work in sales or become a manager. Even if you don't recognize the names of the alumni who now live in your current town, there is generally enough chauvinism among members of a law school that some of those alumni would take a call from you—especially if you first send a letter to them pointing out the connection.

Make a list of every attorney you have ever worked with, cocounseled with, or opposed. Do this if you intend to continue to practice law, whether in your same practice area or not, or if you intend to do contract legal work or move into less traditional legal work. Each lawyer knows numerous other lawyers who also know numerous lawyers, and so on. And, of course, these attorneys know your work, so they can speak personally about you. Even if you want to leave law completely, some of these people will have relevant out-of-law contacts.

Make a list of organizations relevant to the various job areas you want to explore. If you don't know of any organizations, you can find out some names by questioning people who work in those areas. You can also look in Gale Research, Inc's. *Encyclopedia of Associations,* available at most public libraries, to find associations in your choosen industries. Contact these groups and find out if there are local chapters, when they meet, and whom to call. Then attend the meetings. To switch legal practice areas, go to the bar association section meetings in your targeted area (i.e., environmental, probate, family law). Or go to your Chamber of Commerce's programs to cultivate business contacts. Or attend your state's risk management association meetings to meet risk managers. Talk to the people already working in your field of interest—they are great sources of information, useful for confirming whether or not your perception about a field is accurate, and they usually know who's hiring. When James went to the meetings of the local chapter of the National Speakers Association in Texas, he made excellent contacts who gave him not only information about how to position himself as a professional seminar presenter but also several excellent referrals to paid speaking engagements.

Ask the organizations whether they have a newsletter or a job or resume bank. Subscribe to the newsletters—you will learn about the "players" and issues in your chosen area. Write an article that will get your name known. Or if you read an article of interest to you, it might be productive to contact the author to discuss the article; you might find that the author has pertinent information. Reggy sent a letter to the author of an article, the VP of a mid-size company, then followed with a phone call. The author was so pleased to receive feedback and attention, (which is rare unless an article is controversial) and the two men had such a productive discussion that the author invited Reggy to visit at his company. That meeting led to several interviews where Reggy's career interests and skills were discussed. Not long after, a job was created in the author's company to utilize Reggy's skills.

Read legal and trade publications and other business newspapers. Concentrate on local business and legal journals to find out information about law firms and companies in your area of interest and to learn which ones are hiring. If an article indicates that a certain company is growing, contact that company to make a presentation on how your skills can benefit its growth.

• Networking Contact Form

Before you actually begin the process of networking, it is important to prepare a system to keep organized. After all, you will want to remember who told you what about whom so that you don't duplicate efforts, so that you can thank the relevant information source, and so that you don't embarrass yourself when a networking contact calls you back and you can't figure out who they are or why you called them. A relatively simple format to track your contacts can look like the one on page 256.

Of course, to be effective you need to fill in one of these sheets each time you talk to anyone and immediately after you meet anyone at any gathering. Alphabetize by last name of the contact. And for best tracking results, make a new sheet for each "Referred to" name, placing that person's name into the "Contact Name" section on the new sheet. Then file this alphabetically under the new contact's name. If a person you were referred to calls you, you can immediately go to your alphabetical file to

NETWORKING CONTACTS

Name _____

Company _____

Address _____

Telephone _____

Fax/e-mail _____

Referred by _____

Referred to _____

Topics discussed _____

_____

Follow-up?/Date/What done? _____

_____

_____

find the relevant sheet and know who gave you the caller's name and any other pertinent information.

During this period of research, when you are trying to meet and talk to as many people as possible, consider volunteering or doing an internship in a relevant position, such as in a nonprofit, with a mediation program, or in a school. This will give you exposure to people working in your desired field, plus it will give you targeted work experience. For the three years before Sara left the New England area, she volunteered numerous hours at a local humane society—she was on the board of directors and was active on several committees. When Sara moved to the Midwest, she didn't want to take another bar exam or practice law, so she applied for a job at the humane society in her new locale. Even though she was new to the community, based on the references from the staff for her volunteer work, she was offered the job of president at the local humane society. Her paid legal work certainly didn't qualify her for this new job, since she had been a civil litigator in a ten-person firm for five years, but her solid volunteer experience did.

When you meet people who are able to give you information, it is important to ask them for additional names of contacts who might be able to help you. This is the way you build your list. The more people you can talk to, the more opportunity you will have to zero in on a job that really will fit for you, rather than the one you can do, but won't be happy with, that you saw advertised in the newspaper. The newspaper ad is the easy way out, but if the job it represents is a big compromise, you just may be out looking for work again in three months.

RESOURCES

There are numerous books on effective networking. Just keep in mind that you have to do what's comfortable for your style. If the idea of going to meetings and talking to strangers curls your toes, this might be a time to stretch your boundaries just a little.

Networking for Everyone! Connecting with People for Career and Job Success, L. Michelle Tullier, Jist Works, 1998.

The Secrets of Savvy Networking: How to Make the Best Connections for Business and Personal Success, Susan RoAne, Warner Books, 1993. One of the better books on productive "schmoozing." RoAne sets out effective tactics and gives solid tips that never go out of date.

It's Who You Know, Cynthia Chin-Lee, Career Research Institute, 1997. Career strategies for making effective contacts.

• Informational Interviewing

Most job hunters dislike arranging and conducting informational interviews even more than they dislike networking. That's probably because the job hunter perceives that he or she is imposing on the person who gives the informational interview. Well, I won't disagree with that assessment. You *are* imposing on that person's time. But most interviewees know that giving informational time is important; they probably went through the same process themselves to get their current jobs. People generally like to be helpful and like to play matchmaker.

One positive aspect of the informational interview is that it is low stress. You are in control of the interview, and it is not a screening process but a cultivating one. While there is no magic formula for what works best to set up an informational interview, here are three suggestions for what to say on your intial phone call:

1. I'm thinking of a possible new career in _____ and am talking to people in the industry/practice area to gather information to help me in my career decision; or

2. I'm thinking about making a career change and want to find out as much as I can about _____ before I make my decision.

3. _____ gave me your name and said you were very experienced in _____. Since I am investigating making a job change into that field, I would appreciate it if I could ask you some questions.

The following suggestions will hopefully make you feel a bit more at ease when trying to set up and conduct an informational interview, and get you the information you need.

An informational interview is for information. Understand that an informational interview is exactly that. It is for information gathering, research and reality checking—do you really want to work in this industry, are you qualified, can you earn the salary you need? It is not an opportunity to ask for a job, nor is it a time for you to give an interview on your qualifications. You are meeting with your target person to assist your job or career change decision by learning about his or her job, obtaining specific data about an industry, firm, or job, and getting more networking contacts in this or related fields. The added benefit is that if you do decide to move into the target person's industry, you will do so with added knowledge that can be very helpful to your future progression.

Respect your contact's time. When you telephone the target to set up an interview, don't ask job-related questions at that time. Instead, ask what time "next week in the afternoon" or "this week in the morning" would be best for the two of you to meet for "about twenty minutes" so that you can ask some job-related questions. By phrasing your request this way, you demonstrate respect for your target's immediate schedule, by not imposing for more than two minutes when you initially call to set up your visit. You allow your target the freedom to set a time, within parameters you have already established, when she or he has time to meet with you. You also assuage your target's worry about time commitments when you say "twenty minutes."

In order to maximize time during the interview, subtly direct the conversation back to your list of questions if your contact becomes too loquacious. Although the interview is for exploratory research, which means you should allow for some revelatory rambling, you do have a limited amount of time in which to obtain information.

Use prior contacts to make a new contact. If you were given the target's name by another networking contact, be sure to mention that first contact's name when you introduce yourself. While most people are fairly generous with their time, you will generally be given more attention, or you will at least more likely receive an audience, if you are recommended to them by someone they know.

Try to meet in person. If at all possible, arrange to meet with your target in person rather than by telephone. A more memorable and personal connection is made by face-to-face contact. However, it's often difficult to meet in person when you are working full-time since many people won't be willing to see you before or after work. To remedy this problem, perhaps leave a half hour early for lunch, or leave a bit early in the afternoon, or if need be, arrange several informational interviews on one day and take a vacation or personal day off from work. Don't think you must take your target to lunch. Most people don't want to spend an entire hour talking about work with a stranger—even if you're treating.

Be focused, straightforward. Before you go into the interview, have your act together so that you don't waste time—you only have twenty minutes. Identify yourself as a serious job seeker with a clearly defined career objective who is seeking more information about the industry, the company, the job openings. Even if you are really not positive that this particular objective is the one you will eventually pursue, assume you will for purposes of the informational interview.

Do your homework. Before you go into the interview, make a bona fide effort to learn about the law firm or company (read Martindale-Hubbell or Standard & Poor's and annual reports, if applicable, or check the resources listed in chapter 11, on page 296), the person (find articles, ask mutual acquaintances), the industry (read journals or business magazines), and yourself (be able to relate your skills to their field) so that you can ask knowledgeable questions and not have to spend a sizeable portion of your twenty minutes receiving a basic education. This is also good practice for properly preparing for an actual job interview.

Bring a resume or send one ahead. Bring a resume that is drafted with clear objectives and skills related to the industry, company, or law firm so that the other person can see what you have done before and how your skills might be transferable. Even if you haven't decided what you really want to do when you grow up, at least for the twenty minutes of this informational interview you know that you want to do work similar to that done by your target person. For a law interview, bring a chronological resume; for a non-law job, bring a targeted functional resume (see chapter 10 for information on resumes and an explanation of these terms).

Respect time limits. Don't take a minute more time than you have asked for; busy people have other things to do. Unless your interviewee explicitly invites you to stay longer, you must adjourn your interview after twenty minutes. Therefore, you need to pace your questions and guide the answers you receive so that you cover and obtain information on the important points.

Talk less, listen more. Ask well thought-out questions and let the interviewee do 90 percent of the talking. This is not the time for a sales pitch for yourself; instead, ask about opportunities, trends, a particular job, or the organization. Remember, the information you are getting will help you decide if you really do want to pursue this field, plus it will hopefully steer you in a productive direction. You can use a form similar to that on page 256 to record the information you learn during an informational interview.

Ask for other contacts. Be sure to ask for other names to add to your networking list. Also, ask whether you can use the target's name as an introduction to those contacts.

Always follow up. Call any contacts you were given—you never know where they will lead. Besides, if your interviewee talks to those contacts sometime later and finds that you haven't called, it will look like you don't follow through and didn't value the information you were given.

The mandatory thank-you note. Always, always, always promptly send a thank-you note. There are three reasons to do so. One, it's a nice thing to do, but few people take the time. Two, it gives you an opportunity to remind your target person of your existence, just in case the perfect job has come to her or his attention since you two talked. Third—and this is a selfish reason, but why not?—your target feels appreciated by you and that permits you to call again, if you need more information, without seeming to be a "user."

You may want to handwrite your thank-you note if you have legible writing. Keep it short, but remind your target who you are ("thank you for talking to me last Tuesday about selling real estate"), write a sentence or two about the benefits of your meeting ("I now realize that I have much more interest in commercial rather than residential real estate and need to take some classes"), and restate the names of the networking contacts you were given ("thanks also for giving me John Smith's name—I have set up an appointment to meet with him next week"). If you think this industry and the job about which you were inquiring still interest you, close by requesting that you be remembered if the target person hears of any relevant job openings.

Some informational interviewers use the process to excellent effect. Steve was very organized; after he contacted the people whose names he was given by his target person, he would drop that target another note, letting her know that he had talked to the contact "Sam" and what he had found out. He would then drop Sam a note after he talked to the people whose names he'd gotten from Sam, and so on. Because he kept each of his contacts apprised of his efforts and the changes in direction he was making in his job search, after about two months into his search Sam called Steve and said that he had just heard of a job Steve might be interested in. Because Steve kept his name fresh in Sam's memory and had made Sam somewhat "invested" in the results of his job hunt, when Sam learned of a relevant job, he was delighted to call Steve and "matchmake."

Keep it up. Informational interviews are a cumulative process of learning and are also excellent practice for the real job interview.

SAMPLE INFORMATIONAL INTERVIEW QUESTIONS

Breaking into the new field
1. How did you get into this type of work? This job?
2. What qualifications are necessary for this work—what training, experience? Are there any exceptions to these requirements?
3. Can someone learn "on the job"?

What is the work like?
1. What is your average workday like?
2. What are some representative tasks and responsibilities of this job?
3. Does this work require team playing, decision making, managing, etc. (or the opposites of these skills)?
4. What do you like best about your work? Least?
5. What kind of people do you work with? What is the work environment like?

ld readjust your job, what would you change?
he entry salaries in this field? Salary range? Benefits?
d in a growth or declining mode?

npany or firm
this company/firm different (or similar to) others in
lustry?
he company/firm have expansion plans? In which

CES

iring Who: How to Find that Job Fast!, Richard Lathrop,
edition, Ten Speed Press, 1989. Effective techniques on
nation gathering.
Information Interviewing: How to Tap Your Hidden Job Market, Mar-
tha Stoodley, 2nd edition, Ferguson Publishing, 1996.
The Address Book: How to Reach Anyone Who Is Anyone, Michael
Levine, 8th edition, Perigee, 1997. Has websites and e-mail
addresses as well as street addresses if you need to make an
important contact.

CHAPTER TEN

———⊳●⊲———

Effective Resumes and
Cover Letters

Not that the story needs to be long,
but it will take a long time to make it short.
—HENRY DAVID THOREAU

• Resumes

While a resume is a necessary and useful tool, it generally is used only to get you in the door for an interview—it doesn't get you the job. Basically, it is a letter of introduction, to be fleshed out by information that you provide at an interview. In fact, often a personal contact, a telephone call, or a well-written letter are more likely to lead to an interview.

Keep in mind that a resume is a marketing tool that you write to sell a product . . . YOU. The two main reasons that any product is purchased are to solve specific problems for the purchaser or to make the purchaser's life easier and more pleasant.

to every potential employer in a field or industry, employers perceive a resume and cover letter tailored to their needs as evidence of your interest in them specifically. It also answers their question, "Why should I buy you?"

You should obtain relevant information on practice areas, services or products, growth pattern, divisions and subsidiaries, competitors, reputation, number of employees, earnings and profits, and locations. See the resources listed in chapters 6, 7, and 8 to assist you in your research. And don't forget to look at national and local legal papers for law firm information, and at the *Wall Street Journal,* the *New York Times,* or the various weekly news magazines for information about larger companies.

If you have access to the Internet, you can research many of the law firms and companies from information contained in their own websites, other relevant on-line sources, or in research databases. If you aren't "wired," public libraries often have free access to computer databases. Internet directories also will list professional associations in specific fields, many of which have on-line discussion groups or bulletin boards, where you can ask questions and obtain useful information about a specific employer. See the relevant websites in the resource sections at the beginning of chapters 6, 7, and 8.

A resume is a summary that focuses on your skills and achievements—it indicates what you have done, how you have done it,

A **chronological** resume (see example on following pages) is most useful when there is a fairly direct match between your background and the position desired. It is the type most often used for law jobs—this is the format you should follow when applying for a traditional legal position. This resume lists, in reverse chronological order within each category, your employment (with job title and a description of duties), education, and other relevant experience and information. Unless your education credentials are extremely impressive, or you have been out of school for less than five years, put the education section at the end of the resume. Don't use this type of resume for non-law positions. Most non-lawyers do not understand what skills are used in performing the tasks that are described in the typical legal resume. Use a functional resume instead.

A **functional** or **skills** resume (see examples on following pages) is used to display transferable skills (those that you pinpointed in chapter 5) that are applicable to the desired—usually non-law—position. The names of your past employers and your job titles are not as important as the experience and skills gained. Your experience and educational achievements are organized by skill category—"communication skills" or "organizational skills"—rather than date or job title to demonstrate that your experience closely resembles that required for the specific job you are applying for. The resume usually begins with a job objective or summary statement, so that the reader doesn't have to wonder why you are sending your resume. It then focuses on skills and achievements that support that objective and directly indicate your suitability for the job (see chapter 5 for lists of functional skills to include in a resume). Avoid a vague objective such as "I seek a challenging position with a growing company." Instead, your objective might read "Human Resources Director." Remember also that it is important to use action verbs such as "planned" or "coordinated" to describe your experience so that employers can deduce both your skills and what work you actually did.

For lawyers who would like to work outside law, it is very important to have a clear picture of the skills you have to offer the potential employer. Be sure to work through the skills exercises in chapter 5 so that you are clear on which skills you have *and* which you want to use. Then be sure to present those clearly in your resume so that the employer can understand why a lawyer can actually do the work of, for example, a computer account executive. See chapter 5 for a more thorough discussion of this issue.

Remember that a resume is a sample of your work product and as such is reflective of your abilities. Therefore, do not have a resume service prepare a resume for you—these "canned resumes" all have a similar look than an experienced interviewer can easily spot. Ask a friend to proofread your resume for typos and grammar—nothing puts your resume into the "circular file" more quickly than a misspelled or poorly chosen word.

Make your resume easy to read. The average reader will scan your resume in about ten seconds, so don't exclude yourself by making your page look too dense with type or awkward formatting or excess verbiage. Select only light colored or white, good-quality, 8½-by-11-inch bond paper with matching envelopes. Use a readable typeface, such as Times, in at least a 12 point font size, and avoid italics unless you're citing a book title. You needn't have your resume professionally printed; in fact, because you will change portions of the content from one job application to another, it is easier to do it on your computer—but only if you have a laser printer. For those with a small amount of work experience, keep your resume to one page. For more experienced job hunters, try not to go over two pages—and remember to put your name and "page 2" on that second page.

Do not include your photo on the resume. And do not include personal information, such as marital status, health, number of children, age, religion. An employer cannot legally ask you about any of those points, so why give them a chance to exclude you, based on irrelevant-to-the-job-data, before you have even met? There's no need to state "References available on request," because employers will ask for references if they want them. But do have with you at interviews your reference list containing three names, addresses, and telephone numbers, in case it is requested.

Do include awards, both educational and professional, as well as language and computer capabilities, including software packages used. Some people include associations and leisure interests, but be wary. What you see as a plus someone else may see as a liability. In fact, it seems that job hunters always like to travel or windsurf or read—no one ever admits watching Monday night football and drinking beer.

While the preceding basic rules work for paper resumes that are to be read by a human, it's also necessary to be aware of the new developments in electronic processing ("scanning") of resumes that some medium and larger-size law firms and many corporate entities now use. When scanning, the computer relies on "key words" that it has been programmed to find, such as degrees, years of experience, tasks, and skills. These words usually define the requirements of a specific job; for instance, "J.D.," "litigation," "negotiate," "trial," "real estate," are used to scan for a real estate litigator who has negotiation and trial experience. If your scanned resume doesn't contain the key words, the computer passes you by. Therefore, in a resume you suspect may be scanned, try to describe the skills you have developed and use descriptive nouns to recount your experience ("handled *accounts receiveable*" rather than "handled *accounting*.") Additionally, avoid underlining, graphics, shading, and condensed spacing between letters, as they all confuse the computer. Several books are now out on the market that more extensively describe how to prepare an effective scannable resume. If you are applying for a job with a medium to large corporation or a large law firm, read these books. In general, smaller law firms haven't yet delegated the resume review process to a machine. However, over the next several years, many employers will adopt this technology, so it may be useful to prepare your resume with electronic scanning in mind.

What follows are two traditional chronological resumes, one for a junior lawyer and one for a senior lawyer, both of whom are looking to stay in law. After those come a sample format and two sample functional resumes, used by those who would like to transfer their skills out of law. Note that the two functional resumes were developed for the same man. His education and work experience reveal it is the same person, but selectively citing relevant experience from the various facets of his work life makes each of the two functional resumes appear to be for completely different people.

SAMPLE LEGAL RESUME
FOR LITIGATION PARTNER

JANE DOE
0000 Street
San Francisco, CA 94000
(415) 000–0000
e-mail:doe@dot.com

PROFESSIONAL EXPERIENCE

9–93 to present — BUCK & DOE, P.C., San Francisco, California
Managing Attorney/Litigation Partner. Primary management responsibility for firm of 14 attorneys with gross receiveables in excess of $7 million. Negotiate and litigate through trial all cases for a group of companies involved in mining, real estate, banking, and venture capital. Lead attorney in 8 jury trials with recoveries in excess of $150 million

3–90 to 9–93 — NOSE AND HOSE, San Francisco, California
Attorney. Negotiated, structured and documented corporate, business, and real estate transactions. Litigated breach of contract, real estate, and business cases. Lead attorney in 12 jury trials.

6–88 to 2–90 — LAW OFFICES OF M. T. HEAD, San Francisco, California
Attorney. Corporate, business, contract, and real estate transactions and litigation of those issues. Lead attorney in 3 and second chair in 5 jury trials.

9–85 to 6–88 — CROCK AND ROCK, San Francisco, California
Associate Attorney. Researched & drafted pleadings, motions and interrogatories in large individual and class action suits. Argued motions and second chaired 4 court trials.

9–84 to	SUPERIOR COURT of SMITH COUNTY,
9–85	Roe, California
	Research Attorney. Researched, wrote memoranda and legal opinions, and orally briefed two judges in all areas of civil, criminal and appellate law.

EDUCATION

| 9–81 to | Anywhere College of Law |
| 5–84 | San Francisco, California, |

| 9–77 to | University of the Ozone |
| 5–81 | San Francisco, California |

MEMBERSHIPS

State Bar of California, admitted 1984 (only put date if you passed on 1st try)
Bar Association of San Francisco, Litigation Section

OTHER ACTIVITIES

Chair, Board of Directors, San Francisco Gross Humanity Society Member of Board, San Francisco New Wave Orchestra
Active participant, Big Brothers/Big Sisters

SAMPLE LEGAL RESUME
FOR ASSOCIATE

MARY ROE
0000 Street
San Francisco, CA 94000
(415) 000–0000
e-mail: Roe@dot.com

EDUCATION

9–90 to 5–93	Sunshine Law School Pensacola, Florida	Degree: J.D. Top 5% of class [only put if 20%+]

Editor, *Pensacola Law Review*
Article: "Reexamining Tortfeasors: What's Wrong with the System?"

9–86 to 5–90	University of Alaska Juneau, Alaska	Degree: B.A. in Spanish

Graduated *Magna Cum Laude*

MEMBERSHIPS

Admitted State Bars of North Carolina (1993), Florida (1994) and Massachusetts (1996) [only put date if you passed on first try]
Bar Association of San Francisco, Litigation Section

PROFESSIONAL EXPERIENCE

9–95 to present
MILLER, MILLER & MILLER, Portland, Maine
Litigation Associate. Interview and counsel clients. Negotiate and settle business tort, breach of contract and real estate cases valued at $200,000. Research and draft numerous discovery documents and present at court hearings on motions to compel. Take and defend depositions. Researched, drafted and won summary judgment motion, saving client potential judgment in excess of $500,000.

9–93 to 8–95
WAIN AND BAIN, Boston, Massachusetts
Corporate/Commercial Business Associate. (Summer Law Clerk, 1992). Drafted contracts and prepared documentation for corporate, business and real estate transactions. Prepared corporate minutes and bylaws. Researched issues relating to major shopping center lease and drafted preliminary lease clauses. Prepared UCC filings. Interviewed clients.

6–91 to 9–91
LAW OFFICES OF SAM SMITH, Boca Raton, Florida
Summer Law Clerk. Researched and wrote memoranda of law on tort, breach of contract, and real estate issues.

OTHER ACTIVITIES/LANGUAGES

- Board of Directors, American Association of Appraisers National Committee. Coalition to Save the Forests
- Fluent in Spanish

FUNCTIONAL RESUME
WORKSHEET

NAME _____
Street _____
City/State/Zip _____
Phone (____) _____
e-mail: _____

Objective: _____

PROFESSIONAL SKILLS

(Skill Area, e.g. Managerial) _____
  (Give examples of results or achievements which best demonstrate
  this skill as it applies to the objective)
  A. _____
  B. _____
  C. _____

(Skill Area, e.g. Communication) _____
  (Give examples of results or achievements which best demonstrate
  this skill as it applies to the objective)
  A. _____
  B. _____
  C. _____

(Skill Area, e.g. Technical) _____
  (Give examples of results or achievements which best demonstrate
  this skill as it applies to the objective)
  A. _____
  B. _____
  C. _____

EXPERIENCE

(include relevant volunteer experience and start with most recent)

(Company name) _____, (City/State) _____,
(Years) _____
    (one sentence description of product/service produced by
    company)
    (Position) _____

(Company name) _____, (City/State) _____,
(Years) _____
    (one sentence description of product/service produced by
    company)
    (Position) _____

(Company name) _____, (City/State) _____,
(Years) _____
    (one sentence description of product/service produced by
    company)
    (Position) _____

EDUCATION/HONORS/MEMBERSHIPS/LANGUAGES

(Most recent school name & location) _____,
Degree _____, Year _____
    (Nationally-known honors, if any: i.e., law review) _____

(School name & location) _____, Degree _____,
Year _____
    (Nationally-known honors, if any; i.e., magna cum laude) _____

(Relevant Memberships/Associations) _____

(Languages, if any, and computer skills) _____

1ST SAMPLE
FUNCTIONAL RESUME

JOHN SMITH
100 Jones Lane
Any Town, CA 90000
Tel. ——————————
e–mail:jsmith@dot.com

Objective: to obtain a position as the administrator/manager of a medium–size law firm

PROFESSIONAL PROFILE

Administrative/Management Skills:

- Administered and managed a general practice law firm of 12 lawyers for two years. Firm had billings in excess of $3 million dollars. Formulated and implemented firm policy, hired and fired personnel, budgeted and regulated financial issues, and researched and complied with regulatory requirements.
- Managed several companies with 150+ employees. Developed and maintained budgets, managed and hired and fired personnel, handled regulatory affairs, conducted contract negotiations, and administered corporate and employee business affairs.
- Directed start–up of several multimillion dollar business ventures, implemented policy, formulated strategic and financing planning, and managed sales and research and development programs.

Law Firm Practice Experience:

- Practiced law for four years, concentrating on a general civil practice involving corporate transactions, contract issues, and debt–equity restructuring.

- Appeared numerous times in state and federal court and arbitrated many civil issues to successful conclusion.

Communication Abilities:

- Presented successfully numerous times in California State and Federal District Courts.
- Negotiated mergers, acquisitions and joint ventures of deals in excess of $78 million.
- Taught contract law at local law school, as well as a number of MCLE courses on contracts.
- Presented both prepared and extemporaneous talks to large and small groups.

[If you think one more category would be important, list here]

EMPLOYMENT HISTORY

Partner, Law Offices of Justice Unleashed, Los Angeles, CA, 1990–present. Law firm manager, 1992–present.
CEO/COO, Big Wampum Laboratories, Inc., Los Angeles, CA, 1986–1990.
President, Pollution Unlimited, Inc., Phoenix, AZ, 1984–1986.
Branch manager, Cheatum Well Company, San Diego, CA, 1982–84.
[etc. in descending chronological order]

EDUCATION

J.D., Top Ten College of Law, 1990. Associate editor, Law Review.
M.B.A., No Name University, 1980
B.A. (English), Big Deal University, 1975. Graduated Cum Laude.

OTHER ACTIVITIES/COMPUTER SKILLS

Board of Directors, American Management Association
Member, American, California, and Los Angeles Bar Associations
Board of Directors, Big Brothers
Computer knowledge of Windows '95, WordPerfect, and Microsoft Word for Windows

JOHN SMITH
100 Jones Lane
Any Town, CA 90000
Tel. _____
e-mail: _____

Objective: to obtain a position in executive search, focusing on the health care industry

PROFESSIONAL PROFILE

Business Development Skills

- Directed start-up of U.S. and European direct sales and marketing operations for prominent medical diagnostics company, building sales to over $6 million dollars in three years.
- Developed strategic plan for sales and marketing of worldwide expansion programs for medical products company, increasing sales from $35 million to $50 million in two years.
- Developed and implemented multi-tiered marketing plan for major pharmaceutical company, doubling market share of specific products within two years.

Sales and Communication Skills:

- One of top three out of 130 salespeople nationwide for two consecutive years for large national medical supply company.
- Responsible for direct profit and loss responsibility for six medical product lines.
- Conducted numerous successful persuasive oral presentations before judges and arbitrators.
- Negotiated mergers, acquisitions and joint ventures of deals in excess of $78 million.
- Taught legal research and writing skills to classes of 25 first-year law students.
- Presented both prepared and extemporaneous talks to large and small groups.

[Perhaps one more category, either illustrating knowledge of the health industry, or illustrating the contacts this person has]

EMPLOYMENT HISTORY

Lawyer, Law Offices of Justice Unleashed, Los Angeles, CA, 1990–present. Law firm manager, 1992–present.
CEO/COO, Big Wampum Laboratories, Inc., Los Angeles, CA, 1986–1990.
President, Pollution Unlimited, Inc., Phoenix, AZ, 1984–1986.
Branch manager, Cheatum Well Company, San Diego, CA 1982–84.
[etc. in descending chronological order]

EDUCATION

J.D., Top Ten College of Law, 1990. Associate editor, Law Review.
M.B.A., No Name University, 1980
B.A. (English), Big Deal University, 1975. Graduated Cum Laude.

OTHER ACTIVITIES/COMPUTER SKILLS

- Chair, International Medical Coalition
- Member, Allied Health Association
- Board of Directors, Senior Health Coalition
- Board of Directors, Big Brothers
- Computer knowledge of Windows '95, WordPerfect, and Microsoft Word for Windows

There are hundreds of resume books in print, including numerous for specialty areas, such as advertising or health care. I've listed a sampling of the legal and general resume books in the resource list below.

RESOURCES

In many cities across the country, the Chamber of Commerce sponsors a weekly program with a guest panel of business leaders who will discuss hiring and job hunting ideas, as well as critique resumes from audience members.

Best Resumes for Attorneys, Joan Fondell and Mary Jo Russo, John Wiley & Sons, 1994. Sets out and critiques sample legal resumes in many practice areas, as well as cover letters, interviewing techniques, and thank-you letters for both junior and experienced lawyers.

Better Resumes for Attorneys and Paralegals, David Saltman and Adele Lewis, Barron's Educational Series, 1986.

How to Write Better Resumes, Gary Grappo and Adele Lewis, 5th edition, Barron's Educational Series, 1998.

Better Resumes for Executives and Professionals, Robert Wilson and Adele Lewis, 3rd edition, Barron's Educational Series, 1996.

Resume Power; Selling Yourself on Paper, Tom Washington, 5th edition, Mt. Vernon Press, 1996.

Damn Good Resume Guide: A Crash Course in Resume Writing, Yana Parker, 3rd edition, Ten Speed Press, 1996.

The Resume Catalog: 200 Damn Good Examples, Yana Parker, Ten Speed Press, updated, 1996.

Resumes That Knock 'Em Dead, Martin Yate, 3rd edition, Adams Publishing, 1997.

Conquer Resume Objections, Robert Wilson and Erik Rambusch, John Wiley & Sons, 1994. Covers objections to job history, career objectives, and resume format and information.

Resumes for the Over-50 Job Hunter, Samuel Ray, John Wiley & Sons, 1993.

Resumes for Law Careers, VGM Professional Resume Series, 1995.

The New 90-Minute Resume, Peggy Schmidt, Peterson's Guides,

1996. Contains information on resumes, cover letters, and how to get your resume into the hands of decision makers.

Electronic Resume Revolution, Joyce Lain Kennedy and Thomas Morrow, 2nd edition, John Wiley & Sons, 1995. Information on, and techniques to create, scanable resumes.

• Cover Letters

All resumes should be accompanied by an effective, individually prepared cover letter. This, of course, takes more time, but many employment professionals consider the cover letter to be at least as important as the resume. Therefore, do not use a form letter that you send to every employer, unless you are certain that the requirements are the same for each job. A letter that indicates some knowledge of the employer and how your experience would fit in is usually received with more enthusiasm—it shows you've done some homework. If at all possible, do not direct it to a generic "Dear Madam or Sir": unless you are answering a blind ad, call the employer and ask the receptionist or personnel representative the name of the appropriate contact.

The letter should be succinct, containing no more than three to four paragraphs, and it should include highlights, from your resume, of your strengths and accomplishments. Every word in your letter should answer the question, Why is this person qualified for the position I want to fill and what will she do for me? Relate experiences or results in your past work to the qualities the prospective employer is seeking. Remember, your cover letter and resume are sales documents. Whereas it isn't appropriate to use "puff" words on your resume, it is acceptable in the cover letter to tout your "successful" negotiating skills, or your "excellent" oral communication abilities.

When applying for a job in a different field, some people choose to send only a cover letter, summarizing their relevant skills and experience. However, that can often shortchange the applicant because not as much information can be transmitted by letter only, and an employer usually won't take the time to read a three-page letter.

If you are answering an ad that requests previous salary or you have been requested by the employer to include salary history, *and* you believe the job for which you are applying pays much more or less than you currently earn, you can either ignore the request until it can be discussed at the interview or include a statement to the effect that "salary history will be provided at the interview since salary is negotiable and is secondary to opportunity." Of course, keep in mind that there are employers that will toss out your application for ignoring their request.

On the opposite page is a sample cover letter illustrating a persuasive, on-point presentation for the individual introduced in the "1st Sample Functional Resume" on page 276.

RESOURCES

How to Write Successful Cover Letters, Eric Martin and Karyn Langhorne, VGM Career Horizons, 1994.

Cover Letters That Knock 'Em Dead, Martin Yates, 3rd edition, Adams Publishing, 1997.

Dynamite Cover Letters: And Other Great Job Search Letters, Ron Krannich and Caryl Krannich, 3rd edition, Impact Publications, 1994.

SAMPLE COVER LETTER

JOHN SMITH
100 Jones Lane
Any Town, CA 90000
Tel. _____
Fax _____

Date

B. Swarm, Esq.
Sweat, Swat & Swarm
Attorneys at Law
11111 Short Street
Anytown, USA 00000

Dear Mr. Swarm:

I have extensive experience in managing a law firm and other businesses. I would like to meet with you to discuss the in-depth expertise that I could provide to your law firm if hired as its manager. Since your firm has recently grown rapidly and added a bankruptcy department, it may be time to consider hiring a professional manager. I am enclosing my resume to illuminate my law firm and business management background, as well as my knowledge of the legal marketplace.

For the past two years I have managed a small law firm. I have brought to that position my experience in business management, as well as my academic training as a lawyer and an M.B.A. Previously, I have managed the business of both international and smaller companies, as well as managed small and large employee groups. I have a proven record of fiscal, administrative, and interpersonal achievements.

I would very much like to talk with you to explore further how my expertise might contribute to your law firm. I will phone you next week to arrange a mutually convenient time when we could meet. Thank you in advance for your consideration.

Sincerely,

John Smith

Enclosure

CHAPTER ELEVEN

Interviewing Skills

*A successful person is someone who can go
from failure to failure with enthusiasm.*
—WINSTON CHURCHILL

Okay, so you have now figured out what kind of job you want, you've researched which companies or law firms will provide that work, and you've prepared a targeted resume that demonstrates your abilities to do that job. And now you are scheduled for an interview with a company that may just be a perfect fit! What is your next step? How do you prepare for an interview? And why should you prepare?

An excellent resume and cover letter may open doors, but a good interview is what clinches the job. Only in an interview can a prospective employer get a sense of your communication skills, sense of humor, and ability to establish rapport. In fact, a really great job interview can often overcome gaps in your experience. Many jobs have been created for individuals who present themselves and their backgrounds so well that a prospective employer finds a place for them in the company. Therefore, the person who interviews effectively and confidently greatly increases the chances of a job offer.

In order to interview well, preparation is vital. Just as preparation for a law school exam or a trial or an extensive negotiation is important for a successful outcome, thorough preparation for an interview is often the key to securing a desired position. How do you prepare for your interview?

Understand the difference between an informational interview and a job interview. An informational interview is often more exploratory and less focused than a job interview. Whereas an informational interview is a vehicle for research, a job applicant should be well-prepared before a job interview. In an informational interview, you do not have to sell yourself, since you are attempting to get information. In a job interview, however, you have specific selling points you need to make clear about yourself in a limited amount of time.

Research the company or firm. Use the applicable resources listed in chapters 6, 7, and 8 to find out current developments in an industry or field, as well as specific information about the employer, such as practice areas, products or services it offers, clients and market it serves, anticipated projects, and expansion plans. Other areas to investigate include:

- Billable hours requirements in a law firm
- History
- Management structure
- Company size/number of partners and associates in a law firm
- Current problems
- Company culture
- Goals
- Company income/partner's income
- Reputation

Sources for research into a specific organization include, in addition to those listed in chapters 6, 7, and 8:

- Bar associations
- Annual report
- Better Business Bureau
- Employees, both present and former
- Law school career services office
- Headhunters
- Chamber of Commerce
- Your network of contacts
- Stockbrokers
- Company or law firm websites

If you do your homework, when you are asked questions about why you want to work for this employer, what you can do for it, and how your skills translate to this employer's projects, you will be able to focus your responses appropriately. Nothing impresses an employer more than a candidate who has done her or his homework and shows a knowledge of and interest in the employer and its field. Of course, don't tout your knowledge. Instead, allow your information to flow naturally into the conversation. For example, in answer to the question, Why do you think your lawyering skills translate to this job in stock brokerage? you might answer, "With the increased emphasis in the brokerage industry on personal relationships, and specifically, your company's current focus on directly counseling clients rather than just selling stocks, my previous experience and abilities in developing close working relationships with my clients, interviewing them for information, and then using that information to counsel them about effective action would be very useful."

Be aware of the interviewer's role and interests. Most interviewers' questions are intended to find out about your current readiness for the job, your skills and achievements, your motivation and drive, and whether you will fit in with the company and its goals.

In a large firm or company, your first interview may be with a professional interviewer in the Human Resources Department. To this interviewer, it is important to present your experience and skills clearly and candidly, since the purpose of this screening interview is to exclude candidates who don't have the minimum qualifications or who have some easily perceived background or personal problem.

The key interview is the one with the decision maker, the individual who has hiring authority or who will be your superior. In this interview, you will want to present your achievements, experience, and skills, to illustrate your fit with the company, *and* develop a personal chemistry with the interviewer. To do this, you must be able to discern what the interviewer needs from a person who would fill this job, then illustrate your ability to fill those needs.

Be sure to watch for both verbal and nonverbal reactions and respond accordingly. If your interviewer frowns when you are explaining a point, perhaps she or he hasn't fully understood, and you need to clarify your point. If you are not sure what the interviewer's reaction means, decide whether to ask if you might elaborate on something you have said. Awareness of the interviewer's reactions may also alert you to problem areas. If the interviewer seems uncomfortable with an answer, you can try to assuage the concern. If you are given a less than positive reaction and are not sure why, find out. There may just be a misunderstanding, or it might be a legitimate concern you need to alleviate.

Anticipate the questions you may be asked and then practice answers. In most interviews there are some standard questions about your background and skills. But some interviewers like to delve more deeply or broadly into your experience and interests. And some like to toss out oddball questions to see how you handle yourself in a completely unprepared, extemporaneous situation. If you are prepared for any number of questions, you should feel more at ease during the interview. Here are some questions you should be ready to answer, whether you are interviewing for a legal or non-law job (convert the word "company" in the following examples into "law firm" when applicable):

- Why have you chosen this industry/company/practice area?
- What other industries/companies/practice areas are you considering? Why?

- What do you know about our company? What would you like to know about our company?
- Why would you like to work for our company?
- What will you be able to contribute to the growth and success of our company?
- Why should I hire you?
- What interests you most about our product/service/practice area?
- Which aspects of your previous positions have you liked? Disliked? Why?
- Aren't you over (under) qualified for this position?
- What is your greatest strength? Your greatest weakness? Why?
- What is your greatest accomplishment?
- What does success mean to you?
- Why don't you want to be an attorney?
- Why would you, an attorney, want to work in this [non-law] position?
- If you could start all over again, what would you do differently? Why?
- What salary are you looking for?
- What is your present (or most recent) salary? What is your bonus?
- Give me some examples of your leadership capabilities.
- Tell me several qualities you possess that have contributed to your success.
- Give me some examples of your creativity.
- Are you detail-oriented? Give me some examples.
- Why would you be a good (manager, trainer, etc.)?
- How do you react to pressure? To deadlines?
- Tell me something about your interests and hobbies.
- Which magazines and books have you read recently? What industry-related publications do you read?
- Are you involved with any professional associations?
- Have you taken courses to enhance your understanding of this industry?
- How would you describe yourself?
- Can you travel?
- Are you a team player?

- Why would you be willing to take less salary in this job than you earned in your last position?
- What computer software are you familiar with?
- Can you describe a major problem you encountered and how you solved it?
- What do you expect to earn next year? Five years from now? Ten years?
- Do you use drugs? Do you drink?
- What recommendations could we expect from your former employer?
- Why did you leave your most recent employer?

Develop and practice several anecdotes that illustrate your skills. It is easy to say "I am a good writer" or "I am able to clearly explain complex concepts in more understandable terms." But the interviewer won't necessarily remember your bald assertions. A better way to impress him or her is to tell a fifteen- to thirty-second story that illustrates how you utilized your skills. Your story also allows you the opportunity to show off your verbal skills. For example, instead of "I am able to explain complex concepts," you could say, "When I was given the assignment to prepare a comprehensive memorandum to explain to a client all of the possible outcomes he might expect if he filed a lawsuit, I first drafted an outline. Then, when I fleshed out the outline, I made sure that I avoided legal jargon and terminology, explaining each item as concisely as possible. The client phoned my supervisor to tell her that he was able to make an intelligent choice about the lawsuit because of the clarity of that memo." It often helps to prepare two or three such anecdotes for each skill, so that you can present the one most applicable to the interview situation. Be sure to rehearse your stories, although not so much that they sound memorized.

Be prepared to ask questions to determine if the position is a good fit for you. While you can ask any number of questions, you will always want to be prepared to ask at least several. This shows interest in the position and attentiveness to what was already discussed. You also want to determine if you actually have an interest in further pursuing the job. So if, for example, the topics of responsibilities or advancement or international work or client contact have not been broached, by all means ask about them. However, this is not the time to ask about salary, benefits, vacation, or other questions that indicate self-interest, because, at this point, you are still selling yourself and what you can do for the company. Most businesses react favorably to jobseekers who want to do something for the company, and unfavorably to those who want to know what the company will do for them.

A few questions you may want to be ready to ask, in addition to any that are specific to your situation or interests, are:

- Can you describe a typical day for a person in this position?
- Why is this position available? Why did the previous person leave?
- How long has this position been open?
- How long do most people remain in the position here?
- How long does it take to make partner at this firm?
- Are there defined career paths?
- How many women/minority partners/executives are in this firm/company?
- How much input will I have in developing this job?
- What would be expected of a new person in the position during the first year? In the long term?

Lawyers need to know their transferable skills. It is very important to have a clear picture of the skills you offer a potential employer. This is especially true if you intend to seek a job outside of law. Be sure to work through the skills exercises in chapter 5 so that you are clear on which skills you have *and* which you want to use. Then be sure to present those clearly so that the employer can understand why a lawyer can actually do the work of the position for which you are interviewing. For example, when Clarice interviewed with a computer company to work as a technical writer preparing the Help menus for computer software, she had to overcome the employer's reluctance to hire an attorney rather than a writer. She did so by explaining that she was already a technical writer because, in law school and practice, she was taught technical legal terminology and had to explain that terminology, both orally and in writing, in a simplified and understandable manner to her clients. The employer understood this illustration of her technical writing skills and offered her the job.

If you are not familiar with the location, atmosphere, or culture of the company, make a visit to its office. A visit will give you an opportunity to sense the atmosphere of the place—how people dress, how formally visitors are treated, etc.—so that you can dress and conduct yourself accordingly for your interview. It will also allow you to gauge your travel time so that you can arrive for the actual interview on time.

Try to be as relaxed as possible for the interview, but never smoke (even if offered) or drink. It is easier to maintain your concentration if you do not have to worry about spilling coffee or burning the rug.

Most interviews will begin with some small talk, about the weather, the lastest sporting event, the office decor. Let the interviewer begin the actual interview according to her or his own pace. However, remember that during the interview, you have points you want to make, so, without taking control of the interview, be sure to direct your comments around to those points.

Be careful not to be too pushy, however. I remember one woman interviewing with me when I was still practicing law. She obviously wanted to make sure that she got all of her questions answered and that I heard about all of her capabilities, so she spent the next hour grilling me and filling me in on her abilities. I didn't have much opportunity to ask questions, and when I did, she immediately turned them back to the few topics she wanted to address. Apparently she had read somewhere that she should take control of the interview! She did a great job of controlling our interview, but needless to say, she did not get the job.

If at all possible, try not to discuss salary or benefits issues on the first interview. Wait until the employer is more interested in you, as evidenced by a call-back to a second interview. There are several reasons for this. First, you want to convey that you are very interested in the firm or company and what you can do for it, rather than what it can do for you. Once you convince them of the benefit of hiring you for your excellent skills, compensation discussions may be a bit easier. Second, you don't want to exclude yourself from consideration because your financial expectations are, or previous salary was, either too high or too low. Again, once the employer is interested in hiring you, compensation is often somewhat negotiable. Of course, that is true only to a point. Before you even apply for and obtain an interview for a job, your networking and other research should have informed you about the salary range. Then, only you can decide whether that range is acceptable to you.

• Stereotypes About Lawyers

There are a number of stereotypes that people both in and out of the legal profession have about lawyers. These stereotypes can hurt your job hunting prospects. You need to overcome these stereotypes through your attitude and your responses to questions during the interview.

Lawyers are negative. The public hears of the hurtful cases that lawyers handle and the negative issues they have to address, and then presumes that the purveyors of the bad news are themselves bad news. The best way to overcome this stereotype is to show a positive, can-do attitude. Try to appear upbeat and confident, even if your insides don't feel that way. Nothing turns off an interviewer more than a candidate who has a dismal, whining tone of voice or sour expression.

Never bad-mouth your former employer, job, or field of employment, because the interviewer will anticipate that you might say the same bad things about the job for which you are interviewing after you leave it. Instead, call attention to whatever positives you got from the job—this is also a good technique to use to emphasize your skills. For example, although I greatly disliked the contentiousness of litigation practice, I speak positively about the client interactions, the public speaking, and the nontechnical writing in my legal practice, all of which I use in my current work.

If you are asked, "Why are you leaving your current job or the field of law?" it is extremely important not to say anything negative. Don't tell tales on lawyers or law practice, affirming all the bad things that others think they know. This only reflects poorly on you, as it reaffirms that lawyers are bad—and *you* are a lawyer, whether you currently practice or not. Instead, suggest some other, positive reasons for your departure:

• You reached the goals you had set for yourself, for example completing ten trials, or making partner, or even graduating law school to gain information;

• You want renewed challenge, since you have become very good at what you have been doing, and it has now become repetitive; or

• You have developed a new interest that you want to pursue, for example computer software development or consulting, since you have become so enamored of your computer and so proficient at working with it.

All of these reasons show that you are moving forward, toward a positive change, rather than running away from a negative.

Lawyers are confrontational. Everyone hears stories about the "in-your-face" attitude of various lawyers, so many people presume that all lawyers are contrary. An effective way to overcome this stereotype is to weave examples of your team-playing abilities into your interview. Just as you have developed short anecdotes to illustrate your skills, you should also prepare a few stories about effective group endeavors, settlements, or negotiations. However, never relate a long "war story"—even most other lawyers don't want to hear details of your cases. Fifteen to thirty seconds, using untechnical terminology, is best.

Lawyers are not creative. Unfortunately, many individuals outside of law think that lawyers can only function in the left-brained world of logical thinking. This misconception is illustrated by a humorous quotation from Alan O'Connor: "Since law exercises only the left hemisphere of the brain, to be a good lawyer, you have to be mentally unbalanced." Because you don't have the opportunity on your resume to relate information about your hobbies and interests in any detail, an interview is the time to mention the poetry you write, the furniture that you build, or the pottery that you throw. These outside interests give a picture of you as a complete person, in addition to illustrating that you have more skills to offer than just effective arguing.

INTERVIEWING MISTAKES

✔ Excessive information (rambling stories, failure to cut to the bottom line)

✔ Inadequate preparation—inability to concisely yet fully describe skills, experience, and goals

✔ Violating confidentiality of former employer

✔ Focusing on financial considerations too early

✔ Inadequate information about the firm, company, or industry

✔ Complain about excess hours or stress on a previous job

✔ Improper or unprofessional appearance

✔ Negative comments or complaining about a previous boss, employer, or colleagues

✔ Confess shortcomings unnecessarily

✔ Failure to focus on the employer's needs and concerns

✔ Avoiding a question that has specifically been asked

INTERVIEWING BASICS OUTLINE

1. Listening
   A. Attentive to the environment and interviewer style
   B. Clarify questions/comments of interviewer
   C. Establish appropriate dialogue with interviewer

    D. Look for opportunities to direct interviewer to your skills and accomplishments

2. Responding (Answering)
    A. Make sure questions are understood before answering
    B. Answers are clear, concise, and positive
    C. Answers are supported with concrete examples/specific achievements
    D. Respond appropriately to different types of questions
      1) If directly qualified for position
        a) Provide affirmative answer
        b) Cite example/accomplishments
      2) If only comparably qualified
        a) Give qualified answer
        b) Direct to comparable experience
        c) Cite examples/accomplishments
      3) Lacking qualifications
        a) Admit deficiency
        b) Determine importance of deficiency
        c) Cite ability to learn/give an example
    E. When appropriate, test interviewer's reaction to response
    F. Be prepared to redirect interviewer—not bound to answer only planned questions

3. Probing (Questions)
    A. Information about position, working conditions, job requirements
    B. Selection criteria
    C. Personal views of interviewer about position/candidacy
    D. Information on the employment process

IMAGE TO PROJECT ABOUT YOURSELF

1. You are qualified for the position with direct/comparable experience.
2. You have set meaningful goals for yourself in life and have gone about reaching them in a planned way.
3. You are in charge of your own destiny, and have made good decisions for yourself.
4. You are realistic about your abilities and potential.

5. You make a total commitment to every task and do the best job possible.
6. You have received positive feedback from supervisors and fellow employees.
7. You have a positive outlook about career, jobs, companies, managers, life.
8. You are clear on what you want to do and can express it in terms of the company/interviewer's needs.

• The Thank-You Letter

Always send a thank-you letter, no more than 24 hours after the interview, while the interviewer's mind is still clear on your qualifications and before he or she has seen hundreds of other candidates. This letter is another opportunity to keep your name in front of the employer and to demonstrate your follow-up and writing abilities. Whereas a thank-you letter following an informational interview may be handwritten, the interview thank-you letter should be prepared professionally, on good business-type stationery. Make it brief.

✔ Paragraph 1 should thank the employer, reminding him or her of the date of the interview.

✔ Paragraph 2 should reiterate why you are uniquely qualified for the position and reemphasize anything from the interview that was particularly positive.

✔ Paragraph 3 should reassert your interest in the company or firm and the particular position that you want.

RESOURCES

Sweaty Palms: The Neglected Art of Being Interviewed, H. Anthony Medley (a former lawyer), Ten Speed Press, revised 1992. Ageless techniques.

Adams Job Interview Almanac, Adams Publications, 1996. A comprehensive resource, setting out complete job interviews in numerous fields, accompanied by great advice. Includes a section on difficult interviews and advice for career changers.

Interview Power: Selling Yourself Face to Face, Tom Washington, Mt. Vernon Press, 1995.

Dynamite Answers to Interview Questions; No More Sweaty Palms!, Caryl Rae Krannich and Ronald Krannich, 2nd edition, Impact Christian Books, 1994.

Conquer Interview Objections, Robert Wilson and Eric Rambusch, John Wiley & Sons, 1994.

The Legal Job Interview, Clifford R. Ennico, Biennix Corp., revised, 1994.

An Insider's Guide to Interviewing: Insights from the Employer's Perspective, 1996, $6. Order from the National Association for Law Placement, 1666 Connecticut Avenue, N.W., Suite 325, Washington, DC 20009; (202) 667–1666, www.nalp.com/.

The Essential Book of Interviewing: Everything You Need to Know from Both Sides of the Table, Arnold Kanter, Times Books, 1995,

Job Strategies for People with Disabilities, Melanie Witt and Joyce Lain Kennedy, Peterson's Guides, 1992.

Following is an example of an interview for a job outside of law. Note how the candidate brings the interviewer's attention back to the candidate's relevant skills and experience and ties that experience into the job at hand. The candidate also lets the interviewer know that some pre-interview homework was done.

NON-LAW INTERVIEW

INTERVIEWER: Good afternoon, Ms. Jones. Please come in and sit down.

MS. JONES: Thank you. (sits down)

INTERVIEWER: Would you like a cup of coffee or tea?

MS. JONES: No, thank you. Your offices are very beautiful. I'm sure the employees enjoy working in this environment and that your clients enjoy coming here.

INTERVIEWER: We are very fortunate to have found an excellent decorator. It was quite expensive redoing the offices, but we are very fortunate to have a number of very successful clients to whom we sell a lot of product, and that allows us to provide such a nice environment. But in working with our clients, we like to think we help them to become even more successful. Of course, we all work very hard and are very service-oriented towards our clients.

MS. JONES: I agree that providing efficient and effective service to the client helps keep clients happy. When I worked for Wright and Day during the summer of 1994, I was very conscious of completing assignments on time, or even early. For example, I was assigned to research and write a memoranda on complex tax issues. The assigning partner asked for me to complete the project within two weeks, but I put the due date on my personal calendar to be one day earlier, then planned my work around the earlier date. I was also given a fair amount of client contact and always tried to return phone calls immediately and treat clients as I would like to be treated.

INTERVIEWER: Good. You are trained as a lawyer and the work experience you have has been in law firms. Why do you believe you are qualified to be an account representative with this computer company?

MS. JONES: I have been interested in computers and the computer industry for years. When I first entered law school, I thought I wanted to become a patent attorney and service computer company clients, but by the end of my last year in school, I realized that I eventually wanted to be more directly involved in the computer industry rather than just working with it.

When I was in college, I took several computer and technology courses. I am very comfortable working with computers and can use various software programs adequately, including Word Perfect for Windows and Lotus 1,2,3. In law school, I took all of the courses offered in patent and copyright law, with consideration as to how those applied to computer and technology issues.

Then during the past year, while working for the law firm of Wright and Day in Baton Rouge, I did legal and factual research on several new patent applications, including an extensive and complex memo for a prominent computer company. I attended a number of meetings and negotiations with that computer client and became somewhat familiar with their products. I realized that I would prefer to handle those products after they were completed rather than be involved in the legal documentation during their development.

INTERVIEWER: Why are you interested in account representative work?

MS. JONES: I am a very good communicator and work well with diverse groups of people. While in college, I excelled in debate, winning an award for the most persuasive presentation. And in law school, I took a trial advocacy class in which we learned to make concise and convincing presentations. Since that time, I have often been complimented by my clients on my clear and effective explanations of complex concepts. I would like to combine my excellent communication, persuasion, and interpersonal-relation skills with my knowledge of computers and legal issues related to that industry. A computer account rep position would incorporate all of those skills and knowledge. When I was researching which companies I wanted to contact, I noted that your company is growing rapidly and is very proactive in cultivating new clientele, so I felt that it would be productive to meet with you.

INTERVIEWER: Where do you see yourself in five years?

MS. JONES: I would like to be a senior account representative, with some management responsibility. I believe, in addition to the skills I previously mentioned, that I have management abilities, as evidenced by my supervising the preparation of legal documents and oral presentations of twenty law students during law school and three paralegals at my law firm.

INTERVIEWER: How did you like law school and law practice?

MS. JONES: I found the first year of school somewhat difficult, but once I adjusted to the new jargon and way of thinking, the next two years were much easier. Both in school and in practice, I enjoyed the challenge of learning new material. I was also involved in several school and bar association activities and developed a close group of friends, and that made both my schooling and work much more fun.

INTERVIEWER: What activities have you been involved with?

MS. JONES: As a third-year student, I was in charge of supervising the preparation of legal papers and oral arguments for twenty second-year students. Currently, I am involved with a non-profit group on whose behalf I do some fund raising and negotiating of various issues. I am interested in now becoming involved with relevant computer associations.

INTERVIEWER: What are you looking for in a job?

MS. JONES: I want to work for a company that is growing, offers a stimulating and challenging work environment, allows its employees increasing responsibility, and rewards employees according to their merit. My research shows that your company has recently opened offices in several of the Pacific Rim countries, and its financial statement shows very good profits. I believe that I can contribute to the profitability of your company based on my skills and previous training.

INTERVIEWER: Are there other questions you have for me?

MS. JONES: Will your firm be conducting second interviews or will a hiring decision be made on this first interview, and if so, when will that decision be made?

INTERVIEWER: There will be second interviews. If the hiring committee would like to meet you, we will contact you by the end of next week. Thank you for coming in. (extends her hand to shake)

MS. JONES: Thank you for your time. I am very interested in meeting other members of your company and pursuing these discussions further. (rises, shakes hands, and leaves)

In the above interview, Ms. Jones directly responded to the interviewer's concern about her perceived lack of qualifications to be an account rep by demonstrating parallel experience and skills. She deflected the implication that she "was just a lawyer" by exhibiting knowledge of and interest in the computer industry. Unless this employer is so narrowly focused on the fact that Ms. Jones *is* a lawyer, the interview exhibited her as a well-qualified candidate who should be given serious consideration.

Conclusion

In order that people may be happy in their work,
these three things are needed: they must be fit for it;
they must not do too much of it; they
must have a sense of success in it.

—JOHN RUSKIN

By the time you have read this far, you should know a lot about yourself, the career options and resources available to you, and the techniques for pursuing those various alternatives. Many of you are ready to move forward, anticipating and perhaps even somewhat excited about the challenges ahead.

Yet some of you may still feel hesitant. Now, then, is a good time to reexamine your motivations for making a change. If those motivations haven't yet become strong enough to catapult you forward—and you currently have a job, haven't been asked to leave, or have sufficient savings to tide you over for a time— maybe it would be beneficial to let all of the ideas and thoughts you have generated while reading this book "brew" for a few weeks or months. After that period, it's possible that everything will fall more understandably into place and you will then be ready to take the next step, whether that means reevaluating your present work or making a more radical career change.

People always ask me what they should do to find that special job they'll enjoy. I respond that job hunting is not unlike jumping out of the open door of an airplane, 10,000 feet above the ground. If you know you have thoroughly prepared—you have firmly strapped on your parachute, learned everything possible about what you need to do to achieve a soft landing, and conditioned yourself physically and mentally to succeed—you are then ready to take a deep breath, step out, and begin your adventure.

So too with a job hunt. After you have completed a thorough self-assessment, examined some of the career alternatives that will fit for who you are and what you want, and spent the requisite effort to research the various options, talk to those who are knowledgeable, and develop an effective written and oral approach to your job hunt, your next step is to take a deep breath and move resolutely forward to meet any challenges head on. You can do it. Although both are great adventures, job change is really much easier, more interesting, and far less dangerous than parachuting. And your rewards last longer.

Perhaps the greatest risk of all is to do nothing.
—ANONYMOUS

Index

About the Author

HINDI GREENBERG graduated in the top 10 percent of her class in 1974 from Hastings College of the Law in San Francisco, clerked for two courts, and was a business litigator in a major San Francisco law firm, a five-person firm, and in a corporation. She quit full-time practice in 1984 and, during the next six years, did contract legal work for other lawyers. In 1985 she started Lawyers in Transition^{SM} in San Francisco to help attorneys obtain satisfying career choices in and outside of law and assist law firms in retaining the best associates. She does this both by presenting programs for organizations and through consultations with individual lawyers or law firm groups.

Hindi is nationally known for her expertise on attorney career satisfaction and options and has presented repeat programs for the American Bar Association and state and specialty bar associations and law schools nationwide. She has been interviewed by major legal and general publications, including *Time, Business Week, U.S. News & World Report, Forbes, USA Today,* the *New York Times, California Lawyer* Magazine, as well as CNN, NBC, ABC, and PBS television. The *Los Angeles Times* called her "the Ann Landers for lawyers."

She has published numerous articles on career satisfaction, career options, and contract lawyering in legal and business publications nationwide. She wrote a chapter in *Breaking Traditions: Work Alternatives for Lawyers,* published in 1993 by the American Bar Association, is a co-author of *Beyond L.A. Law: Breaking the Traditional "Lawyer" Mold,* published in 1997 by NALP/Harcourt Brace, and has now written *The Lawyer's Career Change Handbook,* a comprehensive career and resource guide.